LIEUT.-COLONEL A. T. PATERSON, D.S.O., M.C., V.D.

THE THIRTY-NINTH

The History of the 39th Battalion Australian Imperial Force

With 36 Illustrations
and 11 Maps.

The Naval & Military Press Ltd

Published by
The Naval & Military Press Ltd
5 Riverside, Brambleside, Bellbrook
Industrial Estate, Uckfield, East Sussex,
TN22 1QQ England
Tel: +44 (0) 1825 749494
Fax: +44 (0) 1825 765701
www.naval-military-press.com
www.military-genealogy.com
www.militarymaproom.com

In reprinting in facsimile from the original, any imperfections are inevitably reproduced and the quality may fall short of modern type and cartographic standards.

Dedicated to the everlasting Memory of Fallen Comrades of the 39th, who by sacrificing their lives in the cause of their country, have consecrated for ever the traditions made by their Battalion.

Battle Honours

MESSINES, 1917

YPRES, 1917

BROODSEINDE

PASSCHENDAELE

SOMME, 1918

AMIENS

MONT ST. QUENTIN

HINDENBURG LINE

ST. QUENTIN CANAL

FRANCE AND FLANDERS, 1916-18

CONTENTS

Dedication

Battle Honours

Foreword, Lieut.-General Sir John Monash, G.C.M.G., K.C.B., V.D.

Message from Field-Marshal Sir W. R. Birdwood, G.C.M.G., K.C.B., K.C.S.I., C.I.E., D.S.O., A.B.C.

Appreciation, Major-General Sir C. B. B. White, K.C.B., K.C.M.G., K.C.V.O., D.S.O., A.D.C., *p.s.c.*

The Writing of the History, Lieut.-Colonel A. T. Paterson, D.S.O., M.C., V.D.

Chapter i.	The Empire's Call	Page	29
Chapter ii.	Outward Bound	,,	35
Chapter iii.	On Salisbury Plain	,,	49
Chapter iv.	Into Action	,,	65
Chapter v.	Winter in Flanders	,,	81
Chapter vi.	Preparing for Battle	,,	95
Chapter vii.	The Battle of Messines	,,	109
Chapter viii.	Summer and Autumn, 1917	,,	123
Chapter ix.	The Battle of Broodseinde	,,	135
Chapter x.	The Battle of Passchendaele	,,	151
Chapter xi.	Holding the Line in Belgium	,,	163
Chapter xii.	The German Offensive, 1918	,,	179
Chapter xiii.	The Allies Advance	,,	203
Chapter xiv.	Still Advancing	,,	223
Chapter xv.	Peace	,,	243
Lest We Forget		,,	251
Decorations and Recommendations		,,	265
Nominal Roll		,,	275
Index		,,	353

ILLUSTRATIONS

Lieut.-Colonel A. T. Paterson, D.S.O., M.C., V.D.	Frontispiece
	Facing Page
Ballarat, Victoria	32
H.M.A.T. A.11, "Ascanius," with 39th Battalion A.I.F., on Board at Port Melbourne	34
Lieut.-Colonel R. Rankine, D.S.O.	40
The Band	42
In Camp	50
Amesbury, Salisbury Plain, England	58
N.C.Os. of the Battalion, Neuve Eglise, Belgium	66
Half Past Eleven Square, Armentieres, France	73
In the Front Line at Houplines, France	74
Near Armentieres, France	85
The Scouts, "No Man's Land"	102
Officers of the Battalion, Neuve Eglise, Belgium	110
Battle of Messines and Key Map, Ground at Messines won by the 39th Battalion	116
"A" Company, Bouillancourt, France	118
"B" Company, Bouillancourt, France	124
"K" Track, Broodseinde Ridge	138
The Animals of the 39th Battalion Played their Part, too	146
Passchendaele	152
Casualties on the Menin Road	160
St. Yves Avenue, Ploegsteert	167
General Sir W. R. Birdwood Presenting Decorations to Members of the 3rd Division at Neuve Eglise, Belgium	174
"C" Company, Bouillancourt, France	182
The Somme	185
Battalion Headquarters, Marett Wood, France	190
"Ici" returned to his owner at Ribemont, France	194
The Sunken Road, Marett Wood, Mericourt, France	197
A Parcel from Home	198
N.C.Os. of "B" Company, Armentieres, France	204
Towards Bois l'Abbe from Villers-Bretonneux, France	207
The Scouts of the Battalion, Bouillancourt, France	212
"D" Company (with "Ici"), Bouillancourt, France	220
Officers, Battalion Headquarters, Bouillancourt, France	226
Lieut.-Colonel R. O. Henderson, D.S.O.	236
Near Gillemont Farm	239
The Battalion's Last Parade, Bouillancourt, France	246

MAPS

		Facing Page
Map No. 1.	Houplines—l'Epinette—Armentieres ...	80
Map No. 2.	La Chapelle d'Armentieres—Cowgate—Rue du Bois	94
Map No. 3.	Battle of Messines	122
Map No. 4.	Ploegsteert Wood	134
Map No. 5.	Battle of Broodseinde Ridge	150
Map No. 6.	Battle of Passchendaele	162
Map No. 7.	The Somme, Morlancourt	202
Map No. 8.	Amiens to Gressaire Wood	222
Map No. 9.	Bray-Sur-Somme to Roisel	242
Map No. 10.	Roisel to Hindenburg Line	242
Map No. 11.	Showing Towns, Villages, Camps and Trenches, associated with the Battalion's Activities in France and Belgium	250

FOREWORD

Lieut.-General Sir John Monash

G.C.M.G., K.C.B., V.D.

—◆—

IT is an especial pleasure to me to have been given the opportunity of writing a few words by way of introduction to this story of the 39th Battalion of the Australian Imperial Force, because I had the privilege of being intimately associated with this fine battalion since the days of its earliest war training.

It was on Salisbury Plain, in the late Summer of 1916, that this battalion of Victorian "diggers," together with its sister battalions of the now celebrated Tenth Australian Brigade, underwent its final preparation for war, arduous in its physical toil, and tense in the expectation of high performance. The 39th being one of the twelve Infantry Battalions of the Third Australian Division, with the command of which I had then been entrusted, there are few who had a better opportunity of forming for it high hopes of a memorable career in the theatre of war.

These hopes were not belied, for the Thirty-Ninth, from the day of its entry into the battle zone, early in December, 1916, until the conclusion of hostilities, heaped victory upon victory, and daily added glory to its laurels. The battalion played a prominent, not to say predominant, role in all the really decisive battles of the last two years of the war, and such memorable names as Messines, Broodseinde, Passchendaele, Amiens, Bray, Clery, and Bony bear evidence of the high place which it has achieved in the annals of the Great War.

It was indeed a privilege to command such men; there can be no greater honour than to have gained their confidence, and to have enjoyed the loyal and devoted performance which they brought to every task assigned to them. It was at Messines that the Thirty-Ninth laid the foundation for its great tradition, and although in the months that followed, the personnel changed considerably, owing to the constant wastage of war, the soul and spirit of the battalion was ever enhanced to still finer records.

The story of such a unit of the Australian Imperial Force is one of high endeavour, of sacrifice and of devotion to duty. It enshrines the deeds and the sufferings of those who composed its ranks. I commend it, and the tale it tells, to the respectful homage of the Australian public, and of the posterity of those heroic men who made of the Thirty-Ninth the battalion which it was.

John Monash

LIEUTENANT-GENERAL.

Melbourne,
    Victoria.

MESSAGE FROM

Field-Marshal Sir W. R. Birdwood

G.C.M.G., K.C.B., K.C.S.I., C.I.E., D.S.O., A.D.C.

—◆—

I WELL remember the 39th coming over from Victoria to England to undergo its training, and then coming across with the 3rd Division to join the A.I.F. in France, where it arrived in time to take part in all the heavy fighting that went on in front of Ypres in 1917 and in those combats which we can never forget for Passchendaele Ridge of 1917.

The following year saw the battalion fighting in all the operations on the Somme and in front of Albert and Amiens, while later on the 39th took its full share in the final glory of forcing the Hindenburg Line, and working up by the St. Quentin Canal. Throughout the whole time of the existence of the battalion it never failed to show that magnificent spirit which actuated the whole of the troops who upheld the honour of Australia during the war, and I feel confident that the people of Victoria will never lose their pride in the men they sent forth to represent them.

FIELD-MARSHAL.

Simla,
    India.

AN APPRECIATION

Major-General Sir C. B. B. White

K.C.B., K.C.M.G., K.C.V.O., D.S.O., *p.s.c.*

—◆—

HOW quickly the past recedes into oblivion. The people of Australia, than whom none were more solicitous for their soldiers in the days of the Great War, have been so engrossed in the economic conflict of the present times that they have almost forgotten the Australian Imperial Force and its valorous deeds. Therein they have been in danger of losing an ideal and an inspiration. The events of the past few years and the courage displayed by the Australian people are, however, evidence of a response to the challenge of the past and it is not too much to say that the spirit of the people of to-day is the spirit of the Australian soldier of 1914-1918.

It is well however that we should keep our beacon lights burning. There has not yet been a word painting of the Australian soldier which has really lit a torch of lasting inspiration. Dr. C. E .W. Bean has written a work which as a military history stands alone and has set a standard for the future. Its truth, accuracy and detail make it a bible—an old testament record of the days of the A.I.F. From its source there will some day arise a new testament which will enlighten and inspire future generations.

This little history of the 39th Battalion is a stepping stone to that ideal. In simplicity it portrays the life and recounts the doings of a battalion of the Australian Imperial Force which nobly and with complete self-sacrifice sought to effect faithfully every task which it was set. The spirit of the men permeates every page. The little details of daily life will recall memories to other than men of the battalion. But the modest and simple recital of battle experiences, full of heroism, courage, fortitude and devotion must make the heart of every reader glow with pride. When the last page is turned we will all find ourselves saying—"Well done 39th! We would have been proud to have been one of you."

Brudenell White

MAJOR-GENERAL.

Melbourne,
   Victoria.

THE WRITING OF THE HISTORY

Lieut-Colonel A. T. Paterson

D.S.O., M.C., V.D.

—◆—

THIS History of the Thirty-Ninth Battalion, Australian Imperial Force, has been written as a tribute to its members who made the supreme sacrifice, and to those who gave their services willingly and cheerfully to their country during the best years of their lives.

After the cessation of hostilities, when the battalion was billeted at Bouillancourt-en-Sery, France, I thought that the task of collating necessary information for such a history should be commenced.

Officers, Non-Commissioned Officers, and Men were all invited to contribute—to tell of battles, camps, billets, and shipboard incidents of which they had personal knowledge.

Lieutenant P. V. Allan was relieved from his other duties and embarked upon the task of weaving the diverse information thus gained into a chronological story; and only those who later analysed his efforts know with what ability and enthusiasm he applied himself to the work. He laid the foundation on which this history has been built. The following members of the battalion materially assisted him:—Lieutenant J. S. August, Private J. Cleary, Sergeant B. R. Davies, Private H. E. Gazzard, Private H. B. Harris, Sergeant A. H. Hobba, Private F. A. Hoy, Sergeant F. H. Hubbard, Lance-Corporal M. C. Ireton, Lieutenant H. J. James, Sergeant C. Loxton, Lieutenant F. J. McEwan, Lance-Corporal A. E. Parrish, Lieutenant W. R. Powell, Lieutenant H. J.

Price, Lieutenant F. M. Shaw, Private J. Sheehan, Captain J. Stewart, and Sergeant G. E. Watkins.

Owing to the peculiar conditions which existed during the early post-war period, no attempt was made to complete the history until one member of the battalion revived the enthusiasm by donating £10 to a Battalion History Fund. A bank account was opened, other members were informed of the project, and the publishing fund rapidly grew to the gratifying total of over £600.

I then formed a Publication Committee, the members being Lieutenant G. S. Browne and Lieutenant G. H. Watkins, Sergeant A. Brooksbank and myself. Frequent meetings were held by these committee-men and their careful work and whole-hearted endeavours have contributed in a great measure to any success which the book may attain. They have been tireless in their ambition to make this record worthy of the battalion.

The difficult and less interesting work of compiling the Roll of Honour and Nominal Roll was undertaken by Company Sergeant-Major H. Johnson, who has been most self-sacrificing in effort and time in his endeavour to present only the most accurate records. Without his services and the valuable co-operation of the staff of Base Records, Melbourne, this history would not have been authentic.

For the voluntary efforts of many friends and well-wishers I am most grateful, and on behalf of the members of the battalion desire to express my thanks and appreciation to Field-Marshal Sir William Birdwood, Lieutenant-General Sir John Monash and Major-General Sir C. B. B. White.

Mr. Justice Russell Martin, Dr. C. E. W. Bean, Captain L. L. Beauchamp, Captain Roy Lamble, Lieutenant H. J. James, Lieutenant P. Neilson, and Charles Barrett, Esq., consented to revise the history prior to publication. Their efforts have added to the value of the book.

Corporal H. J. Sennett has kindly contributed pencil sketches which add a charm to the book.

Lieutenant J. S. August is responsible for the production of six of the maps embodied in the History, and for the adaptation of five others, which were generously donated for our use by the Fortieth Battalion Association. In the work of location, identification, photo-lithography and final revision, he was most ably assisted by Sergeant G. E. Watkins and Corporal A. B. C. Aldred.

In a task of this kind it is possible that the names of some who have contributed some features to the history have been inadvertently omitted. To any such I am just as grateful. Only the good feeling and happy co-operation of a number of friends of the old battalion have made this book possible.

I should like to add a few personal remarks as the commanding officer of the battalion in the field. Having left Australia with, and having been in command of the 39th when the safety of Amiens was threatened by the onrush of the enemy, during the Summer of 1918, I had every opportunity of seeing the men under all possible circumstances—when victory appeared far off, when it actually was achieved, and afterwards. Their fortitude, courage, and bearing have left an indelible impression on my mind. I am proud to have commanded such men, and happy in the knowledge that so many of the members of the battalion are amongst my most intimate friends to-day.

Naturally I have esteemed it an honour to have been the historian of the battalion, and trust that this history will be received by the members of the unit and those near to them as a worthy record of a worthy battalion.

A. T. PATERSON,

LIEUTENANT-COLONEL.

Ormond,
Victoria.

CHAPTER I.

The Empire's Call

Now's the day, and now's the hour:
See the front o' battle lour, —BURNS.

IN retrospect 1916 stands out as a crucial year in the World War. The allied nations had come to realize that early hopes of a speedy victory must be replaced by a determination to fight out to a finish the long and bitter campaign to which the previous 18 months had been but a prelude.

With all the enthusiasm of a young pioneering people, Australia had made an early answer to the Empire's call to arms.

That sense of moral obligation and burning patriotism possessed by an entirely volunteer army had already stood the stress and strain of battle and privation in the rigorous Gallipoli campaign.

Early in 1916 the depleted units of the Australian Expeditionary Force had been transferred from Gallipoli to play an equally arduous part alongside the seasoned armies in France.

Great Britain was making a tremendous effort to stimulate recruiting for the new Kitchener armies; the various Dominions were fully seized of the necessity of replenishing their own warwasted units in France. Australia went further than that in her determination to help the Allied cause. It was decided not only to maintain a steady flow of reinforcements to the fighting troops but also to form a new division—The Third.

The unconquerable tenacity and the fighting spirit of the Anzacs had inspired the people in Australia with a unity of sympathy and of purpose. Entirely of their own volition, keen, intelligent volunteers offered themselves at the various country recruiting centres for service abroad with the new division.

A battalion of the 10th Infantry Brigade was raised in each of the Ballarat, Bendigo and Seymour districts (Victoria) and in Tasmania.

On February 21, 1916, the 39th Battalion, A.I.F., was located at the Show Grounds, Ballarat, under the command of Lieut.-Colonel R. Rankine, D.S.O.

Ballarat is situated 74 miles north-west of Melbourne, the Capital of Victoria. As a city it is second only to Melbourne in importance, and for sheer beauty and advantages of climate it challenges any city in Australia for pride of place. Famous the world over for its production of gold, Ballarat has played an important part in the development of Australia. In no other period in the history of the continent has there been such expansion in population and such remarkable progress as during the gold-digging era.

Men of all callings and stations in life were brought together for a common purpose at the Ballarat Show Grounds camp. All traces of social distinction quickly vanished and these men and boys from the professions, from stations and farms, from offices and factories, and from schools and colleges were all intent on learning the grim business of war.

The early days of the battalion provided all with new and lasting experiences. Who can forget the issue of uniform—the attempted dodging of fatigue duties—being "picked" for guard—the inter-company night raids—the first taste of army "stu" and "bully" beef—church parades and their mournfully rendered hymns—the lively concert parties—the parcels from home—the doctor's lectures—the "awkward squad"—the embarrassment of being such a hero on the first visit home—all such episodes, and many more—who can forget them?

With its open spaces and beautiful park lands Ballarat provided excellent recruit-training grounds. The congenial surroundings and the salubrious climate made one glad to be alive—even while a recruit.

Ballarat literally adopted the men of the 39th. Concert parties were provided in the camp, entertainments for the troops were given in the city, sports meetings were held, and most welcome of all—throughout the whole of the period of intensive training, the homes of the people were thrown open to the men during their hours of recreation.

Fresh air, good food and plenty of it, and the healthy warmth of the Autumn sunshine coupled with the benefits of carefully-graduated military exercises made an astonishing difference to the physique of the men. Discipline crystallised gradually into a habit, but when off duty the troops were all the more eager to enjoy the hospitality and entertainment provided by Ballarat. The dry humour of the men often found ready expression in the everyday incidents of the camp.

At Ballarat friendships were formed which stood the test of the years to come. All will re-trace with pride and pleasure the making of these friendships in camp. But how they have lasted!

Towards the end of April there was "talk" of embarkation. The first "whisper" of this made the men stiffen up; they began to look on life more seriously. Soon, however, embarkation became a subject for camp jokes—suffering the same fate as every other military secret divulged only in low tones after "lights-out."

On May 15 the 39th entrained for Melbourne to take part in the 10th Brigade march through the city. The 37th Battalion (Seymour) and the 38th Battalion (Bendigo) also marched. Unfortunately the 40th Battalion (Tasmania) had not at that time left their island home for the mainland and therefore could not participate.

Starting from the Spencer Street Railway Station, the column proceeded through the city and received a rousing reception from the thousands who had turned out to do honour to the 10th Brigade. The saluting base was at the foot of the steps of Federal

Parliament House, Sir Ronald Munro Ferguson (now Viscount Novar), Governor-General of Australia, acknowledged the salute of the troops. It may be mentioned that the influence and example of the Governor-General, who was himself a graduate of the Royal Military College, Sandhurst, were greatly felt and appreciated in the military training establishments in Australia during the war.

Only those who have taken part in an embarkation march with their own unit through their own capital city in war-time can fully realize the thrill and emotion which it all causes—the cheers and faces of the crowd, the bands playing, the fixed bayonets, the tramp of feet in step, the feeling that one has the privilege of serving with real men.

After the march the battalion returned to Ballarat to undergo the "finishing touches" of training in Australia.

The battalions of the 10th Brigade—in common with the other battalions of the A.I.F.—were distinguished by colour patches worn upon the sleeves of the tunics of the men, about $1\frac{1}{2}$ inches below each shoulder. The colours of the 10th Brigade battalions were elliptical in shape, the foundation colour—red—being common to each unit. The distinctive battalion colours were:—37th Battalion, black over red; 38th Battalion, purple over red; 39th Battalion, brown over red; and 40th Battalion, white over red.

A few days before embarkation, the citizens of Ballarat gave the battalion a farewell concert in the Coliseum. Neither trouble nor expense had been spared in making the function an entire success; and the men of the 39th are most grateful to their foster parents—the people of Ballarat—for their many kindnesses and "home touches" during the days of the camp.

The last fortnight was busy for all ranks, this being the time of final leave. Training had to continue, and the details ordinarily associated with "shifting house" were multiplied a thousand times when camp was struck.

Ballarat, Victoria

On May 25, the battalion baggage guard, lustily cheered by all who remained, left for Port Melbourne.

May 26 was the last day in camp. A concert party chased away the sadness of the last night. The next morning saw Ballarat and the camp astir early. Reveille was at 2 a.m.

The battalion, headed by its band, marched through the streets at 3 a.m. whilst thousands of people lined the route. The onlookers and the men of the battalion, true to their national tradition, tried to stifle their emotion. However, sadness seemed to be in the air. Scenes of touching incidents along the route made this short march an unforgettable experience for all.

Despite the posting of a guard on station entrances to keep the public from the platforms, people swarmed in. The authorities could afford to interpret instructions liberally enough to be indulgent to those who had done so much for the departing battalion. The first troop train left Ballarat for Port Melbourne punctually at 4 a.m. on May 27, 1916.

At 11 a.m. the troop trains drew alongside His Majesty's Australian Troopship A.11, the official designation of the S.S. "Ascanius."

The men were paraded on the pier; rolls called; and embarkation completed.

Immediately the public barriers were removed the people flocked to the edge of the wharf.

Great excitement tinged with high spirits and some sadness prevailed. From every vantage point on shore and aboard, friends, relations, and sweethearts bade each other farewell.

The band played. Messages were written and exchanged under great difficulties. Paper streamers formed a last tangible link between those on shore and aboard.

A sudden bustle of activity became noticeable on board the ship. Cables were slipped; winches grated and grated again; the siren abruptly announced at 1.20 p.m. that the time for farewells had ended. There was singing; there was cheering; there was waving. The khaki-clad figures aboard became more indistinct; the faces ashore became less discernible.

The A.11 was really under weigh.

Down the forty mile stretch of bay before the Heads were reached, the sights were familiar to all. Williamstown, St. Kilda, Brighton, Sandringham, Frankston, Sorrento, Corio Bay, Queenscliff—what memories?

At 6 p.m. the pilot was dropped, taking with him a few letters for home and the sternly prohibited stowaway—the crestfallen and lamented bull-dog-mascot of the 39th Battalion.

Just at dusk the A.11 received a signal-lamp message flashed from the pilot ship—"Good-bye and Good Luck."

H.M.A.T. A.11 was then headed towards the Otway light.

The 39th Battalion, A.I.F., was on its way to the Great Adventure.

H.M.A.T. A.11 "Ascanius," with 39th Battalion A.I.F. on Board, at Port Melbourne

CHAPTER II.

Outward Bound

*Pull out, pull out, on the Long Trail—
the trail that is always new!* —KIPLING.

THOSE who "go down to the sea in ships" know many and varied types of craft, but one class of vessel it is not often given to the average seafarer to voyage in and to know. Those units of His Majesty's fleet of troopships which have carried the Empire's armies over the high seas are types entirely distinct from the mass of ocean traffic. The liners and cargo carriers of a former day, they have an individuality and an atmosphere which are wholly their own. And so it was with the "Ascanius."

On a "trooper" the men live on troopdecks. These are constructed in what formerly was hold space, and are chiefly remarkable for the kind of mess tables which are installed. These tables—which normally accommodate twenty men per table—are placed on either side, along the entire length of the deck, leaving a broad aisle between, in which the arm racks are placed. Long forms provide seating accommodation, whilst directly overhead are hooks from which hammocks and racks for equipment are slung. At either end of the decks are bins in which hammocks are stowed when not in use. The decks are lit by electricity and ventilated by hatchways, and by canvas ventilators arranged on the same principle as the ordinary ship's ventilators.

Each table is numbered and known as a "mess" and for the voyage every man is allotted to one of these messes. Each mess has two orderlies who are usually appointed to the duty for the voyage, and whose work it is to carry the food for every man from the ship's galley, to wash the eating utensils, and to keep the table and its surroundings spotlessly clean. They are generally exempted from all other duties on board.

For the voyage every troopdeck is put in charge of a N.C.O. He is responsible for the order and general cleanliness of his deck, and sees that the men comply with the regulations of the ship.

Officers are given first class, and senior N.C.Os., on most troopships, second class cabins. Canteens are carried on board where biscuits, tobacco and tinned goods may be obtained. Such were the general arrangements on the "Ascanius."

The first days at sea were passed in recovering from the evil effects of seasickness and in settling down to the daily routine of the ship. Sick parades were popular and largely attended during these early days, whereas the number who turned up for meals when "cookhouse" was sounded was remarkably small.

The hour of reveille was 6 o'clock each morning. Every man had to be out and his hammock neatly rolled and stacked in the bin before breakfast.

The mornings and afternoons were occupied in physical drill, musketry exercises and lectures on deck, when sea and weather permitted. Available deck space was governed by the number of troops on board, and the amount of actual training accomplished was correspondingly small. Fatigues were plentiful.

The ship was inspected each day by the O.C. troops and the Captain of the ship, and woe betide any luckless mess orderly who left a spot of grease on his table or a speck of dirt on the floor.

After a time keen competition sprang up between the various troopdecks, and each deck tried to excel in its spick and span appearance when ship's inspection came round.

After the first week at sea the men began to find their sea legs and, having conquered the unpleasant spasms of seasickness, quickly became accustomed to their new surroundings.

The "Ascanius" was soon ploughing her way through the heavy swells of the Bight, and, as day succeeded day bringing the same vista of grey sky and sea, with only now and then the distant sight of a passing ship to relieve its monotony, the sameness of life began to pall a little.

Letter writing filled many of the spare hours. Countless long descriptive epistles were written and the ship's censors found their days busily occupied.

Deck concerts were frequent when the weather was not too inclement, and the 39th Battalion band provided music daily. These band concerts were greatly appreciated. Music on the sea has a charm and a quality entirely unique, and familiar song and dance tunes played on the swaying decks held their listeners enthralled through long hours of the early days of the voyage.

On Sundays church parades were held, when the "padres" delivered stirring soldier sermons with a hatch as pulpit and the deck for church. There could have been many worse settings for a service than that provided by the deck of the "Ascanius" with the clear canopy of the sky for roof and the strong clear winds of the ocean sweeping across.

Boat drills were ordered often during these first weeks at sea, and practice alarms sounded at many unexpected moments to accustom the men to move rapidly and without confusion to their boat stations.

Ocean travelling at this time was accompanied by many perils. German raiders were still plying their piratical business on the high seas, and the trade routes were never quite safe from lurking submarines. When the "Ascanius" was in the Indian Ocean a submarine guard was posted round the ship. Its duty was to maintain a sharp look-out for enemy periscopes and conning towers and to give immediate alarm if one were sighted.

During the first days of this guard's duties, the keen eyes of the sentries saw whole fleets of submarines, but these fortunately materialised into flotsam in the shape of barrels and boxes.

The Marconi installation kept those on board informed of the march of events in the world, and on June 13, there was great jubilation when the news of the Russian success against the Austrians was received.

Only two days later all on board were dismayed by the announcement of Lord Kitchener's death. On the "Ascanius" it created an atmosphere of gloom. Next day an impressive "In Memoriam" service was held on deck, at the conclusion of which the "Last Post" was sounded by the buglers—a soldiers' tribute to a great soldier and a great man.

On the same day the dim outlines of the African coast were seen on the horizon. The first land seen since leaving Australia, it created quite a stir on board, and men thronged the sides of the ship all day. During the afternoon the course of the "Ascanius" took her closer inshore, and a clear view of the coast of Cape Colony could be obtained. The shores were very sandy and seemed to consist of a long line of low dunes receding far inland; in the distance a range of hills was seen against the sky.

A great bush fire was burning ashore and, as the evening advanced, the sky was lit up with brilliant red light, the reflection of which, thrown back on the sea, created a weird yet beautiful effect. Some very considerable expanse of country must have been in flames, for throughout the night as the ship steamed along the coast, sky and sea were lit up quite brilliantly.

The following day brought with it typical Cape weather and the "Ascanius" pushed her way through mountainous seas which swept her forward decks and battered against her sides.

At 4 a.m. on Sunday, June 18, the "Ascanius" entered Table Bay. The men were on deck early that morning and crowded along the rail watching the searchlights which swept across the bay as the ship steamed towards Cape Town. The lights of the city were visible in the distance, and at dawn the great fantastic outlines of the mountains looming against the sky could be seen through the mist.

As the ship neared the docks, the panorama widened and the houses of the city could be clearly seen clustering round the base of Table Mountain. On the left the sharp silhouette of Devil's Peak jutted up into the blue, whilst to the right the grass-covered slopes of Lion's Head looked down on the waters of the Bay.

On the pier a motley crowd of chattering natives and a few whites were standing watching the "Ascanius" as she came alongside and made fast. The natives excited much interest on the crowded decks of the troopship. The Port Medical Officer came aboard and to the disappointment of the men placed the ship in quarantine. The sight of the yellow flag fluttering from the masthead gave the deathblow to long cherished dreams of a brief spell of freedom in Africa. A compensating announcement was made, however, to the effect that route marches would be permitted and arranged during the time the "Ascanius" lay in port.

At 2 p.m. that day the first of these marches took place. The men, eager after their long spell in confined quarters to feel solid earth under them again, scrambled ashore and fell in on the pier. Headed by the band they marched out of the docks and through part of the town, followed by what seemed to be the major part of the native population.

The Cape Town natives are a strange polyglot people. Every type and every colour under the sun can be seen in the streets, their faces varying from pale mustard through cinnamon and brown to pitch black. Representative types of several native races have drifted to Cape Town—Hottentots, Basutos, Swazis and Kaffirs, coolies from Natal sugar plantations—here and there the stately figure of a Zulu, standing out vividly among the rest by reason of his magnificent physique. Scores of little half-clad piccaninnies ran about the streets.

These blacks, selling fruit, chocolate and cigarettes, ran alongside the marching ranks, and amid much chaff from the "diggers" succeeded in disposing of their stock at prices which were often ruinously high.

This first view of Cape Town created lasting good impressions, due chiefly to the extreme cordiality which marked the reception of the Australian troops by the people of the city. Magazines, chocolate, fruit, cigarettes—anything which the people could think of and buy on the spur of the moment—were thrown to the men, and every possible expression of welcome and goodwill was extended to them as they passed. Every Australian who has halted awhile at South African ports on his journey to Europe will have memories of the warm-hearted welcome given to him.

The march, practically the first exercise for the legs for three weeks, was not a long one, but the men returned to the ship feeling tired and hungry. When limbs have been confined to the narrow spaces of shipboard for long, it takes little to fatigue them.

Two other Australian transports lay at anchor in Table Bay when the "Ascanius" arrived, the "Medic" and the "Demosthenes" with H.M.S. "Laconia" as guardian escort. Yet another troopship was expected, and on her arrival the ships, including the "Ascanius," were to leave port as one convoy.

The following day, June 19, the men on the "Ascanius" were marched out to the seaside suburb of Green Point, situated on the shores of Table Bay. Accompanied by the inevitable following of black boys with their trays of goods for sale, the men marched to the Point by well made roads, lined with pretty villas standing amid gardens of luxuriant foliage, and thence to a near-by common where they halted for dinner.

About 3.30 p.m. the march back to the docks was commenced. When the men arrived the "Ascanius" was in the midst of coaling. Her decks were covered by a black carpet of fine dust which had penetrated to the remotest parts of the ship. The work of coaling was continued through the night, and the din of the winches and the ceaseless chatter and shouting of the Kaffir workmen as the bunkers were being filled made sleep impossible.

Lieut.-Colonel R. Rankine, D.S.O.

For Tuesday, June 20, a route march to the Rhodes' Memorial at Groot Schuur had been arranged. The day dawned clear, with a promise of heat in the sky. The men, carrying their mid-day meal with them, assembled on the pier and marched out to the west of the city by the road running round the base of Devil's Peak. As the houses were left behind, many small native settlements were passed. Kaffir washerwomen were busy at their tubs, and a variety of garments drying in the sun covered each bush and rock in the vicinity. Small naked children sprawled on the ground in the shade. Many of them ran excitedly out to the road when they heard the strains of the band. To the right, the slopes of Devil's Peak, clothed by a mantle of sub-tropical trees and shrubs in all their beauty and variety of foliage, towered up into a cloudless sky.

About 11 a.m. the column reached the Zoological Gardens of Groot Schuur and marched through the adjoining park lands. An appropriate welcome was given to the men from Australia by an exceedingly fine specimen of kangaroo which came bounding over the grass to greet his fellow countrymen.

Shortly afterwards the men halted for lunch. The day had turned out to be exceedingly hot, and the last few miles of uphill road had rendered a rest both necessary and welcome.

Continuing its march, the column reached the magnificent memorial erected to the memory of that great Empire builder and pioneer of British Colonisation in Africa, Cecil Rhodes.

The view over Cape Town and Table Bay from the site of the Rhodes' Memorial is particularly fine. A spot sacred to the memory of our greatest Imperialist, it is the goal of many pilgrimages and is regarded as one of Cape Town's most interesting features. On the journey back to the ship the route followed was through Adderley Street and the main thoroughfares of the city, and here again the troops received a warm reception from the people. Many of the men reached the ship laden with tokens of Cape Town's goodwill.

This was the last night in port and accordingly a patrol was despatched into the city to round up any stragglers who might have taken temporary and unauthorised leave of absence. Leave had been entirely prohibited, but certain of the wilder and more adventurous spirits had succumbed to the temptation of a day's liberty and had succeeded in evading the vigilance of the guard on the gangway. One private of the 39th accomplished an ingenious and most successful coup of this kind. Watching his opportunity, he curled himself into an empty coal basket, was hoisted overboard by the winches and deposited on a truck. The effects of his short sojourn in the basket were so marked that, without any difficulty he was able to pass as one of the black stevedores and so make good his escape into the town. During the morning of the 21st the men were taken for a short route march in the direction of Sea Point. They halted on the same common which they had previously visited and made their midday meal of the sandwiches brought with them, supplemented by such articles of food as could be purchased from the black vendors.

Everyone was on board again by 3.30 p.m., and an hour later the "Ascanius" cast off her mooring ropes, and with the band playing, and the crowd on the wharf cheering, she moved out into the bay to join the small fleet of Australian troopships, and dropped anchor alongside the "Demosthenes."

During the morning the "Warilda" had arrived in Table Bay. She was the last ship to join the convoy, and this being now complete H.M.S. "Laconia" sent the following message:—"Transports to be ready to move off at 7 a.m., 22-6-16."

At 7.30 a.m. on the Thursday morning H.M.S. "Laconia" steamed out of Table Bay, followed by the four troopships "Medic," "Demosthenes," "Warilda" and "Ascanius." The shores were shrouded in mist and the convoy crept out to sea unseen.

The Band

Facing Page 42

All the stragglers had rejoined the ship with the exception of two who were still missing at the hour of departure.

The pleasant interlude afforded by the brief stay at the Cape had been full of interest, and had benefited the troops in no small measure; physically in enabling them to obtain much needed exercise, and mentally in refreshing and stimulating minds jaded by the monotony of a long voyage. Their behaviour had been in every respect exemplary, and the Chief of the Cape Town Police complimented them on their discipline. This thoughtful action of his was much appreciated by all ranks.

On leaving Table Bay the convoy entered Atlantic waters, and the danger from enemy craft became greater. More stringent precautions, which the ship's guard had orders to enforce, were observed. Lights on deck were strictly forbidden. Deadlights were fastened over the portholes in the evenings, and through the hours of the night the convoy followed its course silently and in total darkness. During the day the men drilled and worked beside their boat stations in order to minimise delay and confusion in the event of an alarm.

At Cape Town a naval gun had been mounted on board and naval ratings put in charge. They were always standing by for instant action, while a vigilant look-out was maintained by the submarine guard.

Despite these ominous precautions the utmost confidence was felt in the ships. The White Ensign fluttering from the jack staff of the "Laconia"—a symbol of the powerful and ever present protection of the British Navy—inspired everyone with a sense of complete security.

On June 24, the convoy entered the tropics, and from that day on the weather grew steadily warmer and the sea smoother as equatorial waters were neared. All day long the sun blazed down out of the blue tropic skies. The ocean's surface was like a vast sheet of glass unbroken save where the bow of the "Ascanius" threw back rippling waves.

The men lived on deck—dressed only in singlets and shorts. Their faces and limbs became tanned by exposure to sun and salt air. The atmosphere below became intolerably close, and at night the decks were crowded with hammocks slung from every possible point. Some men slept peacefully suspended from a spar many feet above the level of the deck, while others preferred the greater security of a hatch cover. Advantage was taken of the dry atmosphere to wash clothes, and every day the ship was gaily bedecked from stem to stern with shirts and a variety of clothes waving in the wind.

As the voyage proceeded the heat became still greater. Flying fish skimmed the surface of the water all day and at night the phosphorescence of the sea glimmered faintly like liquid fire along the ship's sides.

Each evening the sun went down in a gorgeous blaze of colour. The western sky at sunset became a wonderland of reds and greens and saffrons, succeeded by the delicate changing shades of the short tropical afterglow. Then with almost startling suddenness night would come.

On Saturday, July 1, the convoy crossed the Equator. The time honoured deep-sea ceremony was not observed on the "Ascanius," and indeed had it been, the salt-water monarch Neptune would have found that to initiate 1600 men into the mysteries attending the crossing of the line was a somewhat tall order.

The following day, July 2, the first and only death in the convoy took place on the troopship "Medic." All the ships stopped their engines and hove to, as the body of an Australian artilleryman was laid to rest in the deep waters of the Gulf of Guinea.

The next day brought the startling news that an enemy raider was abroad in these waters. A passing vessel wirelessed a warning and stated that she had actually been pursued by the enemy craft. The utmost watchfulness was observed on every ship, but the voyage proceeded without any abnormal event to mar its tranquility.

A somewhat amusing incident happened on the "Ascanius" about this time. Some food provided for the men's dinner was found to be tainted, and a mock burial of this undesirable item was arranged. The soldiers marched round the ship exhibiting the "corpse" on high, after which it was solemnly lowered overboard to the accompaniment of hymns chanted by the assembled "diggers." Apart from this one instance the food for all ranks was exceedingly good.

On July 6, the rocky shores of the Cape Verde Islands were sighted, and on the following day the convoy anchored in the harbour of St. Vincent, the capital of the Portuguese colony of Cape Verde. These islands are barren and mountainous. The climate is unhealthy and the rainfall exceptionally small. There is a dearth of vegetation on the slopes of the hills—cactus being almost the only form of flora which can withstand the arid nature of the soil. The harbour was full of ships when the Australian convoy arrived, many of these being German vessels interned by the Portuguese authorities. His Majesty's cruisers "Ophir" and "Kent" lay at anchor. The troopships were quickly surrounded by a small fleet of rowing boats full of a variety of goods which enterprising black and half-caste vendors sold to the soldiers by the medium of baskets in which the articles purchased were hauled up to the deck. Native diving boys provided much entertainment for the soldiers, and reaped an abundant financial harvest by displaying their skill in recovering from the water coins thrown from the ships. Two days were spent at St. Vincent during which the men amused themselves by fishing over the ship's sides. The harbour was full of fish and many good hauls were recorded. Swimming was unfortunately an impossibility, the water here being infested by sharks.

On Sunday, July 9, the convoy left St. Vincent and entered on the third and final stages of its voyage. The crews of the

British warships manned their decks and "cheered ship" as the troopships steamed out—a warm-hearted and typically British way the Navy has of expressing its feelings.

From this time on life-belts had to be worn continually by everyone on board, since the perilous waters of the Bay of Biscay and the English Channel were near.

On July 12 the "Demosthenes" developed engine trouble and was compelled to leave the convoy and put in at the nearest port in order that necessary repairs might be effected.

The Bay of Biscay was entered during the morning of Sunday, July 16, and during this most critical period of the whole voyage still greater precautions against disaster were observed. The men had to be near their boat stations all day, guards and look-outs were doubled, and the guns of the escorting cruiser covered every passing vessel until her identity and good intentions had been established.

On the 16th, a wireless message was sent from the "Laconia" stating that the rendezvous would be reached at 5 a.m. on the 17th. At this point a destroyer escort was to meet the convoy and conduct it into port. At 6 a.m. on the 17th the long low outlines of four destroyers glided out of the fog and took up position—one in front of each transport. T.B.D. "Larne," No. 57, was escort for the "Ascanius," and with this additional protection she proceeded to her destination.

Early in the morning of Tuesday, July 18, the rocks of Land's End could be seen dimly through the Channel fog, and the sides of every ship became lined with men eager for their first glimpse of England. A cold breeze was blowing and the sea was choppy. Numerous destroyers and torpedo boat patrols were steaming to and fro engaged in their duty of guarding the South Coast. During the morning the Eddystone Lighthouse was passed, and the cliffs and green fields of Devon made a pleasing picture after the long weeks at sea.

At 11 a.m. the "Ascanius" dropped anchor in Plymouth Sound and lay there until early in the afternoon, when she moved to Devonport, where the long 52 days' voyage came to an end.

Disembarkation was at once proceeded with, and the men were rapidly transferred to troop trains which were waiting alongside the docks. They entrained in two sections, the first train leaving at 5.30 p.m., and the second an hour and a half later.

It was midsummer in England and this railway journey took the men through the loveliest countryside in the British Isles. Devon, with its hedges and lanes, its trim fields and its pretty quaint villages seen in the soft glow of the long English twilight, impressed the men from overseas very greatly: and they leaned from the carriage windows gazing with appreciative eyes at the changing panorama of wooded valleys and purple moors until at last darkness curtained the view.

The trains stopped at Exeter for a short time, and here refreshments—provided and served by the Mayoress of Exeter and lady helpers—were ready for the hungry men.

The battalion detrained at Amesbury, on Salisbury Plain, shortly after midnight and marched two miles to No. 7 Camp, Larkhill, where, after hot drinks had been served, the weary men lay down to sleep.

The fourth phase of the journey had come to an end.

CHAPTER III.

On Salisbury Plain

*What have I done for you,
England, my England?
What is there I would not do,
England, my own?* —HENLEY.

SALISBURY PLAIN has been the theatre in which many of the stirring parts played by British soldiers in the wider arenas of Flanders and Picardy have been rehearsed. The arrival of the 3rd Australian Division in England saw the establishment of many large Australian camps on the Wiltshire Downs; and within a few weeks the camps of Larkhill, Bulford, Tidworth and many others were garrisoned by Australian soldiers. Soon the training which proved the foundation of the Division's future prowess in the field was in full swing.

The many large camps which covered the wide expanse of Salisbury Plain were in every respect well-constructed and made as comfortable as circumstances and local conditions would permit.

The Division arrived in England at a time when the English climate, usually so trying, was at its best; and the training throughout the Summer months proceeded under ideal conditions.

Larkhill is situated near the famous prehistoric monument of Stonehenge, two miles from the village of Amesbury, and some six or seven miles distant from Salisbury City. In 1916 Larkhill was a veritable town of soldiers, and indeed a bird's eye view of the camp was more like a city than a military encampment. As far as the eye could see, stretched streets of huts, with here and there the gaudy front of a camp theatre or cinema palace; small booths and shops lined the roads which were always busy with military transport; Y.M.C.A. huts and camp churches could be seen among the buildings.

Surrounding the camps, the plain stretched away for miles on all sides—great sweeps of gently undulating downs on which men marched, drilled, dug trenches and won imaginary battles all day long.

No. 7 Camp, in which was quartered the 39th Battalion, was in every way comfortable and commodious. The quarters consisted of long huts, wide and spacious, well lit, warmed and ventilated, each accommodating thirty men. They were not merely sleeping places. They were also living rooms in which the men could sit comfortably and read, write letters, or while away the evenings yarning round the stove. The "beds" were made up of bed boards on trestles—each bed comprising three six foot boards supported by two low trestles and surmounted by a straw palliasse. There were forms and tables in each hut, while shelves and hooks on which clothing and equipment could be hung lined the walls. Two large mess rooms, each capable of seating two companies and each having its cookhouse and sculleries adjoining, provided messing accommodation for the battalion. In these, excellent meals were served and partaken of in comfort and under conditions of marked cleanliness. In the centre of the camp was a well-stocked canteen, with recreation rooms, containing writing tables, pianos and a supply of periodicals and newspapers from home. Here the men could spend their evenings pleasantly—reading, writing or listening to the concerts which were from time to time arranged.

An adequacy of ablution sheds, with water laid on, adjoined the huts; and excellent shower baths, hot and cold, could be indulged in as often as the men wished.

Each camp in Larkhill was equipped in a similar manner, every unit being self-contained, and not dependent on any other

In Camp

part of the camp for anything necessary to the comfort and well-being of its men.

There were several large camp theatres in Larkhill, where variety entertainments and occasional blood curdling melodramas were staged. These were well patronised in the evenings, as also were the cinema theatres and the Y.M.C.A. concerts.

The 39th quickly settled down in its new surroundings, and before many days had passed, the usual military routine was established and training continued from the point where it had ceased at Ballarat.

The first "red letter day" at Larkhill came with the arrival of a record Australian mail on July 22. This brought the first news from home for about two months, and nothing could have been more welcome to the men than the big bundles of letters which were distributed to their eager recipients by the camp post office man. All the spare time during the succeeding days was occupied in answering the numerous letters received, even men who had hardly ever put pen to paper in their lives being stimulated to descriptive effort. Among these latter, the following example may perhaps be taken as typical. An up-country member of the battalion who could not remember having written a letter in his life, addressed his brother briefly and to the point as follows:—

"Dear Bill,
O.K.
Jim."

A slight outbreak of measles which occurred on the second day in Larkhill resulted in the camp being isolated for four days, and it was not until this ban of quarantine was removed that the men were able to visit the adjacent country. Stonehenge attracted many sightseers. This ancient temple of the Stone Age was quite near to the camp, and in the Summer evenings numbers of the men walked over to gaze on the massive stone slabs which had witnessed many ancient rites, and which have so well withstood the wear and tear of countless centuries. A police constable well versed in the history and legends of Stonehenge was always on duty there, and he had a large and interested audience of Australians to listen to his recital of what is known as to the origin and building of this strange temple of prehistoric Britain.

On July 27 a furore of excitement was created in the battalion by the announcement that four days leave would be granted to all ranks commencing from the following morning. The majority of the men had relatives in the United Kingdom whom they were anxious to visit, while those who had no such ties of kindred were eager to see the sights of London and other cities of the British Isles.

Before dispersing to the various destinations the men were taken in a body to the London Headquarters of the Australian Imperial Force in Horseferry Road, Westminster. Leaving the Station at Waterloo, they marched through the streets of the city, crossing Westminster Bridge and passing the Houses of Parliament and Westminster Abbey. It was a memorable day for many, and the short march from the station to the Australian Headquarters formed a fitting introduction to London, affording as it did an early opportunity to view and admire the nation's greatest landmarks in history and architecture.

On arrival at Horseferry Road, that well-known rendezvous of Australian soldiers in London, the men were given as much information regarding accommodation, railway travelling, and sight-seeing, as would be useful to them during their leave; after which they were dismissed, some to catch North-bound trains from the great railway stations, others to seek hotels and consult the theatre bills.

That first leave with its varied and interesting experiences can be passed over briefly. Many other furloughs, longer and more memorable, fell to the men of the battalion later on, and whole volumes could be written dealing with the many adventures which came the way of the heroes of this story while holiday-making in England.

Suffice it to say that for four days the men filled every moment of their time seeing the great show places of the metropolis; gazing at the masterpieces of the National Gallery; standing under the great dome of St. Paul's; visiting the Royal tombs in the Abbey; inspecting the Crown jewels in the Tower; wandering along shady paths and well-kept lawns at Hampton Court—until at last it was time to go back to the less attractive but more important business of soldiering.

On the return to camp, training began in grim earnest. It may well be said that the training of the battalion did not commence until it reached Salisbury Plain. The preliminary military instruction the men had received in the camps of the Commonwealth had formed little else but the ground-work. Now they had to begin to learn the business of modern war, the use of new weapons and the mysteries of attack and defence in trench warfare.

The battalions of the 10th Brigade were keen and ready for hard work, and it certainly was hard work. Before an infantryman can take his place as an efficient soldier in a front line trench under modern conditions of warfare he has much to learn and many experiences to undergo. He must learn to kill with bullet, bomb and bayonet; to defend himself against poison gas and other such weapons as German "Kultur" had introduced into war; to dig trenches; put up barbed wire entanglements; master the hazardous duties of scouts and patrols. These and other details of training too numerous to be mentioned here were included in the battalion's daily routine at Larkhill.

Early in August a Light Trench Mortar Battery was formed in the Brigade. To this unit the battalion contributed two of its officers and a number of non-commissioned officers and men, all of fine physique and admirably fitted for the special work. Shortly after this the first reinforcements, which had up to then been training with the battalion, were transferred to the 10th Training Battalion, there to continue their preparation for active service until such time as they were required to fill gaps caused through casualties.

Apart from the ordinary routine, attention was given to the training of specialists. In this category were classed scouts, bombers, Lewis gunners and signallers. They had to learn their special duties in addition to mastering the work of a trained infantry soldier. Much of this training was carried on under Brigade organisation, bombing and signalling schools being instituted for this purpose. Bombing provided much excitement, and especially so when the practices were carried out with live bombs. The bomb at this period of the war was regarded as the principal weapon in trench warfare. The rifle had, under the new conditions of the modern battlefield, fallen from the priority of place which it was to regain later, and bombing in 1916 was a highly important part of the infantryman's training. The initial practices were carried out with dummies which were superseded at a later stage by live bombs. The bombing instruction in the 39th Battalion was under the supervision of Lieutenant L. Roberts, and never failed to create great interest among the pupils.

Lewis gunnery was another subject in the training syllabus which claimed much attention. Lieutenant J. Stewart as Lewis Gun Officer supervised the training. The Lewis gun, which later played so great and decisive a part in the operations at the front, was coming to be recognised as a weapon of undoubted power and possibilities. In addition to the personnel of the Lewis Gun Sections all men in the battalion were taught to handle and use the gun. It was new work and therefore held a greater fascination and interest than it otherwise might have done, the keen spirit in which the men tackled their work making progress rapid.

On August 26, all ranks were inoculated against typhoid fever. The resulting swollen arms put a majority of the men out of action for a few hours, but the training was only interrupted for a brief day. On the 28th the troops set out on a march to the village of Nether Wallop, twelve miles away, to practise a tactical exercise and billeting scheme under conditions akin to active service. These conditions were rendered more realistic and correspondingly uncomfortable by the co-operation of the elements. Rain in torrents fell during the two days' absence from camp. The available accommodation at Nether Wallop was totally inadequate, and the men slept under haystacks and in barns and cowsheds. As a foretaste of life on the western front, this experience was admirable and instructive, but it was a very weary and wet battalion which returned to Larkhill on August 29.

After undergoing, on September 4, a second para-typhoid inoculation, the battalion left camp the following day to carry out its second tactical operation. This took the form of a night march to the village of Orcheston where the 37th Battalion, which had been training there, was relieved. The 39th bivouacked in the open, and for two days the men were taught and practised construction of trenches. Those engaged in specialist training remained at Larkhill during these manoeuvres to carry on work in their respective branches.

Despite the unsettled weather, the operation was in every respect a complete success and much valuable experience was gained.

The inevitable monotony of camp routine and training was relieved during the leisure hours by walks in the surrounding country and visits to the picturesque villages for which the south of England is so justly celebrated.

The villages of Salisbury Plain are among the most beautiful that England can boast. Most of them consist of groups of tiny thatched cottages half-hidden among spreading oaks and elms. Church towers centuries old rise among the trees, and on Sunday mornings the bells from a score of these villages sound melodious chimes over the plain.

Before the far-reaching influence of the war came, these country villages had slumbered from year to year in the unbroken peace of their rural surroundings. Now, the tramp of battalions from the other side of the world resounded on the roads where once Cromwell's Ironsides had ridden; and men from Australia passed to and fro gazing with undisguised interest and curiosity at the beautiful country-side.

Salisbury, with its stately old cathedral and narrow streets of historic houses, was sufficiently near for occasional visits, and, when opportunities presented themselves, numbers of the men went to the city.

During the afternoon of September 20, an inspection and march-past of the 10th Brigade took place close to Stonehenge. The inspecting officer was the Divisional Commander, Major-General John Monash, V.D. After the march past he complimented the members of the Brigade on their turn-out and soldierly bearing.

Shooting practices were carried out on the local ranges, notably at Durrington, a village nestling in a hollow about a mile distant from the camp. This form of instruction was varied slightly by field practices at figure targets.

About this time it became known that His Majesty the King was to review the 3rd Australian Division at Bulford on September 27, and the few days prior to the review were occupied in a preparatory rehearsal.

There ensued much cleaning and polishing of arms and equipment, the "diggers'" democratic Australian comments on Royal reviews being terse and humorous. Yet, despite the manifest disapproval of ceremonial parades, there was not a man who would willingly have been absent from this review, which promised to be unprecedented as a military spectacle in the history of the Australian Army.

On the morning of the 27th the country roads of Salisbury Plain were full of Australian soldiers marching to the rendezvous at Bulford. Tidworth, Larkhill, Rollestone and all the other camps on the plain sent their quotas, led by the bands of their respective units. Artillery and infantry could be seen moving over the Downs on all sides, towards the place of assembly. The review was held, near to the village and camp of Bulford, on an open stretch of meadowland, sheltered along its entire length by pine woods.

On the fringe of the trees an enclosure had been railed off in which stood a flagstaff to mark the saluting base.

Along the opposite side of the field the division formed up in line of battalions in column, a great stretch of khaki-clad humanity as far as the eye could see. Behind the railings at the saluting base a large crowd had congregated, in which were many wounded Australian soldiers and nursing sisters from Hospitals on Salisbury Plain. Someone had brought a small kangaroo, evidently a regimental mascot, which caused much amusement among the crowd as it hopped to and fro about the enclosure.

The troops sat in little groups on the grass, smoking and yarning contentedly at their ease as they waited, yet ready to be in position at a moment's notice.

Suddenly a bugle sounded a long low note. In less than a minute, officers and men were in position and stood steadily waiting events. There was a stir among the assembly at the saluting base, as two motor cars glided up and came to a standstill. A moment's pause, then the great parade presented arms, and the hand of every officer came to the salute as the Royal Standard was unfurled from the flagstaff, and the massed bands burst into the strains of the National Anthem. The King had arrived.

His Majesty King George V., accompanied by his Staff and the Divisional Commander, then made his tour of inspection of the parade, after which, mounted on a magnificent black charger, he took the salute as the troops marched past. Led by the batteries of Field Artillery, their guns moving wheel to wheel, the division marched past magnificently. For well over an hour the spectators were held in admiration as the long lines of marching men passed before the King. Overhead an aeroplane patrolled ceaselessly to and fro, seen every now and then amid the rifts in the low clouds.

After passing the saluting base, the men lined the road along which His Majesty was to ride when departing. There they sat eating their lunches of sandwiches and biscuits—a good humoured happy-go-lucky crowd of Australians in high spirits despite the grey skies and the drizzle which was falling.

As the King rode out on his homeward journey, all rose to their feet, thousands of Australians' wide brimmed hats were waved in the air to the accompaniment of a mighty salvo of cheering which echoed and re-echoed across the Downs. The King's face, which had been gravely set all day, broke into a smile as he rode through the great assembly of troops, quieting his nervous mount with gentle caresses. He was very evidently pleased and gratified by the enthusiasm manifested by the men.

After His Majesty had departed, the battalions marched back to camp in the rain which was every moment falling more heavily.

The prevailing impression left by the day's experiences was one of regret that the people of the Commonwealth could not have themselves witnessed this historic review of one of her fighting divisions. The physique, the bearing and the marching of the troops were excellent, and little doubt could have been left in the minds of the onlookers that these men would, when their time came, worthily uphold and add to the highest traditions of the British race.

The next event which broke the routine at Larkhill was a 3rd Divisional Sports Meeting, which was held near Durrington. All troops in camp were granted a holiday, and the meeting was in every sense a brilliant success. Many mounted events had been arranged, and the transport units of the Division, newly equipped with horses and mules, entered many of their animals

Amesbury, Salisbury Plain, England

in the jumping and riding competitions. These mules, the majority of which had just arrived from South America, caused great excitement among the spectators by their display of gymnastic prowess, and occasioned no little distress and discomfort to their unfortunate riders. A novel touch was afforded to the programme by an airman from a neighbouring aerodrome who executed brilliant and hair-raising feats a few feet above the heads of the crowd.

During the morning of October 2, the battalion left camp and marched to a trench system N.W. of Bustard Inn to undergo a course of four days' training in trench warfare. Rain fell heavily during the march-out, and the condition of the battalion when it reached its destination was, to say the least, damp. The men were quartered in bell tents for the night. They were fortunate in being the reserve battalion, since the other battalions of the Brigade were in the trenches for the night. During the next day the weather became worse, and, consequently, when night fell on October 3, the battalion was not in the best of spirits.

During the night an alarm was sounded. Every man had to turn out in full marching order, ready to take an active part in the tactical scheme if necessary.

The rolls were checked, and the men were then allowed to go back to their tents. As the rain continued to fall steadily throughout the following day, the operations were terminated and the battalion returned to camp at 7 p.m. on October 4. The scheme was to have been extended until the 6th, but the adverse weather conditions upset all pre-arranged plans, and rendered the effective progress of the operations impossible.

The weather during the following week was cold and wet, and the greater part of the training was done indoors. On October 11, a Brigade tactical scheme was carried out near the village of Woodford, in the Avon Valley, but, with the exception of this no field work was done by the battalion until October 17.

On the morning of the 17th, the unit left camp at 10 a.m., in pouring rain, on a six mile march to the trenches at Bustard, to carry out another four days' trench-warfare scheme. The original intention had been that the 39th and 40th Battalions should occupy the trenches that night, but as the whole system was flooded and the men were wet through, this plan was abandoned, and after a hot meal the 39th "turned in" under canvas for the night. The 37th and 38th Battalions were more fortunate in being allotted billets for their men. It was still raining the following morning, but after breakfast the sky cleared and the battalions marched off to occupy the trenches—the 39th on the right flank and the 40th on the left. Some of the traverses were in a very sloppy condition, but the ground had dried considerably, and the men were able to make themselves moderately comfortable for the night.

The general idea of the operations was the carrying out of an attack and defence scheme, and word was passed round among the men holding the trenches that the attack was to be expected in the morning.

The whole of the arrangements were carried out under conditions resembling those of actual warfare. Telephone lines were laid, trench discipline strictly observed, and, except that the fire from "enemy" guns was purely imaginary, the whole effect was one of great realism.

At 3 a.m. on the morning of the 19th a rocket was fired as a signal that an attack was to be delivered by the 39th.

The men in the front line scrambled over the parapet and took a system of trenches in front of them at the point of the bayonet. Star-shells were fired at regular intervals to give light to the attacking party and heighten the effect. Communication was established with Brigade Headquarters within two minutes of leaving the attacking trench. The Brigadier complimented the 39th on its smart work during the progress of the scheme.

During the evening of the 19th the 37th Battalion took over the trenches from the 39th, which withdrew and occupied again the tents in the reserve position.

It was a tired body of men that turned out of their tents the following morning. They had not had the chance to shave for three days, and the majority of the men had not even had a wash during that time. Those who did observe the niceties of toilet had been compelled to use the water in their water bottles for the purpose. As one of the men graphically described the situation "Robinson Crusoe wasn't in it." During the afternoon the battalion marched back to camp.

On Monday, October 23, a special course of training was inaugurated in which the whole battalion, including the specialists, took part. The idea was to train every man in the use of every arm used by infantry. Lewis gunnery, bayonet fighting, and bomb throwing were practised assiduously for twelve days, and during this training the men made their first acquaintance with gas masks.

On November 9, Brigadier-General W. R. McNicoll made a detailed inspection of the battalion, and expressed his pleasure at its turn-out and at the improvements which the months of hard training had effected.

On the 13th, the battalion participated in a fourteen mile divisional route march in which all units took part.

The administrative staff of the battalion was now hard at work preparing for its approaching embarkation for France. Clerks were working in the offices late every night making out the embarkation rolls and the many military documents which had to be sent to Headquarters before a unit goes overseas.

On Saturday, November 18, definite orders were received from 10th Brigade Headquarters to the effect that the battalion would embark at Southampton on the 23rd.

The intervening days were fully occupied in making the final preparations. Steel helmets and gas masks were issued to every man, and on the eve of departure 150 rounds of ammunition per man were issued.

The first snow of the Winter had fallen, and during the last few days of training, the men felt the cold very keenly. On the last Sunday in camp they marched through snow four inches deep to Rollestone rifle range, where the final Lewis gun practices were fired.

On November 20, the first units of the 3rd Division left for France, marching out of camp amid lusty cheers from their comrades, who were to join them at the front very soon afterwards.

The spirit pervading the battalion on the eve of going into action is worthy of comment. The men, hardened in physique by the months of strenuous training and resolute in determination to uphold the name of their battalion, were eager to match themselves against the soldiers of the enemy. They were not ignorant of the hardships and trials which awaited them, but these were discounted by the confidence the men had in themselves and in their leaders. It is this spirit which, permeating the ranks of the A.I.F., has been the foundation of the reputation gained by Australian soldiers in the Great War.

At mid-day on Thursday, November 23, the battalion left Larkhill and marched for the last time down the road to Amesbury, where trains were waiting to convey the troops to Southampton.

The quays of Southampton have witnessed many moving scenes in the drama of war. From them the majority of the men of the British armies departed on their way to the battlefields of France and Flanders. From those first tense days of August, 1914, up to the conclusion of hostilities, the great pageant of Britain's martial power had passed—for the most part secretly and silently—through the precincts of the town. From these wharfs the first British Army sailed for France—the men who, a few days later, fighting against stupendous odds, were to retreat so stubbornly down the road from Mons. Here again the turbaned regiments of the Indian Army embarked for the front; and now stalwart men of the Australian Forces thronged the quaysides on their way to join their compatriots in arms among the allied armies.

During the afternoon of November 23, 1916, the men of the 39th Battalion sat resting on their piled-up equipment in one of the many large covered sheds beside the Southampton Docks. Alongside the wharf, with steam up and the Blue Peter flying, lay the Admiralty Channel Transport "Princess Victoria."

Embarkation officers hurried busily to and fro among the groups of waiting men, and the crowded dock-side presented a scene of great animation. Suddenly, sharp orders rang out and the men rose quickly, donned their equipment, and for the succeeding half hour streamed up the narrow gangway. As each stepped on board he was handed a lifebelt which he had to fasten on, as soon as he had taken off his equipment on the troop deck below.

At 5.30 p.m., the "Princess Victoria" cast off from her berth and picked her way out through the crowded shipping into the waters of the Solent, bound for Havre.

The old ordered sequence of camp life with its routine and security was left behind. In a few days the battalion would be plunged into the maelstrom of war with all its horrors, its perils and uncertainties.

CHAPTER IV.

Into Action

*And nearer—clearer—deadlier than before!
Arm! Arm! it is—it is—the cannon's opening roar!*
—BYRON.

THE crossing of the English Channel during the Great War was in no way the tranquil affair it had been in the days of peace, when crowded passenger boats steamed busily to and fro between Calais and Dover. True, these same steamers still ran into harbour under the white cliffs of Dover and among the dunes of Calais, and their decks were still crowded. But their funnels and sides, once bright with red and white paint, were streaked and striped with fantastic camouflage devices in dull greys and blacks and blues; and instead of the gay holiday crowds of tourists bound on an Easter or Whitsuntide jaunt to the Continent, groups of men in khaki thronged the decks.

Day and night the Channel transports were conveying their freight of men from the shores of England to the great army bases in France. Day and night, minesweeping fleets scoured the Straits of Dover, and the destroyer flotillas patrolled the Channel, from Ushant to the Nore, in order that the traffic of war might go on, unimpeded by the attacks of enemy submarines or the danger of floating mines. It is only those whose lot it has been to make many cross-channel voyages during the war who know how much the nation and our armies owe to the vigilance of the Navy.

Under these conditions the transport "Princess Victoria," bearing the 39th Battalion to fulfil its destiny on the battlefields of France, crossed safely over those perilous waters and entered the harbour of Havre in the early hours of the morning of

November 24, 1916. True November weather had prevailed during the crossing, and the boat had pitched and plunged wildly in the heavy seas that were running.

Disembarkation was not proceeded with until 7.30 a.m. The men had a long march in front of them, with a wearisome train journey after that, and consequently it was necessary to give them every opportunity of resting. As soon as it was light, the ship's rail was crowded by men anxious to have a first glimpse of the country which above all others stood out in the eyes of the world as the theatre in which the fate of civilisation was being decided.

Typical little groups of French people stood watching the men coming down the gangways. Dock workers in dungarees, with the inevitable cigarette between their lips, little ragged urchins begging for pennies, here and there the horizon-blue kepi of a poilu, and mingling with the crowd the khaki of an occasional British soldier.

The band had struck up a stirring march tune, and, laden like beasts of burden with a vast miscellany of equipment, the men marched out through the docks and into the streets of the city. This was the first glimpse they had of a French city, and the early stages of the march were full of interest. The cafes with little tables and chairs set out on the pavement caused some comment. The hurrying crowds chattering in a strange tongue, the unfamiliar names on the tramcars, the unintelligible cries of vendors in the streets, all went to heighten the curiosity and interest of the marching soldiers.

The battalion marched out through the seaside suburb of Saint Adresse, past pretty villas, and past beaches which in Summer-time are thronged with bathing machines, to a large rest camp at Sanvic. The last stages of the march were very arduous. The road mounted up steep hillsides, and the men, laden with equipment and arms and still feeling the effects of a rough Channel passage, found the journey an undertaking of almost herculean magnitude. Many dropped out along the route unable

N.C.Os. of the Battalion, Neuve Eglise, Belgium

to keep even the moderate pace set by the leading files; and when the battalion finally halted in front of the tents of the rest camp, the men were unfit for anything save food and rest.

One man, rendered curious by his experiences on the march, weighed the total equipment he had carried from the docks and found that it turned the scale at 122 pounds.

That same evening orders were received that the battalion would entrain for the front the following morning. Having already an inkling of the exhausting journey that was to follow, everybody turned in early to snatch a few hours of much-needed rest.

The morning of November 25 dawned cold and wet. Reveille was sounded early, and the men packed up their blankets whilst the cooks accomplished culinary miracles with bully beef and potatoes.

At 9.30 a.m. the 39th left Sanvic to march to the Gare Maritime, Havre, the dockside railway station, from which all traffic for the war zone began its journey. The march was no pleasant experience. The route led the battalion for the greater part through mean dirty streets, slippery and wet, while the steadily falling rain made the departure from Havre a somewhat depressing experience. On arrival at the station the battalion formed up in companies under the shelter of the sheds and eyed with mingled feelings a long train of trucks, each truck bearing the interesting inscription—

>   Hommes 40
>   Chevaux 8

Judging by appearances it seemed that the "Chevaux" had the better of the bargain. A Y.M.C.A. hut was discovered which dispensed free cocoa and biscuits to the men. It was their first introduction to the Y.M.C.A. in France, and a very satisfactory one. A canteen which sold bread and tinned foods was also doing a brisk business, and when the men finally got aboard the troop trains every truck was well provisioned for the journey.

Railway travelling in France during the war was always a painful process. Frequently a troop train would take twenty-four hours to cover a distance that any self respecting goods train in peace time could accomplish in six. This, however, is readily comprehensible when one pauses to consider the enormous mass of traffic which the military railway authorities had to handle. Supply and ammunition trains held precedence on the lines, and troop trains suffered accordingly.

For the better part of two days the trains conveying the 39th pursued their journey to the front, putting the miles behind them with ponderous slowness, and halting with exasperating regularity at intervals of twenty minutes or so. The first day was interesting enough, and the men were quite content to watch the panorama of country slowly unfolding before their eyes, or to stroll along the line beside the train. It was their first view of the French landscape, and although the railway journey through Normandy to Flanders does not include much picturesque scenery, it held many features of interest. Every building which could boast a turret or tower was pronounced unhesitatingly to be a "chateau" and thus many an unpretentious country house attracted unwonted attention.

The weather was still cold and gloomy, the cattle trucks were, if anything, more so; and when the first stirring of interest had gone, the journey became tedious beyond description.

It is related that at one stage the train was in sight of three windmills for six hours when it only required a three mile trip to have lost sight of them.

During the frequent halts hot water was obtained from the engine driver and the men made tea in their mess tins.

There was an abundance of rations on board the train, and on this score the men suffered very little discomfort. Had the weather been warmer and the quarters less confined, the journey might have been tolerable. As it was, when they at last reached their journey's end at 2.30 on the morning of the 27th, the men were very tired and their limbs cramped and stiff by the long sojourn in the crowded trucks.

The battalion detrained at Bailleul in the Department du Nord, an old town distant some twelve kilometres from the shattered city of Armentieres and the centre of a group of villages which formed an extensive billeting area for resting troops and units undergoing training.

The 39th had travelled from Havre in three trains, and through the early hours of the morning the detraining troops thronged the station yard at Bailleul.

Motor lorries were lined up along the road outside the station; into these the men climbed and were transported to their first billets in the village of Merris, five kilometres south-west of Bailleul. Arriving there about 4 a.m., they were allotted billets in the barns and buildings of local farmhouses, and, in a few hours, were fraternising with the villagers and drinking hot coffee in the tiny cafes and estaminets. Linguistic difficulties never prevented the interchange of ideas between troops and the civil population in France. The majority of the local people had sufficiently mastered the intricacies of the English tongue to understand and to be understood by the soldiers, and it often happened that a "digger" struggling valiantly to express himself in French would be astonished by being addressed fluently in his own language in reply. Especially was this so with the children, many of whom spoke English remarkably well.

At Merris, for the first time, the 39th heard the sullen growl and rumble of the guns, and had its first glimpse of war when German observing aeroplanes came across the line and the little puff balls of shrapnel burst with dull "pops" among the clouds, as British anti-aircraft batteries opened fire on the enemy.

Merris had been occupied by the Germans during the days when the armies of Von Kluck rolled down towards Paris in 1914, and the memory of that time lived vividly in the minds of the local folk. Our men were told many stories of the enemy invasion of this quiet village and saw the devastating effects of shell fire on the broken walls of a nearby hospice which had been maintained by sisters of a religious order as a refuge for imbecile women. Enemy soldiery had turned these miserable creatures out of the hospice to make room for troops. For many days they wandered at random over the surrounding country until they were eventually collected and brought back to their asylum.

There was a distinct feeling of war in the air during the stay at Merris. The men knew nothing of the conditions under which war was being waged in the forward area. They did not know how far the enemy was away from them; it even seemed feasible in the electric atmosphere of danger and excitement of those first days on the front that murderous foemen might be lurking in the deep shadows of the village streets at night. This feeling of uncertainty was accentuated by orders that men were not to leave their billets unless fully equipped and armed, with a few rounds in the magazines of their rifles. Officers carried loaded revolvers, and generally an air of suppressed excitement prevailed.

Small box respirators, the newly devised protection against enemy poison gas, were issued to the men at Merris, and for some days they were exercised in the adjustment of these masks until proficiency had been attained. The box respirator afforded complete protection against gas, provided that it was adjusted with sufficient rapidity. It consisted of a face piece attached by a rubber tube to a tin container filled with chemical granules. The air passed through a valve in the bottom of this container, through the filtering chemical, and, cleared of the poison, entered the lungs, to be exhaled in turn through another small valve attached to the face piece.

At the conclusion of their gas training the men passed through testing chambers containing concentrations of lachrymatory and the more deadly chlorine gases. This was to assure them of the absolute efficacy of the masks.

Other forms of training—bombing, Lewis gunnery, and scouting also received attention during this period.

Lieut.-Colonel R. Rankine was evacuated sick, and Major G. S. Armfield took command.

At 9 a.m., on the morning of December 2, the battalion left Merris to march to Armentieres. It was in many ways a memorable march, taking the battalion for the first time into close proximity to the trenches.

The men marched along the cobbled roads lined by tall trees, which in Summer make a pleasant avenue of leaf and branch. Packs were filled to their utmost capacity, blankets and steel helmets fixed to the outside, and haversacks crammed with iron rations and such oddments of kit as could not be wedged into the packs.

At 2.30 p.m. the battalion passed through the village of Nieppe, past an ancient church with a gaping shell hole in its walls, and then through the main street of Pont de Nieppe, a long straggling village of factory workers' houses and small shops. Here the battalion was met by a guide from a New Zealand regiment, and, continuing the march, crossed the River Lys where a panorama of the war-broken city of Armentieres unfolded before the men's eyes.

The boom of the guns sounded unpleasantly close, as the city was entered, and on every side the men saw evidences of the havoc and destruction of war. The greater part of the population had deserted the city, except a few people who still lived in the houses, and gained a livelihood by keeping small cafes and postcard shops. The great weaving factories were all closed, but a few breweries still carried on their business.

This part of the front was quiet. The city itself was shelled, and the people who lived in it had become familiar with bursting shells and poison gas. War to a great extent had lost its terrors for them, and they went about their daily business with a strange fatalistic shrug of the shoulders and with the

Half Past Eleven Square
Armentieres.

murmured "C'est la guerre" which greeted each fresh misfortune or trial.

The billets were scattered over a considerable area. Battalion Headquarters was situated in a large house known as the Chateau Rose, with "B" Company's billets adjacent to it. "A" Company was billeted in the Lock House, and "C" and "D" Companies in a large factory on the northern edge of Armentieres, near a square known as "Barbed Wire Square." During the early days of the war the military authorities had made the city as impregnable to assault as was humanly possible, and had placed obstacles at all points of tactical importance to impede the enemy's advance. "Barbed Wire Square" was filled entirely with barbed wire and was nothing more nor less than a mass of entanglements.

The 39th became the battalion in support of the units holding the front line, and was known officially as "C" battalion. Working parties had to be supplied daily to do certain essential work in the trenches. Enemy shell fire was constantly damaging portions of the defence line, and the necessary repairs were always done by men drawn from the ranks of the battalion in support. The men who were engaged on this work were the first of the battalion to come under fire, and many of them will still recall their first experience of building up broken parapets, revetting the sides of fallen-in trenches, and laying duckboards in the morass of Flanders mud, with the sinister whine of shells passing overhead.

It was hazardous work, and on December 5, the battalion received its first casualty when No. 1339, Private J. R. R. Lindsay, was wounded by a shell splinter.

The following day the 39th lost its first officer when Lieutenant Basil White died of wounds received through the premature explosion of a Newton Pippin rifle grenade. He was in charge of a working party when he was fatally wounded. A keen and efficient officer, he was universally popular in the battalion and his untimely death was deeply regretted by his comrades.

The enemy had made frequent use of gas in this sector of the front, and as dusk was approaching on the night of December 6, the strident alarm of the Strombos Horn sounded over Armentieres. It was the battalion's first gas alarm, and as it happened, a false one. Nevertheless it sufficed to emphasise the necessity of being constantly on the alert.

The 3rd Division was already in action, the 37th Battalion being in the front line on the right of the Brigade Sector east of Armentieres and beyond the village of Houplines. Houplines was little more than a heap of ruins. Its streets and houses had long been demolished by continued enemy shelling, and among the piles of debris the British artillery had found good positions for their guns. The 39th was to take over the line from the 37th on December 9; and during the preceding days the acting C.O. and officers of the battalion were engaged in making active reconnaissance of the forward defence and support line systems of the sector they were to occupy.

When a relief of trenches was being carried out it was the custom for the specialists (i.e., bombers, Lewis gunners, etc.) of the relieving battalion to take over on the day preceding the actual relief, from the specialists of the battalion holding the line. This method helped to ensure the smooth working of a relief with a minimum of confusion and a maximum of safety.

Accordingly on December 8 the specialists of the 39th Battalion went into the line and relieved those of the 37th.

The battalion was keenly excited at the prospect of making its debut on the battlefields at last, and spent the time immediately prior to going into action, conjuring up round the billet fires of Armentieres, visions and anticipations of the days to come.

On the night of December 8/9 the battalion left its billets and marched through the wilderness of broken bricks and mortar that once had been Houplines.

The front was quiet and the night still, save for the occasional deadly rattle of a machine gun or the shattering report

Facing Page 74   In the Front Line at Houplines, France

from a nearby gun hidden among the ruined houses. Intermittently star shells soared in graceful curves through the air, illuminating the surroundings vividly for a few moments, then suddenly disappearing to leave the night blacker than ever. Guides from the 37th met the battalion; and, led by them, the men threaded silently through the labyrinth of communication trenches leading up to the front line. The trenches were floored with duckboards—lengths of wood joined together by laths and forming a causeway over the mud and slush in the bottom of the trench. Nearly all trenches in this sector were paved with duckboards; but, however well they were laid, it was always necessary to exercise caution in negotiating them. It was not by any means an uncommon occurrence for a man to slip on the projecting end of a duckboard and to be hurled off into knee-deep mud by the other end unexpectedly springing into the air. Gum boots had been issued to each man at "Tissage Dump" in rear of the trenches, and very necessary they proved.

Pursuing a devious course through the support lines, the battalion at length reached the actual front line where the 37th Battalion was "standing to" in readiness to hand over the line.

A strict mode of procedure governed the relief of a unit in the line, a description of which may prove of interest.

Let it be supposed that "X" Battalion is under orders to relieve "Y" Battalion which is holding the line in front of Armentieres. On receipt of these orders the company and specialist officers of the relieving battalion at once make a reconnaissance of the sector to be taken over, and all available information is gleaned from the unit holding the front.

Prior to the relief, the two adjutants and specialist officers from both units meet in conference, when all information regarding the enemy and local conditions is given to the incoming unit.

On the appointed night "X" Battalion moves off in the formation ordered, the guides are met at a named point and each platoon is led by its guide to the portion of the front allotted to it.

The men of "Y" Battalion are standing to arms on the fire step of their trench; and, as "X" Battalion files in, the men line the parapet alongside the garrison about to be relieved.

Meanwhile the officers commanding companies and platoons are making a tour of inspection and taking over such stores as are kept permanently in the trenches.

On word being given, the men of "Y" Battalion leave their posts and file quietly out of the front line.

The time necessary for the completion of a relief depends upon the circumstances of the moment. It may happen that heavy shelling is encountered while the relieving unit is approaching the line; the guides may be late in arriving at the rendezvous; the enemy may have learnt of the hour of relief and consequently may have attempted a raid, in order to inflict losses on the troops while the relief is in progress. A thousand and one unforeseen contingencies may arise against which the troops have to be on their guard.

The relief of the 37th by the 39th was completed on December 10, without any untoward incident; and thus the men of the battalion found themselves facing the enemy lines with only the narrow mysterious strip of No Man's Land between themselves and the Hun.

The Houplines Sector was a quiet one. For months the opposing forces had occupied the same trenches keeping a wary eye on each other. Except for occasional raids and artillery "strafes," nothing worthy of note had happened on this part of the front for some considerable time. With the advent of the 1916 Winter, however, there came about a gradual "livening up" in the Houplines trenches. The men of the 3rd Division had had the offensive spirit carefully fostered in them, and they were by no means content to sit and look at the enemy wire waiting for something to happen. Consequently within a few weeks of their first occupation of the line, raids and minor operations became the order of the day, and artillery fire on both sides was brisker all along the front.

The first days were occupied in learning something of the new conditions of life which surrounded them, and the men quickly adapted themselves to trench routine. They had to learn the routes from one place to another, as it was an easy thing to lose oneself in the maze of zig-zag trenches. They had to learn also the principles and methods of dug-out construction, and in fact acquire all the knowledge that could be useful to them in the performance of their manifold duties or in promoting their comfort and security.

Life in the trenches, once the early novelty had disappeared, followed a daily ordered routine. The night hours were the most arduous. In the darkness of those winter nights patrols from both sides crept silently about No Man's Land, and on many nights raids took place. Under cover of darkness, also, working parties had to be organised and sent out to repair wires broken by shell fire. Night in the trenches holds a multitude of sinister possibilities, and from dusk to dawn everybody in the front line is in a state of preparedness for any eventuality. An hour before daybreak, everybody "stands to," lining the parapet in fighting order and with bayonets fixed, waiting for an attack. As soon as it is fully light "Stand down" is ordered, and all men not detailed for duty during the day prepare for "turning in." Before they do so, the morning meal is brought up in "dixies" or petrol tins from the cookhouses in rear.

By day, while the men are in their dug-outs, sentries are on duty keeping vigil over the parapet. They are the eyes and ears of the sleepers, and maintain a careful watch for enemy movements, in order to guard against surprises.

During the morning the duty and fatigue parties for the ensuing twenty-four hours are told off. Rations for the day have to be brought up from the rear, as well as barbed wire, pickets, sandbags, corrugated iron and other material necessary for the repair of trenches and the construction of dug-outs.

From daylight till mid-day, little or no work is done. During the afternoon minor repairs are effected in the trenches, such as replacing of dislodged sandbags and the re-building of portions of damaged trench. The men clean their rifles, bayonets and ammunition, and the Lewis gunners and bombers are also busy seeing that their respective weapons are in working order.

The C.O. and the specialist officers of the battalion make their tour of inspection of every part of the battalion front, in order to see that everything necessary to the defence of the line is complete.

At dusk "Stand to" is again ordered, and for one hour the parapet is lined by armed men in readiness for a possible enemy attack.

As soon as it is dark, the patrols and scouts leave the lines to pursue their perilous work in No Man's Land. Before leaving, all sentries are warned that a patrol is going out in order that the danger of the scouts being fired on by their own men may be avoided.

The patrols work along the entire battalion front examining the barbed wire, exploring shell holes and ruins for traces of enemy occupation, and finally making their way as close to the enemy lines as possible.

A battalion relies on its scouts for information of the enemy. The aim of their work is the mastery of No Man's Land, and the side which achieves this in trench warfare has an inestimable advantage over the other.

Scouting in No Man's Land is one of the most hazardous phases of trench warfare.

On December 11 the battalion had its first experience of a Minenwerfer bombardment. The Minenwerfer (German trench mortar) had such low velocity that the projectile could be seen approaching in mid-air with a wobbling, erratic flight. It burst with a rending crash and concussion, and when it exploded within the narrow confines of a trench, the effects were often disastrous.

Many incidents, humorous to recall, marked these first days in action when men were keyed up to the highest pitch of watchfulness and expectation.

One dark night a sentry was mounting a lonely guard on the fire step. The night was very still and his eyes strained anxiously through the darkness towards the enemy lines. Suddenly he heard a noise on the parapet and a black shape loomed before his startled eyes. Beads of perspiration rose on his forehead, and calling wildly "They're coming over" he made a valiant lunge with his bayonet at the enemy figure. As the men in the trench manned the firestep, a great black rat, suffering the indignity of a bayonet prick in its sleek body, squealed and plunged into the security of its hole.

On the night of December 12 a small enemy raiding party attempted to enter the battalion front on "B" Company's sector. A few bombs were thrown on both sides, and the deadly clatter of Lewis guns woke the echoes of No Man's Land. The S.O.S. signal to the artillery was fired, and in less than a minute, the guns were pounding shell after shell into No Man's Land. It was thought that some of the enemy might still be lurking in the battalion's trenches, and search parties crawled cautiously round bays and traverses seeking for any unhappy German who might have been so ill advised as to remain in the lines. Visiting officers had exciting experiences that night. They ran a considerable risk of being shot, and it was necessary to answer the sudden challenges of the search parties smartly and to the point.

One of the battalion patrols operating in front of "D" Company's sector was close to the German lines when the barrage opened, and the men had to retreat rapidly through thick mud to escape the curtain of bursting shrapnel. Half way across No Man's Land they became entangled in a mass of barbed wire, and for the best part of an hour they were engaged in dragging each other out of the clinging tentacles of the entanglements. They eventually reached the comparative safety of their own front line without any casualty.

On December 13 the enemy heavily shelled the centre of the battalion frontage which was held by "B" Company, and a few casualties resulted.

On the night of December 16 the 37th Battalion relieved the 39th. The relief was successfully carried out, and the 39th marched back to its billets in Armentieres.

The first tour of duty in the trenches was over. The 39th had received its baptism of fire.

Map No. 1
HOUPLINES—L'EPINETTE—ARMENTIERES

MAP No. 1

HOUPLINES – L'EPINETTE – ARMENTIERES

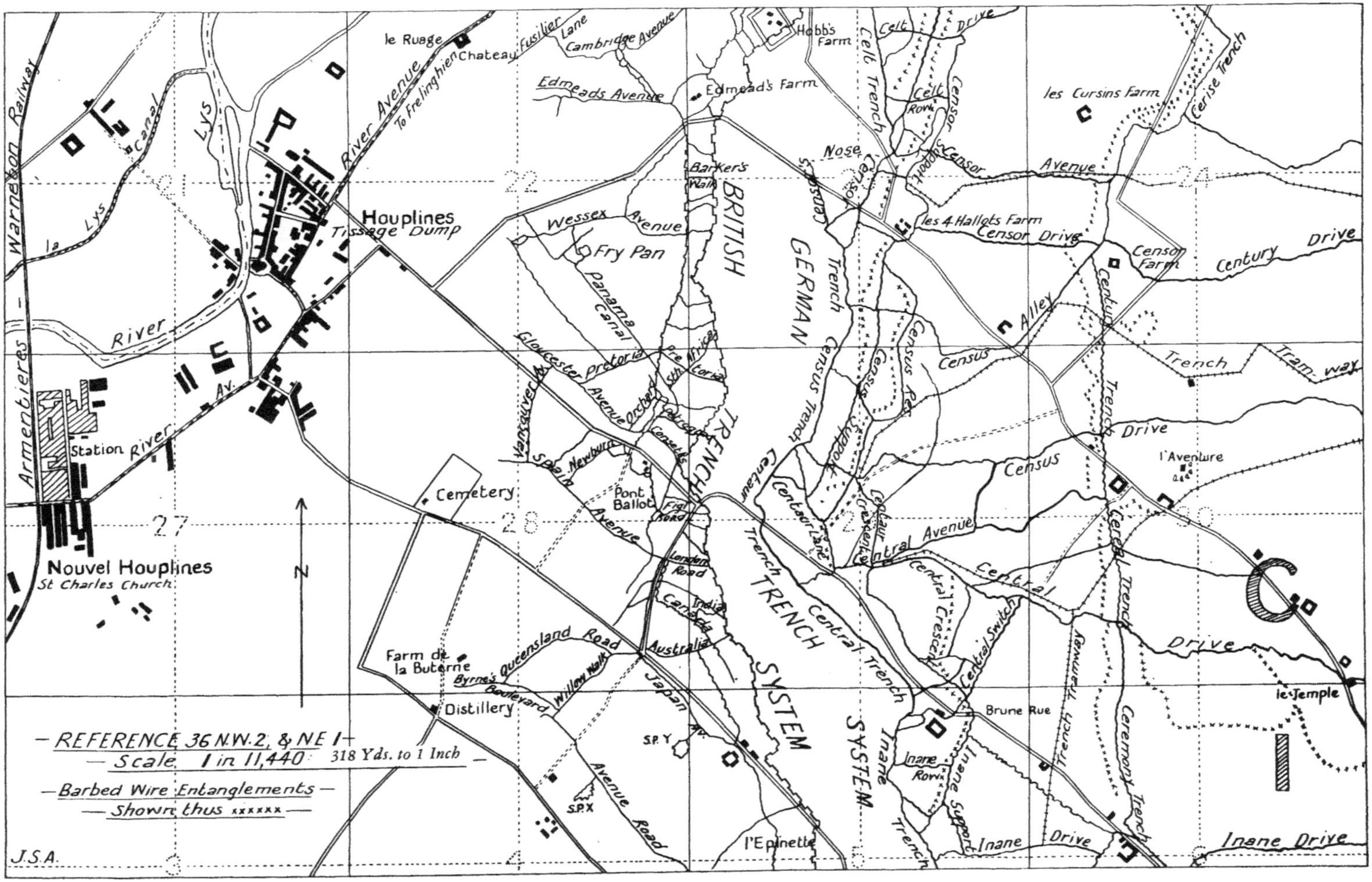

CHAPTER V.

Winter in Flanders

A February face, so full of frost, of storm, and cloudiness!
—SHAKESPEARE.

THE city of Armentieres in 1916 was a typical example of the great number of French and Belgian cities over which the ruthless scythe of war had swept, leaving in place of peaceful industry, desolation.

Armentieres is an off-shoot of that centre of Flemish industry —Lille. In the days of its prosperity its population exceeded 30,000, and it had a moderately large manufacturing trade. Many large textile factories carried on business there, and a host of smaller manufacturing houses represented the paper and flour-milling industries. As large manufacturing centres go, Armentieres was in many respects a beautiful city. The spires of many fine churches—some of them since badly damaged by shell fire —towered up above the houses. Squares bordered by trees and public gardens relieved the monotony of the maze of streets. Walking through the city it was difficult for a passer-by to imagine it as it had been, to people its deserted streets and squares with the bustling crowds of former days, and to visualise the streaming throngs of factory workers coming from their toil at dusk. And at night one could imagine the brilliant lights of the electric trams.

But in 1916 a tragic silence reigned everywhere, only broken now and then by the echoing rattle of a limber or transport waggon over the cobbles, or by the shattering roar of a shell exploding among the houses. In the public gardens, where once bands had made gay music and children had played on the well-kept lawns, the grass grew long and weeds choked the flower beds.

In the streets a rubble of broken bricks and glass covered the pavements, broken lamp posts lay in the gutters, telegraph poles leaned threateningly over the streets, their wires twisted and tangled in confusion. The tram lines were hidden by the unswept dust of two years; and in the factories great masses of machinery lay rusting in idleness. The houses were deserted, some of them wrecked and shattered, others still intact and just as their former inhabitants had quitted them.

It was in the heart of this deserted city that the 39th lived during the intervals between tours of duty in the front line. The billets were not the most cheerful places in the world, and the few cafes and estaminets which still remained open in Armentieres were well patronised by the men. In these places the universal dish was fried eggs and potato-chips. Flemish ingenuity could, apparently, devise no other. But the principal attraction of these dingy cafes lay in the glowing stoves which they all boasted. The weather was daily becoming more severe, and in the evenings a cheerful fire drew the men like a magnet. Not that Armentieres was lacking in the amusements of the civilised world; for an enterprising Y.M.C.A. had opened a cinema theatre. A factor which added considerably to the comfort of life was the installation of baths by the military authorities. These were arranged in what had been a brewery. The great brewing vats were filled with hot water, and a complete change of underclothing was provided for the men. These baths were one of the most striking features of life on the front. It was impossible for the majority of the men to obtain a regular bath elsewhere; while, if the washing of clothes were attempted, the garments were frozen hard long before they were dry. The army baths took the dirty clothes of the men each week, had them thoroughly washed and fumigated, and re-issued the following week. The garments of course changed owners, but that was a minor consideration.

On December 20 the 39th Battalion again relieved the 37th after a four days' respite in billets, during which the usual working parties had been daily supplied. The relief was carried out quietly and without any undue attention from the enemy; and the battalion settled down to the prospect of Christmas in the trenches. This sojourn in the line was marked by very little activity on either side; possibly the Christmas spirit had something to do with this. At any rate the battalion was able to eat in comparative comfort the plum puddings which had been sent by the Australian Comforts Funds, and which had been carried up to the trenches by the ration parties on Christmas Eve.

Festivities in a front line trench are, as the reader may imagine, an impossibility; and so Christmas passed unmarked by anything outside the ordinary routine of the trenches. Minds travelled back over the leagues of dividing ocean to the Homeland; and during the hours of a night watch on the firestep many a man saw visions of the land he had left and recalled the Christmas picnics and excursions of past years.

During this Christmas in the trenches the enemy brought a slight innovation into play in the form of searchlights. These swept over and brilliantly illuminated No Man's Land to the considerable inconvenience of patrols and scouts. Artillery and machine-gun fire was ranged on these lights, but without success, and for many weeks scouting was an operation more dangerous than ever.

New Year was passed in somewhat happier circumstances The battalion was back in Armentieres and such festivities as the front permitted were freely indulged in. Many happy parties gathered round billet fires and in the cafes, but New Year was heralded in a somewhat sinister manner by the boom of the guns.

The battalion went into the line again on January 3, and the following day the enemy attempted to raid the left of the sector together with part of the adjoining frontage, held by the 40th Battalion. This raid was easily repulsed and the enemy failed to penetrate any part of the line. The 39th by this time knew its sector very well and realised, by the attention the enemy paid to them, the positions which must be regarded as danger spots. The Germans evidently had certain positions of the line marked prominently on their range cards, for day after day shells and minenwerfers exploded in the same places.

Near Armentieres

A favourite target of the enemy was what remained of an orchard. Only a few ragged stumps were left to justify its name, and into it the enemy poured his shells with undiminishing fury. Unfortunately "B" Company's Headquarters and support line were in the vicinity, and, during a particularly heavy bombardment on January 7, much damage was done to the defences of the sector, and many casualties were caused.

On January 8/9 the battalion handed over the line to the 37th, and went back to Armentieres as reserve battalion. During the battalion's last tour a party of three officers and fifty men had been behind the lines in training for the first raid to be undertaken by the 39th.

At 5.45 p.m. on January 9 the raid was carried out. Captain C. L. Giles was in command of it. Lieutenant (afterwards

Captain) P. L. Smith commanded the assault party, whilst Lieutenant W. R. Bingle had charge of the right and Lieutenant W. G. Jewkes the left raiding parties. Preceded by an artillery barrage on the enemy lines the raiders, carrying a large supply of hand grenades, left our trenches and stormed the enemy front line. The venture was successful. Numbers of the enemy were killed, dugouts were blown up and machine guns put out of action, while valuable information was gleaned from the documents captured in the German trenches.

This being the first operation carried out by the 39th, great excitement was evidenced among those not participating, and as "zero" hour approached and the barrage opened, the feelings of the men were working up to fever pitch. Questions were being asked on all sides, and the general anxiety took the form of such expressions as "I wonder if they've got any Fritzes"—"They must be in now"—"Was the wire cut?"

Then came the good news that the raiders had returned and that the operation had been a success.

The battalion's casualties numbered 17 N.C.Os. and men killed and wounded, and one officer—Lieutenant W. G. Jewkes—wounded. Lieutenant Jewkes died the following day, to the deep regret of everybody in the battalion.

From this date up to the 22nd of the month the battalion periodically relieved, and was relieved, by the 37th Battalion in the same sector. No operations worthy of note took place on either side during the period. The weather was extremely cold. The 1916-1917 Winter was the most rigorous in the memory of the Flemish peasants, and Australian troops suffered greatly. "Trench-feet"—a disease consequent upon frost-bite, which, if neglected, resulted in mortification and often in the loss of the feet—was very prevalent. To combat it, the feet had to be well rubbed with whale oil, and socks changed daily. The men wore cardigan jackets, fur and leather jerkins and great-coats, and this additional clothing, with fighting equipment buckled on over it, made it difficult at times for two men to pass each other in a trench.

Coke fires in braziers provided a little warmth, but lights had to be used with the utmost caution.

On January 5 the first quota of reinforcements, 45 strong, arrived from England. Casualties had thinned the ranks of the battalion, and these men were badly needed.

Between January 19 and January 26 large working parties of men were nightly engaged in laying cables behind a sector of trenches to the right of Houplines. The cables had to be buried to a depth of six feet. The task of excavating the frozen earth was a most difficult one, and as the work had to be done in the open without the shelter of any cover, enemy machine guns took their toll of the working parties.

On January 25 the battalion received orders to make an inspection of a sector of trenches called Rue du Bois, then held by the 25th Battalion of the Northumberland Fusiliers, and on the following evening the 39th relieved the English troops.

This was the first time the battalion had taken over the line from an English regiment, and the men were rather curious to know how the "Tommies" carried out reliefs. This one was completed without a hitch; and apart from the Northumberland regiment leaving behind them a quantity of rum there was nothing to distinguish it from previous reliefs.

The new sector lay to the east of la Chapelle d'Armentieres, a village lying on the outskirts of the city, to the south of Houplines. The battalion frontage contained a salient, the point of which was only 30 to 40 yards from the enemy trenches. It was a hot corner, and was continually peppered by the German minenwerfers.

On the night of taking over the line in the Rue du Bois sector the enemy's artillery was abnormally active on the battalion front. There were eight minor casualties, and a defensive position known as Burnt Farm was badly damaged by shell fire.

The following day, January 27, was the Kaiser's birthday, and enemy gunners celebrated the auspicious occasion by putting down a heavy bombardment on the British lines.

Lieut.-Colonel R. Rankine, who returned on December 14, was again evacuated sick, and did not re-join the battalion. The temporary command passed to Major G. S. Armfield.

Meanwhile the 10th Infantry Brigade had been preparing for a very extensive raid. On January 8 each battalion had sent a party of 50 men to the Ecole Professionale in Armentieres to undergo a course of special training and instruction. In addition, the 10th Field Engineers had sent a number of sappers to attend the course. Lieutenant E. Fleiter and Lieutenant L. Grondona had charge of the party from the 39th Battalion. Every man was thoroughly practised in the use of the weapons he would employ, bayonet-men in bayonet fighting, bombers in the use of the Mills and phosphorus and lachrymatory grenades, and the sappers in demolition work with gun-cotton and Stokes shells. Each morning the party was taken in motor buses to a field near the town of Steenwerck, where a facsimile of the German trench system had been dug. Over this ground the raid was rehearsed daily until each man understood the features of the ground and the part he was to play. The sector to be attacked resembled an oblong box divided by a cross. The parties of the 39th and 40th Battalions were to work down the communication trench in the centre and then spread out along the lateral trenches in rear, while one party was to push through to the enemy third line to cut off all avenues of escape for the enemy in the front line. The 37th and 38th Battalion parties were to attack on the flanks and work through the German communication trenches on the right and left. It was hoped and expected that in this way numbers of the enemy would be cut off and taken prisoner. A barrage was to be put down on each line of trenches for a few minutes, followed by a box barrage enclosing the entire area on all sides and blocking all the enemy communications. On the day of the raid, the party was assembled in a schoolroom at Armentieres, and, with the aid of blackboard sketches drawn from aeroplane photographs, was put through a final rehearsal. Great care was taken to guard against espionage. The German Secret Service had its agents working behind our lines in great numbers, and especially in the neighbourhood of Armentieres. Sentries were posted round the schoolroom while these final instructions were being given in order to ensure that the enemy would not receive any eleventh-hour warning of the projected attack.

About four o'clock in the afternoon of January 28 the raiding party left the Ecole Professionale and was conveyed in motor buses to within a few hundred yards of the entrance to the trenches.

Before leaving Armentieres the men had removed all badges and titles from their uniforms so that in the event of any of them being captured the enemy would not be able to identify the troops opposing him.

The night was clear and frosty, and the ground was covered by a deep carpet of frozen snow. Before the party entered the trenches the men received sandbags to fasten round their boots to prevent them from falling when crossing the slippery surface of No Man's Land.

The party assembled in the front line twenty minutes before zero hour, where a tot of rum was issued all round, and the various sections were inspected and checked.

Each section had its own particular work to do. There were bayonet parties to attend to any opposition that might be met, searchers to explore the enemy dugouts, sappers to carry boxes of explosives, and scouts to act as guides.

The night was very quiet.

The guns were practically silent on both sides, and only an occasional shell or burst of machine gun fire somewhere on the front broke the stillness. The men waited impatiently and in tension for zero hour; minutes dragged like hours, and it seemed an eternity until with a sudden roar the barrage fell on the German lines.

In a second the party scrambled over the parapet, passed through the wire, and lay down, waiting for the barrage to lift from the enemy front line. The Germans were firing hundreds of Very lights from their trenches, and machine guns were pouring bullets across No Man's Land from all directions.

The landscape for miles was lit up by the Very lights and the flash of the bursting shrapnel. The 3rd Australian Divisional Artillery had just arrived on the front, and this was the first barrage its batteries had fired.

The crossing of No Man's Land was slightly hampered by a little difficulty in traversing a stream which flowed between the trenches. A further delay occurred when the party reached the German wire, which in this locality was very thick and presented a formidable obstacle. The shell fire had not succeeded in cutting it, and the 39th was caught by enfilade fire from machine guns. Many men fell and some confusion and congestion ensued, for a short space, but the sections were soon re-organised.

The German trenches were water-logged and frozen. The ice broke in places and men got a soaking in the cold water. But so far everything went well. Very little opposition was encountered in the enemy front line. The barrage had done its work. Only one party which pushed along the trench towards the right met serious opposition.

Meanwhile each section was engaged in the performance of its special task as rapidly as possible. One searcher party of the 39th, working along the front line and carefully exploring the recesses of dugouts, found a large concrete dugout with two steel doors. The leader of the section attempted to enter, but the heavy doors were securely fastened and all efforts to force them open failed. The occupants were called upon to surrender. No response being made, it was decided to blow in the doors. A demolition box was placed against the doors, and the fuse lit; the little party scattering along the trench to avoid the shock of the explosion. On returning to the dugout, the two doors were found to be shattered, and the dead body of a German could be dimly seen on the floor of the dugout. One of the 39th scouts with torch and revolver crawled through the dark opening to reconnoitre the interior. Switching on his torch, he saw a confused heap of debris in the centre of the place, and the bodies of four Germans. Finding no sign of any other occupant, the scout commenced to search the dugout, a difficult task owing to the ruin caused by the explosion. He found a Very light pistol, several packets of cigars and a few documents. Having taken possession of these he turned his attention to the dead bodies in order to cut from their uniforms such badges and shoulder straps as might serve to identify the unit to which they belonged. While stooping over one of the corpses, he saw a sudden flash of light in a dark corner. He seized his revolver but unfortunately dropped his torch. The dugout was in total darkness, and everything was silent save for the scream of the shells outside. This scout, who had during his training mastered a few words of German, demanded the surrender of whoever might be lurking in the darkness. No reply came and the scout groped about the floor for his torch. Calling to his comrades to come to his assistance, one of them crawled in, and after a whispered consultation they decided to investigate. They advanced towards the direction of the supposed enemy, using all possible caution and prepared to meet opposition at any moment. On reaching the far wall of the dugout they found a small hole through which they could see, in the trench outside, a party of men from their own battalion. The flash of light had come from one of their torches. This incident is typical of many exciting phases of a trench raid.

Other parties of the 39th and 40th had meanwhile pushed through to the enemy third line, searching and bombing dugouts on their way. Half an hour after the commencement of the raid, word reached the 39th that the 38th Battalion party on the left flank had failed to enter the enemy trenches, and that the enemy was counter-attacking. Large numbers of Germans were seen, but they appeared to be retiring instead of attacking. The men of the 39th moved off to intercept them, but before they had gone any distance the red rocket which was the signal to return went up from the Australian trenches.

The journey back across No Man's Land was safely accomplished, each man helping to carry his dead or wounded comrades. Just as the first parties reached their own trenches the enemy artillery opened fire on the Australian lines. One wounded prisoner, the first captured by the Third Division, was brought back by the 39th.

While the centre parties had met with very slight opposition, the flanking parties had been completely held up by thick belts of uncut wire and superior enemy forces. The party from the 37th Battalion, on the right flank, suffered very heavy casualties. Those of the 39th Battalion were also heavy. The wounded were evacuated and the raiders were taken back in motor buses to the school in Armentieres where a well-earned meal was waiting for them.

For gallant conduct during the operation, Lieutenant E. Fleiter received the Military Cross, the first awarded to any officer of the battalion.

At this period trench raids were the order of the day, and half of the 37th and 38th Battalions were undergoing special training for another large raid. The absence of these men entailed a considerable reduction in the fighting strength of the battalions, and for this reason the 39th was relieved on January 31 by a composite battalion drawn from the 37th, 38th, 41st and 43rd Battalions.

The process of taking over was interrupted by an attempted raid on the sector held by "C" Company (commanded by Captain C. R. Hutton) at 6.32 p.m. on the evening of the relief. The enemy's attack was preceded by heavy minenwerfer fire on the front line and support trenches on "C" Company's frontage.

The ground was covered with snow, and the German raiding party wore white overalls, making a difficult target for the rifles of the defenders. The enemy was easily driven back by Lewis guns and bombs of the 39th, and retreated in confusion to their own trenches, leaving many dead and wounded in No Man's Land. Only one German gained entrance to the 39th trenches, and he attempted to remove a wounded "C" Company man to the German lines. He was killed before he could escape from the trench.

The battalion had a few casualties, due chiefly to the heavy minenwerfer fire prior to the raid. Returning to billets in Armentieres, the unit became for a period of four days, the battalion in support.

On the evening of February 5 the 39th relieved the 40th Battalion in the Cowgate Sector, a part of the Armentieres front which was new to the unit.

On the night of February 11/12 a raiding party of the 102nd Brigade, 4th Tyneside Scottish Regiment, made an attack on the enemy trenches from the frontage held by the 39th.

This raid, in which the battalion assisted in minor details, resulted in the capture of seven enemy prisoners. It was led by the Colonel of the Regiment.

The 39th held its frontage in the Cowgate Sector for ten days, during which little occurred to interfere with the customary trench routine.

On February 15, a mixed battalion drawn from the 37th, 38th, 42nd and 44th relieved the 39th, and the battalion returned again to its old billets in Armentieres.

Major R. O. Henderson, of the 38th Battalion, was appointed to command the 39th Battalion, and promoted to the rank of Lieut.-Colonel.

On the 20th the men, after five days' rest, relieved the 40th Battalion in the Rue du Bois sector near la Chapelle d'Armentieres.

Two days later, fifty men from the 39th, under the command of Captain P. L. Smith, carried out a "silent" raid (i.e., without artillery barrage or preparation) against the enemy trenches. Scouts went in front of the party to cut a path through the German wire, and, this accomplished, the raiders crawled across No Man's Land and entered the enemy trenches only to find them unoccupied, water-logged and filled with barbed wire. The party returned to its own trenches without having encountered a single enemy soldier and without sustaining any casualty.

Early in the morning of February 23 a party of Germans attempted a raid on the Rue du Bois salient on the frontage held by "B" Company, now commanded by Captain A. T. Paterson, formerly second in command of "D" Company.

Under cover of a heavy preparatory barrage the enemy rushed the Australian trenches, which were only 40 yards from their own. After a few minutes of hand-to-hand fighting the Germans were driven back to their own lines, leaving their dead and two prisoners in the hands of the company. Severe casualties were inflicted by the Lewis gunners on the enemy as he retired across No Man's Land.

One of the Company bombers—Corporal D. A. Ross—had an exciting experience during this raid. Several of the bombers were resting in a dugout when the German artillery opened fire. The crash of bursting shells awakened them, and they immediately went to their post which was some distance along the trench. Corporal Ross, however, continued to sleep unnoticed by his comrades. He received a sudden and unpleasant awakening by being tapped in the abdomen by a German. There was no alternative but to surrender, and his captor led him for a few yards along the trench. However, the bomber was watching for an opportunity, and seeing the German off his guard for a moment, he dealt him a smashing blow on the jaw with his fist and closed with him. The two men fell into a shell hole where they rolled over and over in a furious struggle. Corporal Ross eventually became the victor, and for his gallant conduct he was awarded the Military Medal.

The Company was congratulated on its splendid defence of the salient.

Both sides suffered heavy casualties in killed and wounded.

On March 2 the battalion was relieved and marched to the West Baths billets in the little town of Erquinghem-Lys, south west of Armentieres, there to receive a brief respite from trench duty in the front line.

Map No. 2
LA CHAPELLE d'ARMENTIERES—COWGATE—RUE DU BOIS

MAP No. 2

LA CHAPELLE d'ARMENTIERES — COWGATE — RUE DU BOIS

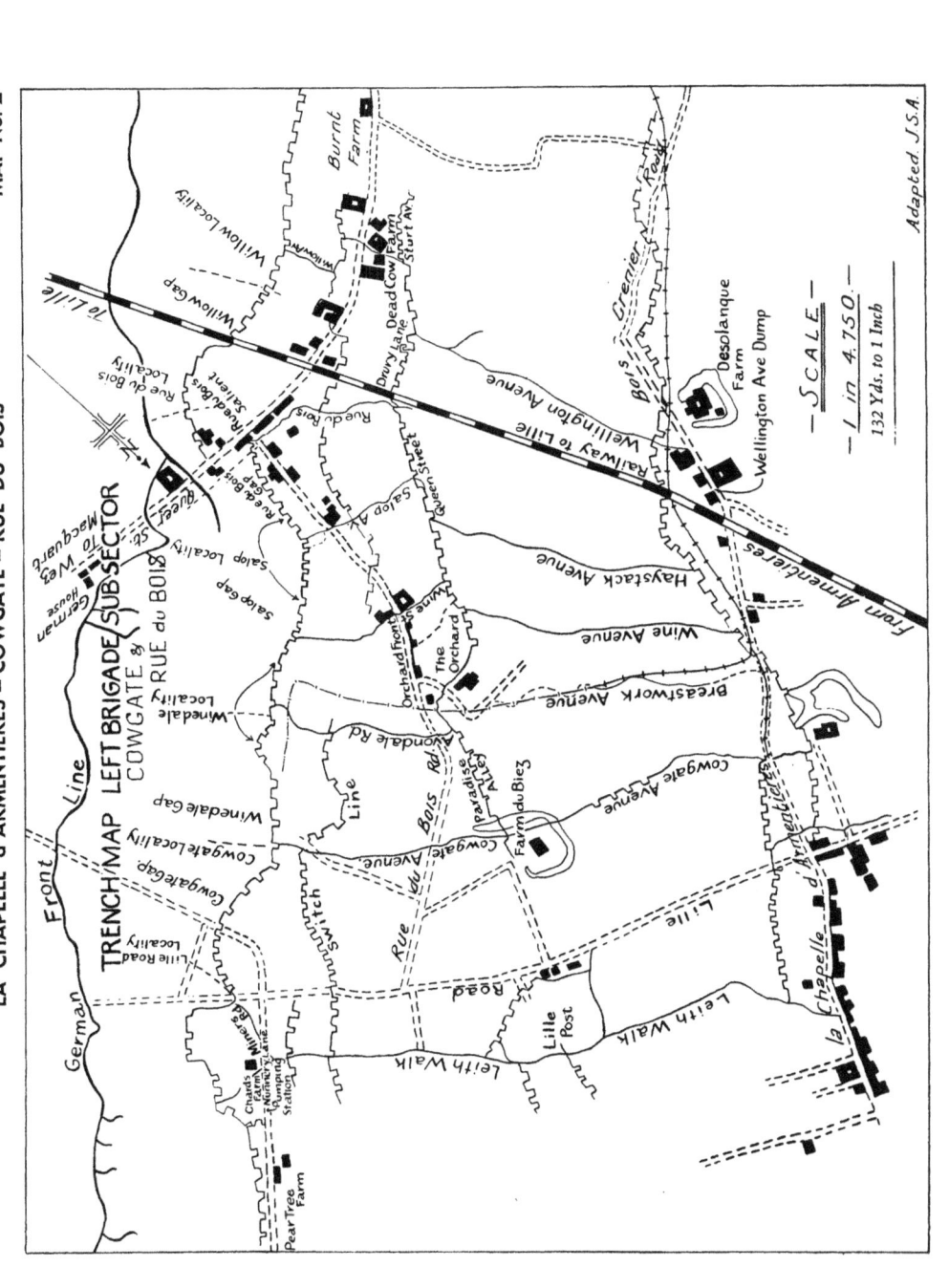

CHAPTER VI.

Preparing for Battle

For now sits Expectation in the air.
—SHAKESPEARE ("Henry V.").

FROM March 2 until March 9 the battalion remained at Erquinghem-Lys, engaged in the work of specialist training. It must not be supposed that, when a unit arrived on the front and went into action, its days of training were over. Every few weeks witnessed the introduction of new weapons; the tactics and methods of trench warfare were constantly changing; the conditions seldom remained the same for long; and thus units had to be incessantly training to cope with each new set of circumstances.

On March 6 the whole battalion was put through a practice cloud gas attack in the trenches of the training area. The enemy had used poison gas very largely on the Armentieres front, and that new weapon of modern warfare was an ever-present menace to troops both in forward and back areas. The wide-reaching effects of the gas necessitated that all men within a considerable distance of the line should maintain a constant vigilance and be prepared to protect themselves by means of their masks at a few moments' notice.

To ensure the proficiency of every individual man, frequent practices were necessary which, when possible, took the form of a sham gas attack. It was not all sham, because actual gas was sometimes discharged.

On March 9 the battalion left Erquinghem-Lys and marched to the hamlet of Nouveau Monde, situated on the outskirts of the old town of Bailleul. Here, for ten days, the training was continued in the Mont de Lille training area.

Nouveau Monde was, from the men's point of view, a distinct improvement on Erquinghem-Lys. After the day's work, a moderately pleasant evening could be spent in Bailleul which, despite its proximity to the front, was very little different from what it had been before the war. It was at this time seldom troubled by German artillery, and only a small percentage of its population had taken refuge in flight. To replace these, had come many scores of refugees from Messines, Neuve Eglise, and other villages, either occupied by the enemy or so close to the line as to become untenable. Thus Bailleul's streets were crowded, her factories running, her shops open and doing exceptional business. On market days the large cobbled square was thronged with stalls and booths from which the country people from surrounding farms and villages sold their produce, and from which travelling cheapjacks disposed of their goods at double pre-war rates. Cinema entertainments and a military pierrot show supplied amusement in the evenings. Thus billeting at Nouveau Monde meant for the 39th a return to comparative civilisation.

On March 16 the Corps Commander, Lieut.-General Godley, visited the area and inspected the battalion at work.

Each army operating on the front had a training area, some considerable distance from the battle-front. To these training areas, the various units were periodically sent both in order to undergo training and to get some relief amid peaceful surroundings from the constant strain of the front line. During the time spent at Nouveau Monde it became known that the 39th Battalion was to march to the training area in the Pas-de-Calais.

On March 21, the first day of the Spring, the long journey commenced at 9 a.m. Early in the afternoon the small village of Grand sec Bois was reached, where a halt was made and the men billeted for the night. The weather was cold, and heavy rain fell during the night, making the conditions and surroundings exceedingly uncomfortable. At 8 o'clock the following morning the march was continued through the town of Hazebrouck, a town of narrow winding streets and cobbled squares, and an important railway junction on the British lines of communication. One mile outside Hazebrouck on the main road to St. Omer the battalion was inspected on the march by the Army Commander, General Sir H. O. Plumer. At 2.15 p.m. the battalion arrived at the village of Ebblinghem, where good billets were available and the men spent a comfortable night. They were tired and footsore, and, although the march was being done in moderately easy stages, the cold weather and the snow-covered roads, had played havoc with the men's marching capabilities.

The chief trouble was blistered and frost-bitten feet. Yet, with their usual cheerfulness under hardship and their dogged tenacity, the "diggers" carried on, and few, if any, fell out along the road. The band was the soul of the battalion. The stirring marches and popular airs which it struck up, braced the men as nothing else could have done, tired though they were.

On March 23, the battalion, passing through Renescure, reached the small town of Arques. Here a network of canals intersected the streets, and heavy barges were seen manned by men of the Inland Water Transport Corps being towed in long rows by small steam river-tugs. This was a phase of the British Transport Services in France which had not been observed by the men before. Shortly after passing through Arques the battalion entered and passed through the ancient and historic city of St. Omer, where the veteran Lord Roberts died in the early months of the war.

The small village of Petit Difques, the destination of the 39th, was reached at 3.30 p.m. By this time the snow, which had been falling all day, was five inches deep. It continued to fall during the succeeding days, and the training had in consequence to be considerably curtailed.

The stay at Petit Difques gave the men an insight into life as it is led in the villages of Northern France. The villages in Pas-de-Calais are generally small groups of tiny two-roomed ramshackle houses, clustering round two or three large farms. They lack the cleanliness of the Australian townships on the one hand, and the tidiness and quaint beauty of the English villages on the other. The farms are for the most part rectangular groups of disreputable buildings, with odoriferous yards in the centre, altogether devoid of any modern improvements. The chief attraction of these villages lay rather in the surrounding country than in themselves. The pastoral lands of Pas-de-Calais are verdant stretches of undulating country, wooded in parts and watered by many small streams—an agreeable contrast to the dreary flats of Flanders.

The peasants of these back areas were different from the peasants of the Department du Nord. The latter were mostly of a taciturn, almost surly, disposition, whereas the people with whom the battalion came in contact at Petit Difques were amiable and hospitable.

The training done by the battalion was confined to tactical exercises, in which new attacking formations were practised, and to the training of the specialists.

On April 2 the largest of these tactical exercises was carried out in conjunction with the other battalions of the 10th Brigade. The Brigade was to attack a series of trenches south-east of the village of Quelmes, and assault and take that village. The operation was excellently carried out, and after the final objectives had been taken, the men were informed that the day's work might be regarded as a rehearsal of a similar operation to be executed the following day in the presence of the Corps' Divisional and Brigade Commanders.

Owing to an exceptionally heavy snowstorm on April 3, the manoeuvres had to be postponed until the 4th. Lieut.-General Godley, commanding the 2nd Anzac Corps, watched the operations and afterwards inspected the troops who had participated.

This event brought the period of training to a close, and the following day, April 5, an advance party, consisting of three officers and 126 other ranks, left by road for Armentieres.

At 10 a.m. on the same day the remainder of the battalion left Petit Difques and marched to the village of St. Martin au Laert, on the outskirts of St. Omer. Here they were billeted in barns and farm buildings for the night. The following day the men marched to the railway station where, at 10.30 a.m., they entrained for Steenwerck, the Divisional railhead for the Armentieres sector. The short period spent in Petit Difques, although not favoured by congenial weather, had been a pleasant break in the trying conditions of trench duty and a welcome relief from the intense strain of the forward areas. The brief rest and change had done the men a great deal of good, and they returned to the front more fit in every way for the strenuous days ahead.

At 1.50 p.m., on April 6, the main body of the battalion arrived and detrained at Steenwerck, and commenced a ten kilometre march to Armentieres which was reached at 4.30 p.m. The party which had travelled by road arrived an hour and a half later. The battalion was billeted in the Blue Factory and in the Hospice.

On April 8 the 39th relieved the 33rd Battalion in the Epinette Sector on the right of Houplines. The relief was carried out uneventfully, and the men settled down to a nine days' tour of trench duty. Very little happened worthy of note on either side. Enemy artillery was active, and there were several casualties. The worst of these bombardments was a barrage to cover an enemy raid on the adjoining sector. Unfortunately most of the shells fell on the 39th frontage, and killed and wounded several men.

The 39th was relieved by the 37th Battalion on April 17. Heavy rain fell during the relief, and the men were thoroughly wet when they reached billets near the Armentieres railway station. During the ensuing days, training proceeded and the usual working parties were supplied. As poison gas was being used by our troops against the enemy, a frequent duty of the working parties was the carrying of cylinders of gas up to the forward trenches. The men who were not employed on these duties spent the days drilling and practising with the Lewis gun, bombs and gas. During the evenings the battalion band played in a disused linen factory near the billets. These excellent musical interludes, so reminiscent of other and happier days, never failed to attract large audiences, not only from the battalion but also from other troops billeted in the vicinity, with a sprinkling of the civil population of the city. Armentieres was still quiet during these days. At times it was difficult to realise that the Prussians were at the gates of the city, and it was easy to be lulled into a sense of false security.

Occasionally an enemy shell would whine through the air and burst among the houses in a cloud of bricks and smoke. But despite the easy target which Armentieres presented to the enemy's artillery, this was rather the exception than the rule. The sector was a notoriously quiet one, and it suited the enemy to keep it so. He therefore did not invite the retaliation of the British guns.

Yet as events proved, this comparative peace in Armentieres was but a lull before a storm. The city was not so lightly to escape the hand of war.

During the stay in billets, the men recorded their votes in the Australian Federal Elections. April 25 and 26 were the polling days, and the votes were taken among the shattered houses of Armentieres in just the same business-like manner that would have been adopted in the polling booths in Australia. All necessary papers had been prepared at the London Administrative Headquarters, and regimental officers conducted the polling. The organisation was in every way admirable.

An important change of the division's sector was now imminent.

During this period a percentage of officers and N.C.Os. were daily reconnoitring the trenches just taken over by the 43rd Australian Battalion in front of Ploegsteert Wood, near Messines.

On April 27 the 39th commenced the relief of the 43rd Battalion, completing it on the evening of the 28th. There was a lively initiation to our new sector. Soon after taking over the line it was notified that a gas attack was to be directed against the enemy early the following morning. Men trained in gas warfare—one of the "special" companies of the Royal Engineers—had all preparations in hand, and, a few hours after the relief the gas was discharged. All the men had their masks on, and, although they could see nothing, the fact that gas was being sent over was known by the hiss as it escaped from the cylinders. Very shortly afterwards a heavy enemy barrage fell on our lines. Shells shrieked through the air, machine gun bullets whizzed overhead or pattered into the sandbags, and the sky was red with bursting shrapnel. The Germans never liked being paid back in their own coin, and whenever it was demonstrated practically to them that the German Empire did not possess a monopoly of poison gas, they became very angry and replied with violent artillery "strafes." The battalion's working parties were kept busy the following day repairing the damage done.

The Ploegsteert Sector was a great change from the comparative quiet of Houplines. The enemy was very active. Patrols had exciting adventures and hairbreadth escapes in No Man's Land, where enemy machine-gun posts and snipers made the work of patrols a business of "touch and go."

One night a small patrol belonging to the 39th crept over the parapet and out into the shadows of No Man's Land to reconnoitre the enemy's positions. Its members were new hands at patrolling, and for some of them this was their first adventure in that sinister belt of ground between the trenches. They were on their guard and looking out keenly for enemy snipers as they advanced cautiously over the broken ground.

The tunnellers had been for a long time driving saps underneath the enemy positions on the Ploegsteert Sector and on Messines Ridge. The entrances to some of these tunnels, or sap-heads, were situated in the trenches held by the battalion, and early in the morning of April 30 the enemy, evidently uneasy and alarmed at the extensive mining of his position, made a raid against the St. Yves sector of the battalion frontage with the object of blowing up the sap-heads. A party of the battalion scouts was just returning from a night reconnaissance of No Man's Land and had almost reached their own wire when they heard the voices of the approaching Germans. The scouts hurried into their own front line and gave the alarm to the officer on guard, who fired the S.O.S. signal to the artillery. No sooner had this been done than the enemy barrage opened.

The artillery fire was most intense and took the form of a box barrage enclosing the area of the enemy's attack. There was a small gap in the front line a little to the right of the communication trench known as Toronto Avenue. This gap was only lightly wired and it was here that the enemy intended to enter our trenches. The raiding party, 80 to 100 strong, carried with it a large supply of bombs and explosives. "C" company's frontage was to the right of the gap and "A" company's to the left. On them the enemy's attack fell, and for a short time a stiff fight ensued. One of the fire bays on "C" company's front was blown in and some of the enemy succeeded in entering the trench. Private F. Waring, of "C" company, at this critical juncture took his Lewis gun into a shell hole in rear of the trench, and bringing it into action, inflicted many casualties among the enemy on the parapet. For this splendid piece of work he was later awarded the Distinguished Conduct Medal. The raiders were eventually ejected from the trenches and returned in disorder across No Man's Land where the Australian Artillery fire played havoc among them. They left behind two dead, a number of picks and shovels, and boxes of explosives. The

The Scouts "No Man's Land"

Facing Page 102

attempt to reach the sap-heads had been completely frustrated, but at no light cost to the battalion.

Captain L. Roberts, the officer commanding "C" company, was killed, together with thirteen other ranks. The wounded numbered two officers and 47 other ranks.

Private C. R. Makeham was taken prisoner during the attack—the first prisoner lost by the battalion.

Several casualties were caused in the support lines and communication trenches by the enemy barrage fire.

The enemy dead were identified as belonging to the 5th Bavarian Regiment, one of them being one of the officers who had led the raid.

May opened with glorious Spring weather. At daybreak and in the twilight the songs of the birds could be heard all round the shell-torn countryside, and often the call of the cuckoo sounded from the trees. Shrubs and trees were bursting into leaf and bud, and a carpet of wildflowers came to cover the scarred face of No Man's Land and to spread a pall of tiny blossoms over the little mounds with their rough wooden crosses where the dead were sleeping. With the breath of Spring in the air, with blue skies above and the beauties of nature, war seemed a sacrilege. And yet the advent of Spring and fine weather only meant that war would be pursued by both sides more vigorously, relentlessly and terribly.

On May 5 a patrol operating in No Man's Land captured a prisoner. The circumstances surrounding the incident are interesting and typical of the adventures which befall a scout in the execution of his duties.

As usual the posts in the front line were warned that a patrol was going out into No Man's Land. This was done by the leader of the party, Private G. E. Watkins. When Watkins reached the post on the extreme right of the frontage, the observer on duty told him that he thought an enemy patrol was out in No Man's Land. The two men peered into the darkness beyond the parapet, but no signs of the enemy could be seen or heard. They fired a Very light, but it revealed nothing. Then a Lewis gun was brought into action and a magazine fired haphazardly into No Man's Land. Having done all that was possible to disconcert any Germans patrolling between the trenches, the little party of five crawled out cautiously towards the centre of No Man's Land. The night was bright, and as they moved forward the leader suddenly saw in front of him a black object coming towards the patrol. He at once concluded that the German patrol was still at work and that it was advancing on his party. Watkins got his men into a convenient shell hole, gave them instructions to await his orders, and then he moved out to intercept the enemy. By this time the moving object had approached so near that Watkins could see that it was a man carrying arms, crawling laboriously across the uneven ground. When he had approached to within 10 or 12 yards, Watkins decided to tackle him. To make absolutely certain that he was an enemy he first challenged him. The unknown at once dropped flat and lay motionless. Believing him to be leading others, Watkins called to his comrades to fire a volley. In the uncertain light the shots went wide. After a moment's pause he drew his revolver and crept over towards the German. Suddenly the latter rose and threw up his hands in token of surrender. He did not show a sign of fight, was disarmed, and escorted back to the 39th trenches. On being questioned he said that he had been out on a patrol with four others and that the fire of the Lewis gun immediately prior to the 39th patrol's departure had killed one and wounded three of his comrades. A patrol went out to verify this information but no bodies could be found, and if the prisoner had spoken the truth it was evident that the wounded Germans had succeeded in regaining their own trenches, taking the dead man with them. This prisoner, a Bavarian, proved to be both intelligent and loquacious.

On the morning of May 6, whilst patrolling No Man's Land, a patrol of the battalion, consisting of Privates C. Cameron, J. G. Pulbrook, J. B. Stephens and Tom W. Martin (Regimental No. 1683), was fired on by an enemy patrol lying in wait behind a hedge. Bombs and rifle shots were exchanged. Private Cameron, the patrol leader, was severely wounded, also Pulbrook and Stephens. The responsibility of protecting the wounded men and driving off the enemy patrol, rested upon Martin. He moved to a position in front of the patrol, threw bombs at the enemy and fired rifle shots. The onslaught was too much for the enemy, who immediately sought safety in flight. Single handed, Martin carried each wounded man, a distance of 150 yards to the wire. With the assistance of men from the front line they were carried to a place of safety. He was awarded the Belgian Croix de Guerre.

On May 6, the battalion was relieved by the 40th and went back to Ploegsteert Wood, where the men found billets in dug-outs and partially-demolished houses. The surroundings here, notwithstanding the devastation of war, were very beautiful and the weather was ideal. The days were sunny and warm, and the Spring foliage clothed the slopes of the low hills and formed a canopy of leaf and branches in Ploegsteert Wood. The crops in the fields surrounding Nieppe and Steenwerck were already high and the pastures rich in lush grass and golden with buttercups and cowslips. It was indeed a change from the utter desolation of the Flanders fields.

With the advent of clear skies came increased activity in the air, and many exciting fights were witnessed high above Ploegsteert Wood. Every day the squadrons of fighting planes could be seen circling and banking in the air, scintillating in the sun as they turned about. Then perhaps the muffled burst of anti-aircraft shrapnel would signify that a German machine was over our lines, and a little later the crackle of machine guns would be heard in the sky, and one knew that somewhere in that great expanse of blue a deadly combat was being waged. Sometimes a blazing mass came falling through the air bearing the pilot and observer to almost certain death. The days immediately prior to the Battle of Messines Ridge were full of activity in the air, and the slopes of Hill 63 gave good vantage ground for the observation of these contests.

A great concentration of artillery of all calibres was gradually being made on this front. Guns were everywhere—in ruined buildings and farmhouses, in excavated positions and amid the trees and bushes, skilfully camouflaged with greenery. A battery of eighteen pounders took up a position in rear of the battalion in the wood and their fire was responsible for many uneasy moments, as the enemy had located this battery's position, and made several attempts to blow up the guns by long range artillery fire. On one occasion the men of the 39th had to abandon their dugouts and take refuge from the storm of enemy shell fire in near-by trenches.

During the evenings the band played among the woods, and the men sat in little groups smoking and yarning. So the days passed in Ploegsteert Wood.

The first adjutant of the 39th Battalion was Captain R. Lamble. On him devolved much of the arduous, detailed work of forming and organising the unit. A keen and able administrator possessing both geniality and the gift of tact, he made an indelible imprint on the 39th.

Only those with military service can appreciate the real importance of the adjutant's duties both in peace and war. While on service Captain Lamble was often busy for twenty-four hours a day. The high efficiency of the battalion owed much to his qualities. In May, 1917, when he joined the Brigade staff the whole battalion regretted his departure. Later he became Brigade-Major.

Captain L. L. Beauchamp was appointed adjutant of the 39th on Captain Lamble's transfer to the Brigade staff. In the new adjutant the battalion was fortunate in having an officer who could ably maintain the standards set by Captain Lamble.

On May 13, the 39th moved to the Catacombs—a great labyrinth of underground passages tunnelled (by Australian miners) into the heart of Hill 63, resembling a subterranean city. "Streets" were laid out in systematic order—each street bearing a name, and on either side bunks had been built in. The whole place was lit by electricity. Here the men lived in absolute security, for the Catacombs gave protection against the largest German shells.

Large working parties had to be supplied each day. The preparations for the assault on Messines were being pushed rapidly forward, and new trenches, tramways, gun positions and dumps were in course of construction in the area, entailing the employment of the bulk of those men who were not in the front line. Many hundreds of truck loads of material were sent along the tramways daily to all parts of the front. The names of Hyde Park Corner, Hunter and Anscroft Avenues, Seaforth Farm, Anton's Farm, Hasted House, Mud Lane, and many other places will recall memories of these Messines working parties to any men who participated in the work.

A raiding party had been chosen from the battalion and sent back to Nieppe on May 20, to undergo special training for a raid which had as its object the obtaining of information as to the enemy's dispositions.

At 1.45 a.m., on the morning of May 30, the raid was carried out under the command of Captain P. L. Smith. The party comprised three officers and 60 other ranks. The customary barrage fire was directed upon the enemy lines, following which the party assaulted and entered the German trenches, these, however, were found to be practically empty. No prisoners were taken although much valuable information was gained. The casualties sustained by the battalion in this operation were exceptionally heavy, numbering in all seven killed and 33 wounded. Most of these were inflicted by the retaliatory fire of the enemy's artillery while the raiders were returning across No Man's Land.

These last days were full of preparation for the coming attack on Messines Ridge, and the atmosphere was one of excitement and expectation.

It was the eve of the Third Division's first battle, and the battalions were waiting eagerly for the day on which they would storm the strong enemy positions—the positions which gave the Germans such an inestimable advantage on that front, and which looked menacingly down on the British from Armentieres to Ypres.

On May 30 the 39th sent a party of two officers and 66 other ranks to a concentration camp at Morbecque. These men were to form a nucleus for the re-organisation of the battalion after the battle.

June opened with glorious weather. The month was to prove full of stirring events.

CHAPTER VII.

The Battle of Messines

And louder than the bolts of Heaven
Far flashed the red artillery. —CAMPBELL.

THE British assault on Messines Ridge had been in preparation for a considerable time. The high ground of the ridge. affording observation over the whole Ypres salient was the key to that portion of the front. As long as the enemy retained possession of it no movement of troops could take place unobserved. The Ypres salient was therefore regarded as the most sinister and perilous part of the entire battle front. The removal of this enemy menace was the object of the attack on Messines. The enemy's defensive positions were known to be of great strength. The ruined town of Messines situated on the southern end of the ridge was nothing less than a fortress of concrete machine-gun posts which presented a difficult obstacle to attacking infantry. It will be appreciated that preparations on an extensive scale were necessary for the projected attack. These preparations had been in progress since May of the preceding year. For eighteen months the engineers had been driving long saps underneath the enemy positions, and long before the attack these had been charged with sufficient explosives to reduce the almost impregnable defences to heaps of debris, and to blow the Messines front line defences sky high. Artillery had been concentrated on a gigantic scale along the eight-mile front of the offensive, and colossal dumps of munitions had been constructed in the forward areas from which light tramways were laid to carry the shells to the battery positions. The enemy, having seen many of the preparations, knew of the assault which was to be launched upon him, and during the days immediately prior to the battle, he brought heavy artillery fire to bear on the British lines and back areas in a vain effort to break up the British concentrations of men, guns and material.

Aerial observation was, to a great extent, made impossible to the enemy by the activity and vigilance of the British aeroplane squadrons, while skilful camouflage of the dumps and other positions made accurate shooting extremely difficult for the enemy's artillery. Thus the preparations for the attack suffered very little from German shelling.

On June 1, the battalion was still stationed in the Catacombs. At 3 o'clock in the afternoon of that day a great dump of trench mortar shells at Hyde Park Corner exploded and shook the ground like an earthquake. The precise cause of this disaster was never ascertained. The effects were cataclysmic. Sheds and buildings within a radius of three hundred yards were blown down; the electric lights in the Catacombs were extinguished; and a great column of smoke and flame shot far into the sky. A Very light store was set on fire, and the coloured lights and rockets mingled with the smoke from the exploding shells. An appalling number of casualties resulted from the explosion. The concussion alone hurled men down, while flying splinters from the exploding mass of projectiles killed and wounded many men working in the vicinity. Fortunately for the 39th the majority of the men were absent on working parties, and the battalion did not suffer as heavily as it might have done. It lost two killed and 19 wounded. The stretcher-bearers of the 39th hurried to the scene of the disaster, and the wounded were quickly transferred to the Charing Cross dressing station. From the clouds of smoke the enemy guessed what had happened and sent shell after shell into the area.

Enemy shell fire was daily increasing over a considerable area of the British lines and the men had many exciting moments in the Catacombs. Shells frequently fell unpleasantly close. On one day a battalion cookhouse and an adjacent New Zealand

Officers of the Battalion, Neuve Eglise, Belgium

Y.M.C.A. hut were hit. The days and nights were full of hard work, and the men spent most of their time on working parties. What leisure hours they had were occupied in writing letters home. About this time there arrived a consignment of boxes from the Australian Comforts Fund, originally intended for Christmas but delayed in transit.

Just as the intense gunfire on the ground heralded the approaching battle, so in the air extraordinary activity on the part of the British fighting and scouting planes suggested the approach of stirring events. Every day squadrons of the British Air Force patrolled over the lines ready to pounce upon and destroy any enemy who ventured to cross. The activity of German aeroplanes was limited to raids on the British observation balloons. During the evening a German plane would sometimes come across in the failing light of dusk and dive suddenly on to the huge "gas-bags," empty its machine guns, and then turn and race for its own lines amid a storm of anti-aircraft shrapnel. Meanwhile the balloon burned in mid-air, and the parachutes bearing the observers floated slowly down.

An observation balloon near the village of Nieppe was a perpetual source of annoyance to the enemy. This position gave excellent observation of the German lines, consequently it was attacked by enemy planes almost daily. Times out of number the balloons in this position were set on fire and destroyed, notwithstanding the mobile batteries of anti-aircraft guns mounted on motor lorries which were sent to protect them. No sooner was one destroyed than another took its place. This expedient, which speaks volumes for British organisation and administration, no doubt annoyed the enemy.

On June 2 the 39th was relieved by the 44th in the Catacombs and moved into billets at Oosthove Farm, on the outskirts of Nieppe, there to make final preparations for its share in the attack. During the relief the enemy heavily shelled the British battery positions and the roads of the back areas without, however, inflicting any material damage.

On the following day, June 3, the German artillery commenced to pour shells into the villages of Nieppe and Pont de Nieppe. Many casualties were caused among the civilian inhabitants and numerous houses wrecked. The enemy directed a great volume of the shell fire against the Nieppe bridge which spanned the River Lys about a kilometre west of Armentieres. Although enemy shells fell dangerously close on both sides of the river, the bridge escaped unharmed.

At the same time a storm of enemy shell fire was concentrated on back areas. Small, out-of-the-way hamlets, which had been regarded as havens of security and refuge by the homeless fugitives from the devastated areas, were swept by the German guns. Up to the last the enemy was vainly attempting to prevent the British attack.

Just before midnight on June 4, the enemy "strafed" these back areas with thousands of gas shells. It is probable that he expected the attack to be launched that night and hoped to cause losses among the troops which would have been concentrating.

The men of the 39th had to wear their respirators for many hours to protect themselves from the dense gas near the billets at Oosthove Farm. Two officers and three other ranks were gassed and had to be evacuated to hospital. Shelling continued during the whole time the battalion was at Oosthove Farm. A hut in the grounds of the farm used by the officers was wrecked by a shell: but fortunately it was unoccupied at the time. On another occasion one of the enemy shells burst through the house adjoining, fortunately without injuring anyone.

The final preparations for the battle were by this time almost complete. Positions had been constructed for the artillery to occupy when the advance was made, and thousands of shells placed in readiness near new emplacements. Under cover of darkness endless columns of motor and horse transport filled the roads, carrying up to the front ammunition, reserve supplies of rations and water, timber, explosives and everything necessary for the success of the operation.

Prior to marching up, the men of the 39th were taken over the route to be followed to the assembly point. This route was officially known as the "Green Route." It led through Ploegsteert Wood up to the trenches fronting Messines Hill, from which the battalion was to launch the attack. The flank of the 39th rested on Anton's Farm on the right, and extended to Seaforth Farm on the left.

On June 4 the Operation Order for the battle was issued, and the platoons were instructed regarding their duties in the attack.

On the 5th, enemy artillery fire increased in intensity. The baths at Pont de Nieppe were hit during the day, and a hail of shells fell in the vicinity of the battalion's billets. The men had to seek safety in the fields near by. One high explosive shell burst between two of the huts, cutting the frail buildings to pieces, smashing the rifles and ruining the equipment.

The working parties on their way to and from the trenches had to run the gauntlet of the German fire, and many were killed or wounded.

On June 6, every man was in readiness for the battle, and equipped with the regulation supply of ammunition, bombs, iron rations (i.e., bully beef and biscuits), a pick or shovel, field dressing, water bottle, sandbags, rifle, bayonet and gas mask. To facilitate re-organisation during the action, the men of each company had distinctive colour patches sewn on to the backs of their tunics.

During the evening one of the "padres" of the Brigade gathered some of the men round him in a field near the farm and held a communion service for those about to go into battle.

After the evening meal the men were informed that the attack would take place in the early hours of the following morning. A letter from the Corps Commander was read telling them what was expected and wishing them good luck.

At 11.42 p.m. the 39th Battalion marched in battle order out of Oosthove Farm on the way up to the assembly point. Simultaneously along the front, scores of other battalions were marching up to the front line.

Shortly after the battalion left billets it encountered a heavy gas-shell bombardment directed against the approaches to the British trenches. Practically every unit on this part of the front was subjected to shelling of great violence during the march up to the trenches to participate in the Battle of Messines. The route from Oosthove Farm lay through Ploegsteert Corner and Anscroft Avenue, and almost from the beginning of the march the men had to wear their respirators. The night was dark and calm and the gas hung about like a heavy fog, while the shells came across in a steady stream. The men groped their way along the narrow tracks, frequently falling over unseen obstacles into ditches and shell holes and often losing the gas masks from their faces in the fall. It became necessary for them to hold on to the bayonet scabbards of their comrades in front to avoid being separated from their units. That difficult march to the trenches was nothing less than a nightmare. Scores of men were falling out gassed, or wounded by the flying shell splinters. The gas shells poured into Ploegsteert Wood and burst with low reports or "pops." They came hurtling through the air at low velocity, falling in a steady shower along the battalion's path. At Ploegsteert Corner a high explosive shell burst in the centre of the leading platoon with disastrous results. It was practically impossible for officers and N.C.Os. to wear their masks effectively owing to the necessity of directing and controlling the men. Major S. E. Tucker, who was in command (the C.O., Lieut.-Colonel R. O. Henderson, having gone ahead earlier in the day to his Headquarters), was overcome by the gas and the senior company commander, Captain A. T. Paterson, took command. Officers and men were overcome every few yards, and the track through Bunhill Row and Mud Lane was strewn with prostrate men coughing and gasping in agony. Captain Paterson eventually reached the Regimental Aid Post in Anscroft Avenue about 2.20 on the morning of the 7th, with only twelve men. Stragglers, dazed and exhausted, gradually dribbled in until the number at the assembly point reached a total of 120 men. Captain Paterson obtained all available ammonia capsules from the Regimental Medical Officer (Captain Ivan Blaubaum) at the Regimental Aid Post and distributed them among the partially-gassed men in the front line. Zero hour was 3.10 a.m., and twenty minutes before "zero" the 120 men were in position in the battalion assembly trenches on the south bank of the River Douve and to the north of Anton's Farm.

Captain Paterson re-organised the battalion, and in view of its diminished strength he went to Headquarters and obtained permission from the C.O. to go to the assault in one wave instead of two. It had originally been arranged that the first wave, under the command of Major Tucker, should capture Douve Farm and Avenue Farm and the second, under the command of Captain Paterson, should go as far as the Grey Farm Line (known as the Black Line) which, after capture, was to be held at all costs.

The assembly trenches being on high ground were free from gas, and during the short period before zero hour the men were able to take off their masks and recover from the exhaustion of the march. The morning was fine and the British forward positions quiet. The men's nerves were taut and strained as they waited for the opening of the barrage which would give the signal to attack.

The battalion's final objective (Black Line) was to the north of Grey Farm, which was situated in the fields about 300 yards south of the River Douve and about the same distance west of Tilleul Road.

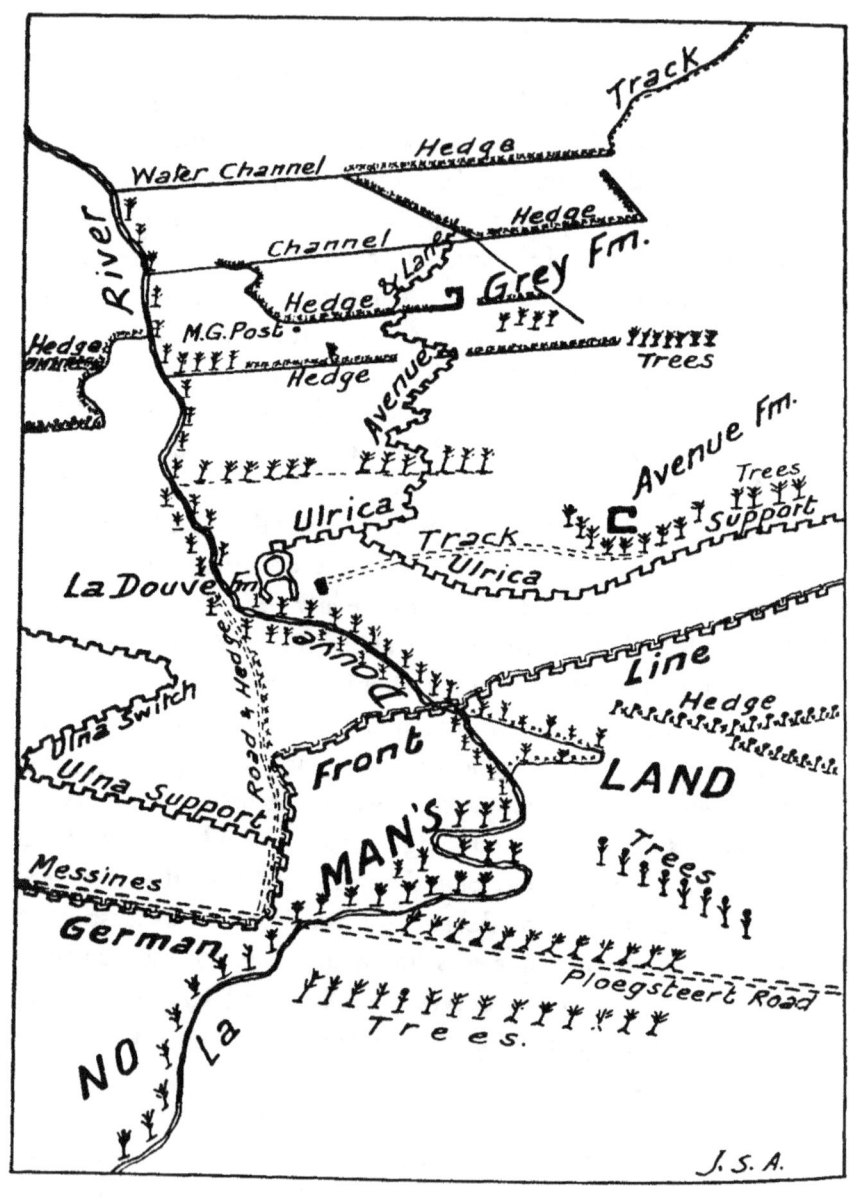

Battle of Messines, Key Map

THE BATTLE OF MESSINES

Facing Page 116 Battle of Messines,
Ground at Messines won by the 39th Battalion

At precisely 3.10 a.m., 19 huge mines were exploded underneath the German positions along the ridge. Their almost simultaneous explosion was like a series of titanic thunderclaps, and the deafening roar and terrific concussion made the whole countryside quake. With one tremendous burst the British barrage opened, and, in less time than it takes to tell, every battery on the front was in action. Guns flashed from Armentieres to Ypres. This was the signal to attack, and the men scrambled over the parapet and advanced across No Man's Land behind the curtain of bursting shrapnel. The 40th Battalion was on the left flank of the 39th, and the 9th Brigade attacked on the battalion's right.

The British barrage was extremely accurate. It fell in front of the attacking infantry—a great wall of flame and smoke in the midst of which huge geysers of earth were shot skywards. At zero hour the enemy's barrage fell heavily in front of his own line. It was a zig-zag barrage and the 39th was fortunate enough to get through gaps without many casualties.

Amid the indescribable turmoil, dominated by the sharp crack of thousands of machine gun bullets passing over the heads of the advancing men, the battalion moved steadily forward towards its objectives. The German front line trenches were found to be badly damaged by British shell fire. From a system of defensive earthworks they had been transformed into a chaotic mass of smashed timber, churned up soil and barbed wire.

The enemy fire was feeble in comparison with that of the British guns, and it was evident that the German batteries were being hotly engaged. The casualties suffered during the advance were principally due to machine gun fire which, as the 39th moved forward, still further diminished its thin ranks. The enemy was encountered when advancing through the German support lines. The memory of the comrades left struggling in agony for breath in the gas-drenched approach-march dispelled any thought of quarter from the men's minds. On the left flank of the battalion the enemy barrage came down on his own front line while it was still occupied by his own troops. Some Germans had taken refuge in their dugouts, and the 39th left flank south-west of La Douve Farm successfully bombed them out of their refuge.

The battalion had captured its first objectives—La Douve and Avenue Farms.

The two inner flanks of the battalion joined up along the line of a track running from the Douve River past Avenue Farm to Ulrica Avenue, and the advance was continued behind the barrage to a point about two hundred yards short of the objective, Grey Farm Line. Here Captain Paterson ordered the men to take cover behind a hedge in a ditch, and flares were lighted to show the battalion's position to the contact aeroplane patrols. Half an hour had elapsed since the attack opened, and the 39th had almost reached its objective.

Shortly after 5 o'clock the final phase of the 39th's advance began. As the British barrage lifted to beyond the Black Line it left unharmed a machine gun post to the north of Grey Farm. This gun, mounted on the roof of a concrete strongpost, held up the battalion's advance and the men were compelled to seek cover in adjacent shell holes. An attempt was made on the right to outflank the gun, but the fire was too intense, and for a time it seemed that this enemy post would stop the advance. It was concealed from the attacking troops of the battalion on the left because of a hedge. The situation was saved by the gallantry of the officer in charge, Captain A. T. Paterson, who, advancing closer, silenced with a rifle the enemy gunner working the gun on the strongpost roof. While the gun was thus temporarily out of action he led those men forward who were near him, rushed the position, and captured the crews and two machine guns.

The battalion thus carried its final objective and then linked up with the 34th Battalion. The task of consolidating the new position then began. Shortly after taking the objective, the strength of the battalion was only 88 men. Although "C" com-

"A" Company, Bouillancourt, France

pany was in Brigade reserve, 272 casualties had occurred since leaving Oosthove Farm.

The work of making the new position secure against an enemy counter-attack was rapidly pursued, and exhausted as the men were, they put all their energy into the task of consolidation. The 34th Battalion was to have taken over from the 39th at 7 a.m., but was unable to do so until three hours and twenty minutes later, when the following receipt was given for the ground won:

> "I have taken over the Black Line of consolidation from my left to the Douve from Captain Paterson, 39th Battalion A.I.F."

10.20 a.m.,   (Sgd.) R. Stewart,
    7th June, 1917.   Captain, 34th Battn.

Whilst waiting for the 34th to take over, digging in was continued with very little interference from the enemy guns. The British aeroplanes, working in liaison with the artillery, were flying at low altitudes over the forward positions. The contact patrols flew over the enemy lines, and whenever the Germans massed to make a counter attack, the location of their assembly point was signalled back to the British batteries which promptly brought heavy shell fire to bear on it. The British superiority in the air was never more clearly illustrated than during the Battle of Messines, and no praise is too great for the gallant and daring work of the pilots during the attack. In the course of the morning one machine was struck by a shell in mid-air and crashed to earth in front of the 39th's position.

Towards mid-day the enemy's artillery fire increased, and all the German batteries from the direction of Comines and Lille seemed to concentrate their fire along the Valley of the Douve and across the top of the ridge. At 11 a.m. the battalion received orders to stand by on the north side of the river below Schnitzel Farm.

Walking back over the shell-torn ground across which the advance had swept, one found everywhere appalling evidence of the efficacy of artillery fire and the stark horror of modern war. The bodies of our own and enemy dead littered the wrecked countryside. Great shell craters yawned in the fields; broken equipment and rifles lay about among the debris, and over all drifted still the smoke of battle.

At this stage the 37th Battalion could be seen coming forward in extended order over the rise of Messines Hill. The enemy seemed to be concentrating a great deal of artillery fire in front of the advance, and every now and then the men would drop to the ground as shells burst near them, only to rise and move forward again.

Stretcher parties were working across the battlefield picking up the wounded, and enemy prisoners were being escorted to the rear. The enemy was firing heavily on Messines village (which had been taken early in the morning by the New Zealanders) and the crest of the ridge was being continually plastered with high explosive shells from which great clouds of black smoke drifted upwards.

The battalion received orders to consolidate on its new position west of Schnitzel Farm, and it was while here that Captain Paterson was wounded. He remained on duty for several hours after being wounded, inspiring his men, but owing to loss of blood, and also the effects of gas during the approach-march he handed over the command to Lieutenant W. Palstra. Earlier in the day this officer had been of great assistance to Captain Paterson, and had throughout the battle shown much resource and devotion to duty. Lieutenant Palstra received a Military Cross for his part in the attack.

For his gallant conduct and skilful leadership, continuing up to the time he fell wounded, Captain A. T. Paterson was subsequently awarded the Military Cross. The work of this officer had a most definite bearing on the battalion's success.

The battalion continued the task of consolidation and the entrenching tool that day in the hands of the "digger" did excellent work. Early in the afternoon troops, going forward to attack, passed through the battalion, thus removing the possibility of a surprise attack. The reserve company, 100 strong, reinforced the battalion, and assisted in digging the new trenches. During the day small parties of men were engaged in "mopping up" the ground over which the attack had passed and in clearing out many deep enemy dugouts which had been overlooked during the advance. Many of these were found to be full of enemy soldiers who with difficulty were prevailed upon to quit their shelter.

That night pack mules were brought up to the south of Schnitzel Farm with hot food for the men.

Meanwhile the attack had progressed successfully in all other localities. The powerfully fortified ridge from the Douve River to Wytschaete had been carried at small cost. Over 7,000 prisoners had been taken, and the cost in British casualties was lower than that of any previous battle fought by the British on this scale. (The cost was about 25,000, June 7—12.)

The 3rd Australian Division formed the right flank of the attack and advanced astride the River Douve. The New Zealand division had attacked opposite Messines and taken that village, the advance being continued by the 4th Australian Division which passed through the New Zealanders. British Divisions had attacked on the left flank opposite Wytschaete with equal success, and thus with comparative ease and slight loss, the enemy was driven out of positions which had been considered almost impregnable.

On the morning of June 8, the 39th was located in an abandoned trench between Ulna Avenue and Douve Farm, and during the day was engaged in digging communication trenches towards Schnitzel and Betlheem Farms. The enemy again tried to counter-attack and used heavy artillery fire against the advanced British positions. His attempts were repeatedly repelled. By nightfall the attacking troops had pushed the work of consolidation sufficiently forward to make them secure in their new positions. Consolidation was continued during the night of the 8/9th under heavy enemy fire, and at 5 a.m. on the 9th what was left of the battalion was relieved by a battalion of the 11th Brigade. The 39th had been over fifty hours in the attack before it marched back to Nieppe.

The men of the battalion had borne themselves magnificently throughout the operation and had carried on gallantly and uncomplainingly despite the large number of casualties which had entailed so much additional hardship and strain. They had greatly distinguished themselves and had responded to all demands. They had captured their objectives, taken many enemy machine guns, trench mortars and prisoners, and done much valuable work in consolidating new positions and in repulsing the enemy.

At Nieppe hot food and baths were waiting for the exhausted troops, and there were also comfortable billets where they could rest and make up for the three previous sleepless nights.

On the 10th the battalion's nucleus returned from Morbecque, full of anxiety regarding their comrades, and the progress of the battle.

When full details of the battle were made known, it was found that the attack had exceeded all expectations and among the troops the general opinion was that, had the success been anticipated, it might have been turned into a victory which might have dealt a smashing blow to the German armies in Flanders, but both British and German commanders knew that a thrust at Messines, with the River Lys and Canal close in front, and Lille forts on the flank, could never be a decisive blow. It was a necessary preliminary to the Battle of Ypres.

Map No. 3
BATTLE OF MESSINES

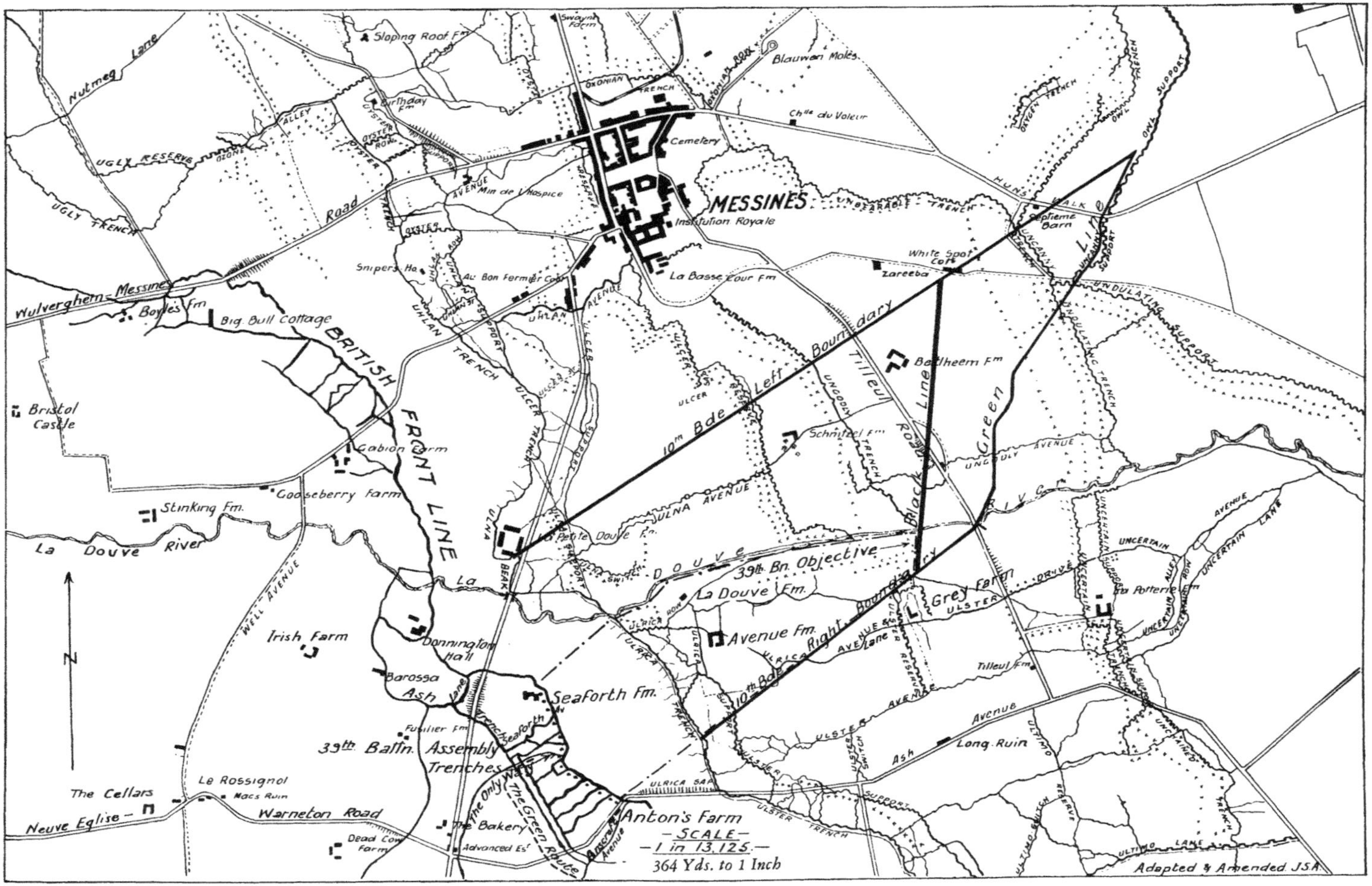

MAP No. 3

BATTLE OF MESSINES

CHAPTER VIII.

Summer and Autumn, 1917

"Take my word for it, if you had seen but one day of war, you would pray to Almighty God that you might never see such a thing again."
—WELLINGTON.

AFTER a day spent in billets at Nieppe the battalion marched on June 11 to a camping ground in the vicinity of the village of Neuve Eglise, and Keepaway Farm, remaining there for eight days as Corps Reserve. The first task was the re-organisation of the thinned ranks of the battalion. The Messines attack had exacted a heavy toll in killed and wounded, and the companies and platoons were greatly reduced in numbers.

To fill the vacancies in the commissioned ranks, non-commissioned officers who had shewn enterprise and ability during the operations were promoted on the field, so that in the Australian Imperial Force, as in Bonaparte's armies, "every soldier carried a marshal's baton in his knapsack."

The time spent near Keepaway Farm was not a period of undisturbed rest. From a corner of the field, about 500 yards away from the shelters and tents, a heavy howitzer periodically fired shells into the town of Warneton. This continued until the third day, when, about midnight, the enemy artillery opened searching fire with the evident object of destroying the big gun. The German 5.9s did not find their intended target, but found the 39th Battalion instead, causing a rush of half-clad men for the shelter of some near-by trenches.

Men of the battalion were daily engaged on working parties, repairing the Messines Road which had been badly damaged by shell fire during the battle. This work was constantly hampered by the enemy artillery and there were many narrow escapes. One morning a waggon convoy of the Army Service Corps came up laden with timber, iron and road metal. The 39th working party had commenced to unload the waggons when suddenly a salvo of shells crashed among the men. The drivers whipped their horses into a gallop, the men scattered to find cover, and the road building material flew in all directions. By good fortune only one man was slightly wounded.

The explanation of the sudden hail of shell lay in the fact that a German observation balloon had "spotted" the group of men and vehicles on the road.

On June 19, a move was made to the De Seule area, situated between Neuve Eglise and the hamlet of La Creche, where infantry training proceeded for four days.

On June 23, the battalion marched to Hillside Camp, near Neuve Eglise, where a halt was made for the night.

The following day the march was continued to La Douve Valley Camp on the southern side of Mount Kemmel—the highest point on the Flanders Plain.

Here eighteen days were passed in special training, the monotony of which was relieved by athletic competitions and sports of every description. These competitions terminated in a Brigade Sports Meeting, in which representatives from each battalion competed, the victory falling to the 40th Battalion for military events, and to the 37th for sports. Cricket matches, into which the men entered with eagerness, were frequently arranged.

The value to the men of this period of recreational training was inestimable; and the mental and bodily fatigue caused by the more strenuous days of the preceding month vanished completely.

On July 10, just after dusk, the support trenches near Boyles Farm, west of Messines, were taken over. The Battalion Headquarters was located in Bristol Castle, a demolished brick building which, in its more prosperous days, had been a civilian post office.

During the night of the 11/12th working parties were sent

"B" Company, Bouillancourt, France

up to the forward positions near Warneton. The German artillery was very active, and the work of filling sandbags was carried on under difficult and hazardous conditions.

The night was pitch dark, and on the way back the guides lost themselves, and had to rely on the intermittent gun flashes and enemy star shells to find the track. About midnight heavy rain fell, converting the wilderness of shell holes and churned-up earth into slippery mud. The enemy guns maintained heavy fire over the area, and the party suffered many casualties as the men, continually falling into old trenches and waterlogged shell craters, picked their way over the broken ground. Boyles Farm was eventually reached at 2 a.m. These experiences are typical of those of scores of working parties which went out nightly from the support trenches.

During the morning of July 16, the battalion came under heavy enemy shell fire. Many of the dugouts were completely demolished. One of these was being used as the battalion orderly room, and many valuable records were thus lost. Several casualties were sustained during the morning. By 11 o'clock, the position became untenable, so a move was made to the top of Hill 63, where the battalion occupied one of the old trench systems.

Just before dawn on July 18, the 39th again became a target for the German gunners. A violent barrage of gas and high explosive shells fell on the battalion trenches for six hours. During this artillery "strafe" the men had their first experience of the latest product of the enemy poison gas factories—Dichlorlthyl Sulphide, or "mustard gas." This new gas evidenced itself by a peculiar odour like garlic.

The effects of mustard gas are particularly cruel. In addition to its lethal qualities it burns severely every part of the body it touches, scalding the skin, affecting the lungs (if inhaled), and being especially severe on the eyes. There were fortunately no casualties, adequate precautions having been observed. The gas lay in trenches and shell holes for several days, and great caution had to be observed in approaching any hollow in the ground. Mustard gas had been first used against other British troops at Ypres, just two weeks before the 39th experienced it.

On the night of July 20, the 39th relieved the 37th Battalion in support trenches on the top of Messines Ridge and on the outskirts of the ruins of Messines. While occupying this position numbers of working parties had to be supplied, and the following fortnight was a very strenuous time, full of danger and hardship. German artillery fire was heavy, and there was hardly one working party which returned without casualties. The weather was very wet, and the rough tracks to the front line were in places knee deep in mud which clung to the limbs of any unfortunate "digger" who stumbled. The trenches were in a very bad condition owing to the enemy shell fire and the wet weather, and the dugouts in which the men lived were often mere holes, dug in the sides of the trenches. Water oozed into them continually, making the interiors muddy and miserable beyond description. It was difficult at the time to obtain timber with which to prop up these makeshift dugouts, and one morning, owing to the concussion from bursting shells loosening the earth on the surface, most of the dugouts collapsed. Some of the men were buried and had to be dug out by their comrades.

Life at the front held many a strange contrast. Within three miles of the enemy lines one could buy for the trifling sum of six sous the Paris edition of the London newspapers. One could visit also a cinema theatre in an old barn or abandoned factory, while perhaps, not far off, a machine gun fired bursts at an enemy bombing plane. It was an excellent thing that life held these contrasts, for they bridged to a great extent the gulf between the horror and hopelessness of war and the cherished things of the outside world which the men had left behind.

Within a few miles of the muddy trenches of Messines and within easy range of the enemy batteries the 3rd Australian Division held a Horse Show on July 22. Marquees were erected, a ring railed off, and an assembly of soldiers and civilians, dressed in their best uniforms and cleanest clothes, attended the event. Bands played gay tunes, displays of horsemanship were given in the arena, and it would have been easy to imagine the war thousands of miles away, had it not been for the thunder of the guns and the fleecy balls of shrapnel bursting overhead as a German scouting plane patrolled among the clouds. And yet within an hour's walk of that scene of animation and gaiety death lurked in every corner of the countryside, and the deadly duel was always being grimly fought.

During July the enemy gun fire swept over the forward and back areas of the British front in Flanders unremittingly. Roads, towns and railways were shelled continuously day and night, and the Armentieres neighbourhood, which had been so quiet a few months previously, became a very active sector of the front. The battalion transport drivers had difficult and perilous duties to perform in taking their limbers up to the front each night along the shell-swept roads approaching the trenches. It stands to the credit of the transport section of the battalion that, however heavy the shelling, the limbers always weathered the storm and the transport never once broke down.

The enemy, during the weeks succeeding his defeat at Messines, commenced a systematic shelling of Armentieres, apparently suspecting that reserves would be concealed there for the approaching offensive at Ypres. Salvoes of high explosive and gas shells were rained into the city day and night, and many civilians were killed. Others took refuge in the cellars of their houses, only to perish from the dreadful effects of poison gas, while some were buried alive under the wreckage of their homes. Eventually Armentieres was reduced to a city of ruins—a place silent and deserted—into which the German batteries still hurled shells in blind fury. Philip Gibbs, the British correspondent, has described this period as "The Agony of Armentieres," and a more fitting term could not have been found for the ruined city.

During the relief of the 9th Brigade by the 11th Brigade, on July 28, the enemy attempted a raid on the front line trenches, preceded as usual by a heavy artillery barrage. The S.O.S. signals from the Australian trenches obtained prompt response from the artillery and machine guns, which, together with the Lewis guns of the infantry, inflicted heavy penalties on the enemy for his temerity. The raiders failed to reach the front line and suffered losses in No Man's Land before they were able to regain their own trenches. After this reverse the German artillery fire increased, and on the following day, July 29, one of the battalion's working parties, while returning from the front line, came under heavy shell fire in the demolished village of Messines, and suffered severe losses. Lieutenant C. P. Christensen, who was in charge of the party, was killed, together with four of his men. Three others were wounded.

Just before dawn on July 31 two battalions of the 11th Brigade launched an attack against The Windmill, and other enemy strong points in front of the town of Warneton. The object of the operation was to capture the strong points and at the same time to form a diversion for the tremendous offensive which commenced this day at Ypres. The 39th at the time was acting as tactical support to the 41st Battalion, and before The Windmill attack, the Lewis guns of the battalion took up positions from which their fire could support the 11th Brigade in the event of an enemy counter attack.

The operation was very successful. The Windmill, which had been converted by the enemy into a miniature fortress of machine guns was captured. Other strong points of the German defence lines were also taken.

Many prisoners were captured by the attacking battalions. The enemy retaliated by "strafing" the British lines, and the 39th came under heavy fire. The battalion had been in the trenches since July 10, and had had a particularly trying time. The weather was continually wet, the trenches were muddy and in parts waterlogged. Constant hard work under enemy fire was the daily routine.

On August 2, two companies of the 39th were ordered to relieve the 41st Battalion, which was holding the recently-captured ground in front of Warneton. They moved off at 10 o'clock on the night of the 2nd/3rd, and after a difficult march under harassing enemy fire, arrived in the front line and took over from the 41st, completing the relief at 5 a.m. The new trenches were very narrow and knee-deep in mud, the weather was very wet, and the position was one of the most difficult which the 39th had been called upon to hold. The line formed a salient on which the enemy guns were concentrated. For 48 hours the men lived in a hell of shell fire. The position was enfiladed by the enemy on both flanks, and heavily shelled from the front. The German barrage was so terrific that it seemed impossible for men to live through it. The enemy counter attacked and attempted to re-take The Windmill and strong points, but, notwithstanding their fatigue and the trying ordeal they had endured, the men showed a determined opposition which broke up the assault.

On August 4, the two companies were relieved, and marched five kilometres through mud and water, and were shelled on their way back to a point where motor lorries were waiting to pick them up. Many were so exhausted that they could not muster sufficient strength to scramble into the lorries. On arrival at Hillside Camp the feet of the majority of the men were badly swollen from standing for so long in knee-deep mud, and their gum boots had to be cut off. The following day several men were evacuated to hospital with trench feet. The remainder of the battalion was relieved the same night, August 4, by the 15th Battalion.

Prior to the relief the enemy observed the 39th Battalion's transport moving off, and opened fire. Great confusion was caused on the narrow tracks, but fortunately the majority of the shells fell into the deep mud and failed to explode. A few casualties were caused by the fire among men and animals, and some of the vehicles were damaged. Heavy shelling continued throughout the relief, which was completed at 5 a.m. on August 5.

The battalion marched from Hillside Camp to Tank Camp, about three kilometres from the village of Dranoutre, and remained in this camp for nine days.

It was about this time that the enemy commenced to send bombing aeroplanes over the British back areas. These attacks took place whenever the weather conditions favoured night flying. Powerful searchlights, increased numbers of anti-aircraft and machine guns were installed in the area to combat these raids, but, in spite of all defensive measures, enemy machines ran the gauntlet of the gun fire and dropped bombs in large numbers on the roads and in towns and villages which the Germans thought were billeting places for British troops. Whilst the 39th was occupying Tank Camp, the enemy bombing squadrons dropped their bombs nightly in the vicinity, and the nights were made very lively by the quick-firing anti-aircraft guns, the vicious chatter of the machine guns, and the tearing crash of the exploding bombs. Fortunately no damage was done, and there were no casualties in the camp itself.

On August 11, the four battalions of the 10th Brigade with three transport sections were inspected near Bailleul by General Sir H. O. Plumer, the Army Commander. This inspection was preliminary to the Brigade's departure to the Army Rest Area. General Plumer expressed himself as highly satisfied with the appearance of the men and complimented the Brigade on its turnout.

On August 14, the battalion left for a training and rest area in the Pas-de-Calais Department beyond St. Omer. Reveille sounded in Tank Camp at 4 a.m. and at 8 a.m. the march to Bailleul railway station began, each man carrying his blankets and full equipment. The battalion left Bailleul at 10.30 a.m.

detrained at Wizernes, and started on a march of 23 kilometres to Ledinghem. During the long march heavy rain fell.

After a night spent at Ledinghem the march was continued on the following day to Zoteux, a distance of five kilometres. This village formed the billeting area. It was a typical French hamlet, ramshackle and dirty, and the billets were by no means all that could be desired. The peasants were at first rather antagonistic towards the soldiers whom they had perforce to accommodate in their barns and houses. However, during the six weeks' stay at Zoteux, the attitude of the villagers completely changed, and the people were sincerely sorry when the battalion left.

On arrival in the rest area an extensive course of training was commenced. An attack on the Passchendaele Ridge was in preparation, and the 39th was destined to play a part in the battle. The main object of this rest at Zoteux was to give opportunities for recreation and the necessary preparatory training, so that in the impending operations every man would be as fit as possible. Route marches formed a feature of the day's work. The weather was fine and the surrounding country pretty. Battalion and Brigade inspections by General Officers Commanding Corps, Division and Brigade were frequent events.

On September 15, battalion sports were held. The day was warm and sunny, and the sports were attended by almost every man. Private M. P. Dunne gained the distinction of being champion athlete of the battalion by winning all the flat races. Prizes were awarded and presented by the Commanding Officer at the close of the day's proceedings.

On September 20, a Brigade tactical scheme was carried out near the village of Senlecques in the presence of the Corps, Divisional and Brigade Commanders. The minor operations of the day were especially interesting, and were marked by great dash and enterprise on the part of the troops. The most exciting of these operations was the rounding up and capture of four large hares which ventured upon the training ground at, for them, an inopportune moment. The fight was short and sharp. The Australians attacked with all the armaments of a modern platoon—tin hats, box respirators, spades, and entrenching tools.

At 8 a.m., on September 22, the 39th Battalion was carried in motor lorries to Drionville to take part in a Divisional review by Field Marshal Sir Douglas Haig. The Commander-in-Chief arrived at 10.30 a.m. The general salute was given, and the Division inspected. Then followed the march past to the music of the combined bands. As was usual on such occasions the "digger" acquitted himself well.

The hour of the 39th's entry into the battle of Ypres and Passchendaele was now drawing near. The vast operation against the enemy in Northern Belgium had commenced in July, followed by greater efforts in September. These attempts were destined to culminate in the battles which took place in October.

On September 25, a four days' march to the battle zone was commenced from Zoteux. The weather was warm and sultry, and dust lay thick upon the roads. For the greater part of the long march the main roads were avoided, and good progress was made. The first night was spent at the village of St. Pierre—a distance of fourteen kilometres from Zoteux.

At 8 a.m., on September 26, the battalion left St. Pierre for Blaringhem. That day's march proved one of the hardest ever undertaken by the unit. The whole of the Third Division was on the move, and the roads were packed with endless columns of men, and motor and horse transport. So great was the congestion that the 39th was able to cover only six kilometres before the halt for dinner was made on the outskirts of the town of Lumbres. It was not until the middle of the afternoon that good progress could be made, and even then at times the 39th had to abandon the main road and move across country. Long before the end of the journey many were utterly exhausted and fell out along the road and were picked up by the transport. The destination, Blaringhem, was not reached until 9 p.m. The battalion had been marching for thirteen hours under the worst conditions, and had covered twenty-seven kilometres. Fortunately, good billets were available. The following two days were much easier. On the 27th the battalion left Blaringhem at 9.30 a.m. and with clear roads ahead covered the distance to the next halting place in good time, and reached St. Sylvestre Cappel at 3 p.m. Billets at this village were very poor in comparison with those which other villages had provided.

The next day the 39th left St. Sylvestre Cappel at 10 a.m., and marched eight kilometres to the village of Winnezeele, near the Belgian frontier. Here tents were provided, and the remainder of the day was pleasantly occupied by a cricket match between the officers and the rest of the battalion. The officers were beaten by 25 runs. Winnezeele was crowded with troops, as units of the First Australian Division were billeted in the vicinity. Three days were spent here in training, sports and final preparations for the battle.

On September 29, the battalion nucleus was despatched to Morbecque, there to remain until the completion of the operations in front of Ypres.

On September 30, the battalion's final preparations for the battle were completed. The Lewis guns were overhauled, bombs and ammunition cleaned, emergency rations issued, and the equipment and arms of the platoons inspected.

A party of officers and N.C.Os. from the 39th was conveyed by motor lorry to the front, and a reconnaissance of the line and its approaches east of Ypres was carried out.

On the evening of September 30, a working party was sent forward through the battered ruins of Ypres to lay cables under the supervision of the Divisional Engineers. This working party was taken to the forward area by motor transport and commenced its task about 9 p.m. In the early hours of the morning of October 1, the enemy artillery opened fire and several shells caused casualties. The 39th party escaped lightly, and continued working until dawn, when the increasing light and shell fire at 8.30 a.m. made it necessary to leave the task incomplete.

On October 2, the battalion left Winnezeele by motor bus and journeyed through Steenwoorde and Poperinghe across the Belgian frontier to Vlamertinghe, a small town on the main road to Ypres. Here the battalion was quartered in huts, and final arrangements for going into action were completed.

It was again the eve of battle.

The next day the approach-march to the trenches fronting Broodseinde Ridge was to take place. Already the first rumbles of the coming storm were in the air. The thunder of the guns resounded on every ridge, the flare of battle rose and fell on the horizon. All through the night a stream of men, horses and guns pounded over the cobbles of the tree-lined road to Ypres, and above all sounded the sinister hum of the enemy bombing planes and the shattering crash of bombs bursting in an adjacent camp. Thus at Vlamertinghe, on the edge of the whirlpool of war into which they would be thrown, the men of the 39th awaited calmly the call to action in their second big battle.

MAP No. 4
PLOEGSTEERT WOOD

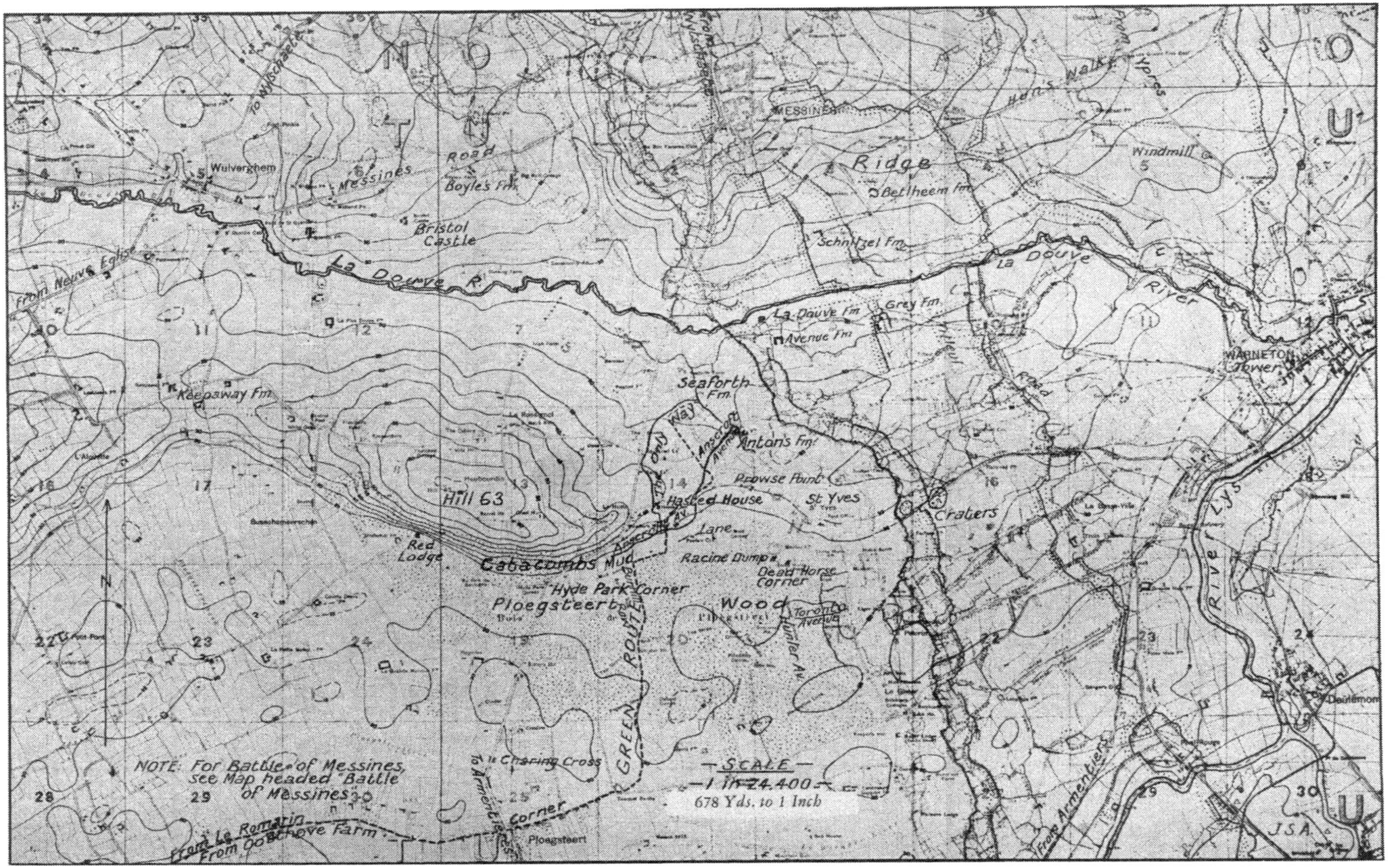

MAP No. 4

PLOEGSTEERT WOOD

CHAPTER IX.

The Battle of Broodseinde

"Nothing except a battle lost can be half so melancholy as a battle won." —WELLINGTON (Despatch, 1815).

TO realise fully the reasons for and the object of the battles in October, 1917, it is necessary to understand something of the events which led up to the British offensive in Flanders. At this time the situations on the Italian Front and in Russia were far from satisfactory. German propaganda, skilfully and cunningly organised, was gradually undermining the morale of certain of the Allied armies. The press of England and France was urging that the British Army should take some action to relieve the tension, and many of the daily newspapers, in their leading articles, suggested that Britain should take over portions of the French Front and thus relieve the hard-pressed French troops. For three years the French Army had borne the main stress of the war. In the Spring of 1917 it had undertaken, under the direction of General Nivelle, a vast offensive beyond the power of its troops, and when this failed the French power of resistance became, for a time, dangerously low. Had the Germans then been able to attack the French, the war might have been lost, at least on land.

It was very necessary for the British to take some action which would have for its object the prevention of the enemy onslaught and which would relieve the tension on the French. It was decided that this action should take the form of an attack against the enemy positions in the Ypres salient, which, although well fortified and defended, were most valuable to the enemy. If the high ground east of Ypres could be carried, it meant that the German right flank would be turned, thus freeing the Belgian coast and clearing the Germans from the submarine bases there.

The great offensive was at first hampered by rain, but, after a pause, the British had during the latter half of September launched two heavy attacks on this sector, with complete success, making strong headway through the enemy defensive systems. These defences consisted of numerous large concrete block houses, placed at irregular intervals in the midst of the low swampy plain, in positions from which they could best command the intervening ground. The armament of these miniature fortresses consisted of heavy machine guns, which could fire at almost any angle, and, even under the heaviest barrage, could maintain a deadly fire upon attacking infantry. These pill-boxes were joined by trench systems garrisoned by rifles and lighter types of machine guns, and formed very formidable lines of defence.

At 4 p.m., on October 3, after an early tea, the 39th Battalion, under the command of Lieut.-Colonel R. O. Henderson, moved on to the main road and turned eastwards towards Ypres. The platoons marched a hundred yards apart in order to minimise casualties in the event of enemy shelling. The straight road, lined on either side by tall Lombardy poplars, was crowded with traffic. Long columns of troops used the edges of the road; strings of ammunition mules, laden with shell panniers, clattered over the cobbles; cumbersome lorries took possession of the centre of the road—followed by ration limbers and waggons. Now and then a little body of infantry coming back from the fighting passed by, their clothes torn and mud-bespattered, their steps dragging wearily, and a picture of the hell they had come from mirrored in the fixed stare of their sunken eyes.

It was almost dark when the 39th reached the ruined walls of Ypres, the "Verdun of Flanders." Here stark devastation lay on every side. Not a building remained intact. As the battalion passed along the streets of the shattered city the darkness increased, and lights glimmered from the cellars of the houses where troops were living. It was completely dark when the battalion cleared the eastern outskirts of the city. Passing out along the Roulers Road, the men halted in a field near Potijze, and rested until 11.30 p.m.

At half past eleven the platoons moved silently in single file into the darkness. The road was followed for a time, and then the battalion turned off to the right and along a duckboard cross-country track known officially as "K" track.

Filing steadily forward, past deserted gun emplacements from which the batteries had moved to positions farther forward, past dumps of ammunition of every calibre, the 39th finally reached ground which had only recently been won from the enemy. Here the duckboards ended, and the only track was a narrow dimly-seen path winding between water-logged shell craters. The ground was very muddy and slippery, and the darkness added to the difficulties of the march. Now and then a flare from the trenches lit up the country for a few seconds, disclosing a desolate waste of mud and shell holes, with here and there a splintered tree, the only sign of vegetation in that wilderness. Shells fell regularly along the track, and wounded men began to drop out.

At 3 a.m., on October 4, the assembly point was reached. Here the four battalions of the 10th Brigade (37th, 38th, 39th and 40th), which were to move forward together, were concentrated. The men sought protection in shell holes, and settled down to wait for zero hour.

This period of waiting before action is always trying to the nerves, and hours seem like days to men waiting with every sense alert to catch the first indications of the opening of battle.

While waiting in front of Broodseinde Ridge for the roar of guns which would give the signal to advance, some of the men slept, lying close together in the shell holes for warmth. It was three hours to zero; the front was comparatively quiet, and it had stopped raining. Suddenly the deafening roar of an enemy barrage rent the night air, and a curtain of bursting shrapnel fell upon the 2nd Australian Division, which was on the right flank of the 3rd Division. The 11th Brigade, on the right of the 3rd Division, suffered many casualties from this enemy fire. It seemed evident that the enemy was about to launch an attack himself, and the thought which was uppermost in every man's mind was "Will our barrage come in time to forestall Fritz?" Time passed slowly, and tense anxiety continued, but there were no signs of the waves of grey clad enemy, which everybody half-expected to see emerge from the shadows of No Man's Land.

Zero hour was six o'clock, and, punctually at that time, the British barrage opened with one colossal burst. The sky was suddenly lit up with a blaze of light from bursting shrapnel, an illumination of awe-inspiring grandeur. From the enemy trenches thousands of coloured lights shot up into the sky, calling for aid from the German guns.

Under the flickering light of the bombardment the battalion filed out from its position in open battle formation. The hum of a British aeroplane could be heard above the roar of the guns, and, as the grey light of dawn increased, this single guardian loomed up through the mists, circled over-head and waited for signs of the success or failure of the operation. In the growing light the waves of attacking infantry were plainly seen. On the left, advancing up the gentle slopes of the ground, was a Brigade of the New Zealand Division. Its cool and orderly advance under the hail of shell fire inspired everybody to greater effort. On the right the battalions of the 11th Brigade moved forward with the same deliberate calmness and precision, notwithstanding the terrific ordeal they had endured prior to the opening of the attack.

Large numbers of Germans were found in No Man's Land, and bodies of enemy dead lay everywhere. It was apparent that the German troops had been massed for an attack against the British positions, and that this purpose had been frustrated in

"K" Track Broodseinde Ridge.

time by the opening of the British offensive. The enemy showed very little fight, seemed dazed by the violence of the bombardment, and was glad to surrender.

The British gunfire formed a "creeping" barrage, so called because of its continual slow forward movement. The attacking troops advanced behind this curtain of fire, keeping as close to it as was consistent with safety. So accurate was the fire, it seemed impossible that a single man in the enemy positions could be left alive. But some escaped, for, as soon as the barrage passed onward, heavy machine gun fire was directed against the Australians from pill-boxes which had not been destroyed by shell fire. Many sections of infantry were cut up by this enemy fire, but owing to the initiative and gallantry of officers and men, the opposition from the pill-boxes was quickly overcome. These concrete strong points were stormed, and their occupants driven out by bombs.

The 37th Battalion, which formed the first wave of the 10th Brigade's attack, soon reached its objective, and the barrage rested for an hour, forming a protective screen under cover of which the 37th commenced to dig in, and consolidate the position which they had won.

While this work proceeded, the remainder of the attacking forces rested, scattered in little groups in shell holes. The men lit cigarettes and pipes, and smoked and yarned with perfect sang-froid as they waited for the resumption of the advance. Many German dugouts and pill-boxes had been found to contain large stocks of provisions, whisky and cigars. It was an odd sight to see these men, in the midst of an inferno of battle, contentedly puffing away at fat German cigars.

As the barrage lifted again, the next wave, composed of the 38th Battalion, pushed on, closely followed by the 39th and 40th advancing in artillery formation. Enemy pill-boxes continued to give trouble as the advance progressed. The German machine gunners always held out to the last against the storming parties, and often their guns did much execution before they were silenced.

The tactics adopted by the attacking parties consisted of rushing the pill-boxes and crouching close to the concrete walls for shelter from the fire of the guns. Phosphorus bombs were then thrown through the loop-holes, and the dense suffocating clouds of smoke and the phosphorus from these missiles quickly drove the enemy garrison into the open.

The 38th Battalion easily carried its objective and thoroughly mopped up the whole of the ground won. At this stage of the battle a further halt of one hour was made to enable the captured positions to be consolidated.

The Germans made no large-scale counter attack, and seemed resigned to the loss of the territory already taken, but they were not prepared to lose much more. Stragglers could now be seen making their way back, from shell hole to shell hole, to Gravenstafel Switch, a strongly fortified trench system. It lay between the battalion's jumping off line and the objective.

As the battle had now been in progress for some hours, the frontage of the attack was known to the German staff. The guns on the flanks of the position were now directed to fire on the storm troops; and because the advance formed a salient, this fire came partly from the rear. Other enemy guns were engaged in counter-battery work and they put a number of British guns out of action.

During this hour's interval the 39th sustained a number of casualties. It was a most anxious period. The men had to wait for their turn, and meanwhile they were subjected to heavy fire without having the chance of retaliating.

Among the many incidents of this period, one calls for special mention. A shell put a Lewis gun out of action and wounded its section commander. Private George C. Black, who was No. 1 of the gun crew, took command, repaired his gun under heavy shell

THE BATTLE OF BROODSEINDE

fire, re-organised the section and subsequently led his gun into action, and did good work throughout the battle.

A heavy task lay ahead of the battalion inasmuch as the German gunners had found the range. The element of surprise had disappeared, and the enemy was waiting in strongly fortified positions. Pill-boxes protected by barbed wire could be seen near the trench systems and they were known to be manned by picked German troops who would fight till the last. Heavily laden with equipment, the men had already marched for some miles over rough ground.

The battalion formed an approximately straight line and waited calmly for the barrage to open. After a delay, which seemed interminable, there was one tumultuous explosion at the rear—the welcome sound of British guns. By the aid of synchronised watches, the first shots from all the guns were fired in unison.

In a few instants shells were hurtling overhead. The whistling sound of the "106" fuses could be heard plainly, followed by high velocity "60 pounders," followed again by shells of heavier calibre. So many machine guns were firing that they created a continuous roar.

It was a wonderful barrage.

The ground in front began to spurt up like geysers, overhead shrapnel was bursting, and in good heart the men went forward. The enemy artillery, in response to the S.O.S. signals, now concentrated its fire on the attacking troops, and, knowing the range, caused many casualties, while machine guns and trench mortars also began to take their toll.

For a time the advance was steady and even. Then big gaps were made in the line of assaulting troops as the enemy gunners brought their fire to bear with yet more deadly effect.

A few minutes later it became apparent that some machine guns required special attention. Though the barrage was compelling the men in the enemy trenches to keep their heads down still, despite the fall of heavy shell fire, the machine gunners in the pill-boxes kept on firing steadily.

The situation called for individual enterprise and considerable heroism.

Corporal William J. Hume, at the head of his section, disposed of one gun. Lance-Corporal Edward J. L. B. Miles silenced another with a Lewis gun and captured the German crew. Private Leslie Morton bombed one gun crew, and in the confusion seized a German revolver, dashed forward, shot the whole of another crew and captured its gun, but in attempting to repeat this performance, was severely wounded.

These acts of heroism were observed and reported. From a distance many other acts of great gallantry were seen, but the individuals could not be identified.

The advance moved steadily forward until enfilade machine gun fire was opened from the left flank. The New Zealanders were bogged in a morass and were thus unable to advance rapidly. They had to force their way through mud feet deep.

The Germans of that sector, knowing that they would not be troubled for some time on their own front, diverted their artillery, machine gun and rifle fire to the 39th.

Shelled from the rear, the front, and the flank, and subjected to heavy machine gun fire from Broodseinde Ridge, the men were in a serious position. As there was practically no cover, the Germans were easily able to "pick off" the officers. For a time there was some confusion. Warrant Officer Leonard F. Hodgetts—his company officers all being wounded—did wonderful work. Under heavy shell and machine-gun fire he re-organised his company and led it forward to the attack. The work of Sergeant Edward Brady in collecting troops and making one fighting unit of them was also highly commendable. This gallant N.C.O. was killed the following week in the Battle of Passchendaele.

The enfilade fire continuing, it was now necessary to advance in a series of short rushes from shell hole to shell hole until Gravenstafel Switch was reached.

Here the Germans fought grimly, firing to the last moment. When they found that their comparatively safe line of retreat, the communication trenches, had been battered in by shell fire, they engaged in a fierce battle with bombs at very close range. They delayed the men of the 39th but could not stop them. The furious fight at this Switch lasted for several minutes.

Finding themselves overpowered, numbers of the enemy jumped out of the trench, and bolted back, but others were taken prisoner and this system of trenches was subjugated.

There were no other lateral trenches in the battalion's sector; but every now and then a party of retreating Germans would be re-organised, and offer stout resistance, firing until they were rushed from the flank, bombed and overwhelmed.

The machine gun fire from Broodseinde Ridge was now hotter than ever, and, being nearer, was better directed, but still that Ridge lay beyond the creeping barrage. German gunners were firing over open sights and causing many casualties.

The signal section and the battalion runners were doing splendid work in keeping communications open. The gallant conduct of Private Charles A. Mann in taking messages backwards and forwards from his company under heavy machine gun fire was conspicuous. The value of this work was further enhanced by the action of Corporal Eric W. Bates who maintained communication, under heavy shell fire, between Forward Battalion and Forward Brigade Headquarters. As the objective was neared, the leaders began to look for big shell craters which might afford sufficient shelter for their men to permit of linking these craters into a continuous line by narrow trenches.

While the men were hard at work with entrenching tools, the 40th Battalion came up, and passed through or "leap frogged" over them. During its approach-march this battalion suffered severely. There being no immediate prospect of a counter attack, many of the 39th volunteered to go forward with them, and this assistance was much appreciated by the men of the 40th—the Tasmanian battalion of the 10th Brigade.

One of the volunteers, Private Robert A. Gerdts, was soon responsible for the capture of a persistent machine gun.

A gallant N.C.O., Sergeant Jonathan W. Gration, showed a fine example by his coolness and devotion to duty throughout the operation. He stormed a pill-box, shot a sniper whose accurate shooting had given much trouble; then, a little later, at the head of his men, he captured a machine gun and thirty prisoners, remaining after that in the front line to assist in the repulsion of counter attacks. He was awarded the Distinguished Conduct Medal.

Lance-Corporal James J. McMahon, with Private William Partridge, rushed a machine gun. Not content with killing the crew, they pushed on further and captured between thirty and forty prisoners.

Captain Douglas F. Middleton was awarded the Military Cross for gallantry and devotion to duty displayed during the whole operation.

Under Captain Ivan Blaubaum, the Army Medical Corps detail rendered splendid service at Broodseinde.

To find a suitable Regimental Aid Post, he "hopped over" with the fighting troops, and finally settled his men in an old shell hole 150 yards behind the battalion.

Protected only by a piece of iron pulled across the shell hole to keep the dressings dry, the doctor and his helpers gave speedy relief to hundreds of casualties.

At night he selected another site, nearer battalion headquarters, so that a light might be used in his work for the wounded.

No praise would be too high for Captain Blaubaum's wonderful work, and Sergeant A. R. Ellis and Private W. Miller earned the admiration of all who saw them darting here and there under fire to facilitate the work of the aid post during a most difficult time.

Meanwhile stretcher-bearers and carrying-parties were very busy. Without the satisfaction of hitting back, it was their duty to go overland, in full view of the enemy, right up to the forward line. Working in pairs, and carrying wounded, they could not rush for safety when they heard a shell or machine gun bullets travelling towards them. Private William Scott, though suffering severely from sore feet, for two days and one night carried wounded men back. Private John Sheehan, himself wounded, assisted in bringing others back until he collapsed in a state of utter exhaustion.

Carrying-parties also, travelling overland, did not enjoy immunity from aimed fire. Theirs was the lot of advertising their presence by carrying duckboards, ammunition and stores. The enemy shelled them heavily and the gallant work of Corporal George H. Stoddart and Private Hector T. S. Aldred was conspicuous under this heavy fire. One carrying party sustained such losses that their loads would never have reached their destination in time to be of service but for the action of Lance-Corporal Frederick I. Phillips. This N.C.O. had shown great coolness at the head of his section under heavy shell fire. He re-organised a special rush forward with the result that the loads reached their objective.

When the objective was taken, and the 40th Battalion was well in front, the work of consolidation proceeded steadily. So many had volunteered to go forward that those who remained had to do much more than their normal share; but the brilliant victory which had been won put all in good spirits.

While the men were digging, many casualties were caused by the fire of machine guns and from the bullets of snipers hidden in Berlin Wood. These enemy posts were afterwards dealt with by the advancing 40th Battalion and the New Zealanders. Prisoners were coming back in large numbers, some under escort, others moving to the rear of the British lines unattended, only too willing to retire from the battle. Once, a crowd of Germans appeared on the brow of a low ridge in front of the 39th's new position. The men seized their rifles and prepared to repel the supposed counter attack, but, perceiving that the party of enemy soldiers had no arms, quickly realised that they had been captured and were, of their own accord, making their way to the rear.

The majority of the prisoners were young Bavarians, still in their teens, with eyes more accustomed to the sights of the schoolroom than to the horrors of a modern battlefield. They were requisitioned as stretcher-bearers to carry the wounded to the dressing stations; work in which they readily assisted, desiring doubtless to make a good impression upon their captors.

Meanwhile the 40th Battalion had met with determined enemy opposition and had to call on the 39th for reinforcements. A party of fifty went forward to fill the gaps in the ranks of the 40th, and eventually the latter battalion carried the final objective of the 10th Brigade's attack, and the position was consolidated. The enemy attempted to counter attack, but heavy fire from the British guns effectively prevented every attempted advance.

The final objective was taken before 11 a.m., and the work of consolidation progressed until nightfall.

The experiences of the night of October 4 were unpleasant. There was nothing to do except to wait through the long hours of darkness and watch the ground in front, ready at a moment's notice to deal with any enemy counter attack. All through the night the guns maintained a violent bombardment of the new No Man's Land, and at times the continuous thunder of discharge and burst was almost unbearable, standing as the troops were, in the muddy trenches with nerves strained to breaking point. Scouts working in front of the line were constantly sending back messages reporting upon the enemy's movements. S.O.S. signals to the artillery flared up, and a few moments later the shells shrieked

The Animals of the 39th Battalion played their part too

THE BATTLE OF BROODSEINDE

through the air with re-doubled intensity, but no counter attack was developed on the front of the 10th Brigade.

Dawn came at last, revealing a scene of utter desolation. Light rains had fallen during the early hours of the morning, adding to the discomfort. The shell fire by that time had slackened somewhat and became intermittent. Dead men, half covered with mud, lay in hideously grotesque attitudes on the ground, and here and there a wounded man who had patiently endured the horrors of the night lay waiting with Spartan fortitude for the stretcher parties to pick him up. Of the men who formed these stretcher parties it is impossible to speak too highly. They worked uncomplainingly hour after hour, often up to their thighs in mud, and amid a hail of shell and machine gun fire.

After "Standing To" until it was fully light, the men had a scanty breakfast, and then turned again to the improvement of the defences. Carrying parties came up with materials for trench construction—barbed wire, timber, and also with supplies of ammunition, bombs and water. Later in the day rations were brought up. Until late afternoon there was very little shelling from either the British or enemy guns. During the morning, German aeroplanes came over to search for the positions of the British troops so as to be able to give the range to the German artillery. The patrols of the British Air Force were on the alert, and the enemy pilots found the odds against them too heavy, and thus the infantry passed the greater part of the day in comparative peace. One or two of the enemy aeroplanes more daring than the rest swooped down on the trenches and emptied their machine guns among the garrisons. But attacks of this nature were few, owing to the vigilance and prompt action of the British pilots. The enemy fire increased in violence during the afternoon until it became a bombardment. At dusk the troops in the trenches stood to arms, half expecting the defeated Germans to follow the barrage with an infantry assault. Just as night fell, another S.O.S. was fired and again the artillery replied with a heavy barrage, which, as no further signals were made, gradually died down, and the fire on both sides steadied to intermittent shelling. At 9 p.m. the shadowy forms of relieving English troops loomed up through the darkness, and soon the narrow trenches were crowded with men waiting for the formalities of the relief to be completed by their leaders. The 198th Brigade of the 66th Imperial Division relieved the 10th Brigade, and the 39th Battalion handed over the positions which it had won to a battalion of the Manchester Regiment. The weary "diggers," glad to be relieved after the hardships of the previous thirty-six hours, filed out silently towards the main road. The ground had been churned up so completely by the shells that every vestige of tracks had been destroyed. The men lost touch with each other in the darkness, and finally, it being no longer possible to keep the platoons together, found their way back to billets independently. Eventually the main road was reached, and passing motor lorries picked up many of the most exhausted and conveyed them to Vlamertinghe, where the majority of the battalion arrived at 3 a.m. on October 6. Here everything had been prepared for the return. The cooks had a hot meal ready, and after a satisfying breakfast, the men lay down to sleep off the fatigue of battle. Despite exhaustion, everyone was in high spirits. The attack had been in every way successful, and the battalion had taken its objectives, thus adding to the laurels won at Messines four months previously. An average advance of two thousand yards on a twelve mile front had been made, and the British forces were thus within striking distance of Passchendaele Ridge.

On October 7, the battalion nucleus returned from Morbecque. Re-organisation was carried out, and the men settled down to await the next move.

After the battle of Broodseinde, the splendid work of Lieut.-Colonel R. O. Henderson, the C.O., was recognised, and, as a result of the following recommendation he was awarded the Distinguished Service Order:—

"For conspicuous gallantry and devotion to duty. When his battalion had reached its objective he personally supervised the digging in and remained in the shell holes with his men. On another occasion, when his battalion was brought up from reserve to replace casualties, he did excellent work in re-organising the various units under heavy fire after many officers had become casualties. He set a splendid example to his men."

MAP No. 5
BATTLE OF BROODSEINDE RIDGE

MAP No. 5

BATTLE OF BROODSEINDE RIDGE

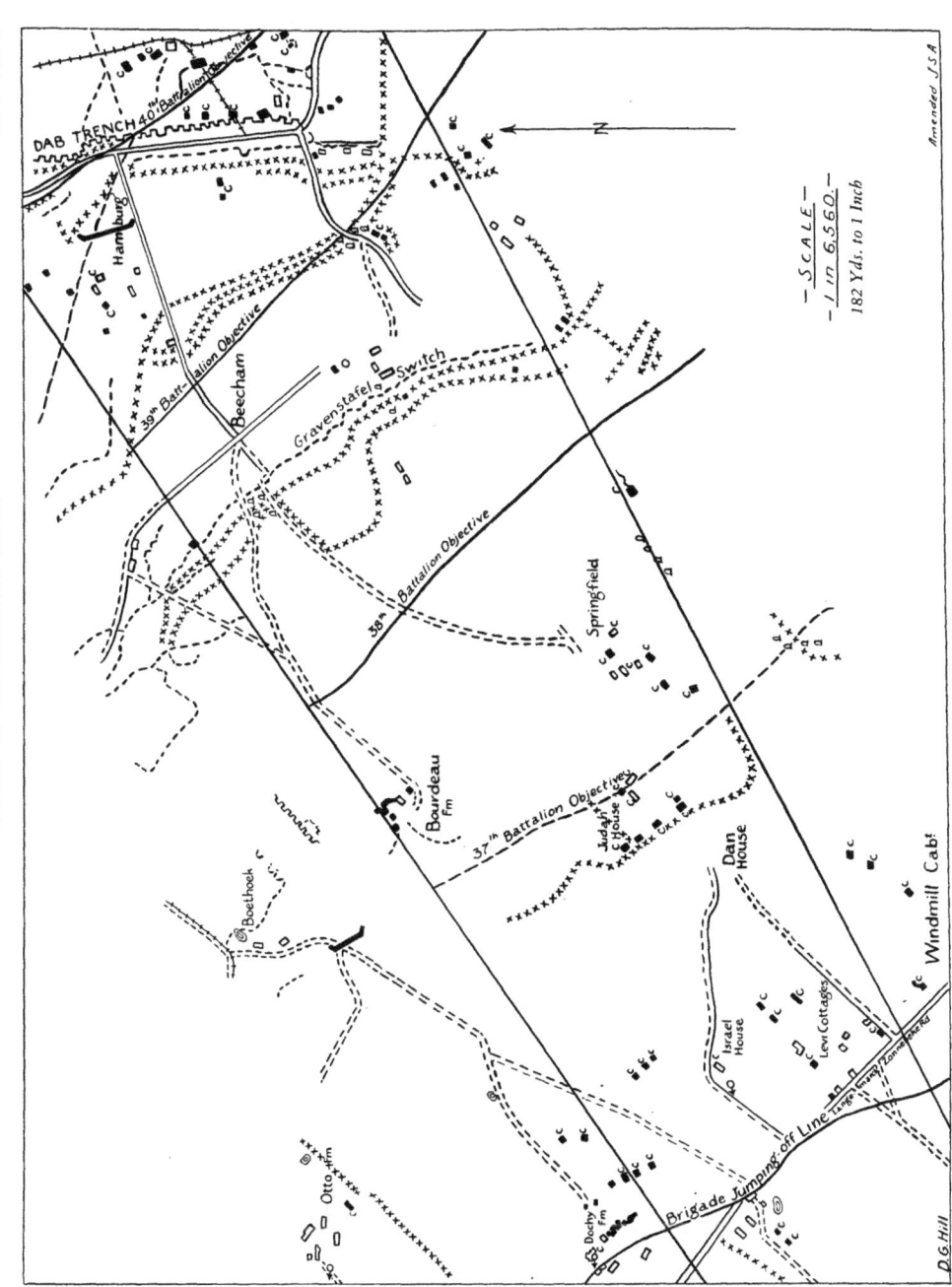

CHAPTER X.

The Battle of Passchendaele

*"Black it stood as night,
Fierce as ten furies, terrible as hell,"*
—MILTON.

ON October 8, only two days after the battalion had been relieved on Broodseinde Ridge, preparations for another battle were commenced. This was really a continuation of the attack made on October 4, the intention being to exploit the success then gained and to capture the enemy positions on Passchendaele Ridge.

The rumour that the battalion was going "over the top" again flew round like wildfire, and when supplies of bombs and ammunition were issued, the men knew that rumour for once spoke truthfully. Although they had barely recovered from the hardships of the fight for Broodseinde, yet every man was in good spirit, and perfectly confident that the forthcoming action would be as successful in its results as the one which had just been fought.

Unfortunately the weather, which had been uncertain since the commencement of the fighting, now took a decided turn for the worse.

On October 9, heavy rain fell, and the succeeding days were consistently wet. But for this adverse weather the story of the fight for Passchendaele Ridge might have had a different ending. In order that the march into action might be shortened, the men were moved forward on October 10 to a position known as Hussar Farm. This was situated near the original British front line and eight kilometres behind the furthest limit of the advance recently made on that sector.

The battalion left Vlamertinghe at 7.30 a.m., and marched through ruined Ypres to the new position. Upon arrival the camp was found to be in anything but a cheerful condition; soon, however, dug-outs and shelters of every description were constructed in old trenches and gun pits, the material used being salvage from debris which lay everywhere. Rusted sheets of corrugated iron, shell and ammunition boxes, pieces of canvas and the waterproof sheets of the men were used to form these rough shelters. Eventually (although not particularly comfortable) the men had at least protection from the weather.

During the day the men were employed on working parties, repairing damage done by enemy shell fire to the duckboard approaches to the trenches.

At 10 p.m., on October 11, the battalion left its improvised camp and began the approach-march. The country lying between the camp and the battle assembly-line had just been won from the enemy, and consequently it was badly broken up by gun fire into a series of shell holes. In many parts, one shell hole was within another. Heavy rain made the ground almost impassable. A duckboard track, known as "K" track, had been placed along the surface, and the whole battalion had to march along it in single file.

Being visible from the high ground, known as Passchendaele Ridge, this track was accurately registered by enemy artillery. During the approach-march the aim of the German artillery was so deadly that shells repeatedly splintered the duckboards. Thus troops were soon forced to pass through mud some of which was carried on to the unbroken portions of track, making the duckboards very slippery.

That was not the worst feature. The night was pitch dark, and presently, the enemy used gas shells, necessitating the adjustment of gas masks by all troops. Only sheer determination saw the men through. They had still another difficulty to face; for

soon they met troops moving in the opposite direction. The going was very difficult and progress slow.

The leading platoons reached the assembly point at 3 a.m. on October 12, having taken five hours to complete a journey which would normally have taken one hour.

The assembly point was a sunken road near Hamburg Farm. Evidently the enemy anticipated the selection of that point, for, just as the rear platoons were coming up, the assembly-line was heavily shelled.

Zero hour was still two hours ahead. Continuous heavy rain fell the whole time and the Germans kept up a bombardment along the sunken road. Little shrapnel was used, and the ground was so soft that shells buried themselves before exploding. But for this circumstance, the waiting troops would have been decimated before the battle began. As it was, heavy casualties resulted. The men longed for zero hour, preferring activity to a passive submission to a heavy bombardment.

At 5.25 a.m., the British barrage opened. At the long-anticipated zero hour the men gladly scrambled out of the sunken road and began to advance. Presently the barrage slackened to mere desultory fire. Our artillery had been unable to find ground solid enough for gun platforms, and many guns were out of action within a minute—hopelessly buried in the mud.

The German artillery was better placed, since it was on high ground which had not been churned up by successive barrages. With practically no assistance from the artillery, the infantry recognised how great was the task ahead; the enemy gunners soon realized that they had little to fear from the artillery, and became very daring. Despite all this, the advance continued, the men grimly forcing their way through the mud, though it was impossible to keep in line. At times men sank in mud to their arm-pits, and had to be rescued by their comrades. Each instance of this kind occasioned the temporary loss of three or four rifles to fire on the machine gunners and snipers.

The advance had not proceeded far when the attacking force was held up by a nest of machine guns and snipers. Discovering that his company officers and senior N.C.Os. had become casualties, Corporal Eric A. Pagels took charge. Although soon shot through the leg, he bravely volunteered to take a message back to Battalion Headquarters reporting the situation. He later returned through heavy shell and machine gun fire with orders.

The advance proceeded, and the few shells that made up the barrage were now falling so far ahead of the attacking troops that they were useless. The German machine gunners became yet more daring and directed their fire very accurately.

The situation was desperate. New Zealanders on the left had encountered a gully so thick with mud that many wounded men were suffocated as soon as they fell. The Ravebeek Creek was in flood and, as its banks had been torn by the shell fire of the past few weeks, it had overflowed and formed a series of lakes. The New Zealanders made very gallant efforts, but it was hopeless to try to advance, and their inability to take Bellevue Spur brought severe enfilade fire upon the 39th.

At 7 a.m., the first objective was reached by the leading troops and for some time men continued to arrive in twos and threes.

Further advance was out of the question, as already the men were being fired on from the left rear.

It was imperative to pass messages back. Private Eric E. Anderson, although wounded twice during the morning of the 12th, continued carrying messages backwards and forwards until the battalion was relieved on the night of the 13th.

Despite the gallantry and determination of the runners, it took hours to get messages to Brigade Headquarters and back again. Something had to be done. Lieutenant Herbert J. James, running grave personal risk from shell fire, established visual communication with Brigade Headquarters.

The men proceeded to dig in, but the task was impossible, as mud oozed in almost as quickly as it was dug out. The shell holes all contained water and below that lay mud as treacherous as quicksand. Lying flat the men patiently set to work. To stand up meant certain death.

At this stage a German 'plane came over flying low, giving the range to the enemy artillery. Shells began to fall right along the line.

The attacking force had been strengthened by the arrival from the sunken road of the reserve company, under Captain Alex. T. Paterson, but the enemy fire caused many casualties. Fortunately the Germans used very little shrapnel, otherwise the forward troops might have been more severely handled by the enemy.

This preliminary objective was held for some hours. For the time being the British artillery had practically ceased firing, while the German guns on more solid ground kept up a steady barrage. Enemy machine gunners and snipers were causing casualties almost every minute. As it would take too long to receive a reply to any message sent to headquarters, somebody on the spot had to take into his own hands the responsibility of dealing with the situation.

Discovering that he was the senior officer unwounded, Captain Alex. T. Paterson decided to confer with Major Giblin, of the 40th Battalion. They had a discussion in a shell hole. Meanwhile the 9th Brigade on the right flank began to withdraw; and Germans could be seen making their way along the New Zealanders' sector, working round to the rear of the battalion's position.

These two officers in conference decided to withdraw to a line in advance of the sunken road which formed the assembly point and starting-off line. It was a serious decision, and they felt the responsibility keenly, especially as it was the Brigade's first reverse. If senior officers further back had not agreed that the situation warranted such a retirement these two officers might have been sent home to Australia disgraced.

Having made their decision, Major Giblin and Captain Paterson at once began to carry it into effect. They had first to satisfy themselves that every man knew what was to be done, otherwise men who had fought gallantly might have been isolated, and there was a large number of wounded to be considered. These men could not possibly be deserted. The ground was so heavy and the enemy fire so accurate that at least an hour passed before all ranks were acquainted with the proposed operation.

Meanwhile carrying parties under Sergeant William R. Powell came up to the front line with fresh ammunition. This gallant N.C.O. then proceeded to make dumps from which the men, as they fell back, could replenish their supplies. Lance-Corporal Albert E. Parrish showed a calm disregard for personal safety in organising carrying parties and keeping dumps supplied.

As most of our rifles were choked with mud, there was little chance of effective resistance. Efforts were now concentrated on rescuing the wounded, including men of the 66th British Division, who had relieved the battalion on October 9, and who had been lying wounded in the open for four days.

Captain Paterson now called for volunteers to help him bring in the wounded. Meeting with a ready response, he ordered the volunteers to leave their rifles in the shell holes and to go forward with him to search for wounded. At first the Germans misunderstood the work of rescue and turned machine guns on our men; but to the enemy's credit, as soon as he discovered that they were bringing in wounded, he deliberately ceased firing on them. The Germans also came out into the open to collect their wounded. All had to take their chance, however, with shells.

The conditions were so desperate and the sufferings of the wounded, including the men of the 66th Division, were so terrible that the Germans actually assisted by pointing out half-buried men to the searching parties, and the men of the 39th reciprocated wherever possible.

The wounded having been collected, the remnant of the battalion made its way back towards the original starting-off line. The ground, which had been won at so great a cost, and held with the left flank "in the air," had now to be given up. This was a disappointment, after such hard fighting. There was only one alternative, namely, to be surrounded and captured, and this would have meant the taking of the wounded as well.

The conduct of Lance-Corporal Arthur E. Guyett was conspicuously gallant, as was the unselfish devotion to duty of Corporal A. A. Olin.

For his cheerful leadership, even under such dismal conditions, Private Edward J. Mellish deserves special mention. When all his N.C.Os. were either killed or wounded this private soldier organised two sections of men, placed himself in charge, and throughout that day and the next continuously urged them to greater efforts. Utterly disregarding his own safety, he made many trips forward to rescue wounded.

The troops retired to a line approximately 100 yards in front of the jumping-off point, which was on the crest of the salient.

All ranks proceeded to consolidate this position, determined to hold it at all costs. The battalion successfully maintained this line until relieved on the following night.

The men were considerably cheered by the arrival of a ration party, under Corporal William J. Hume. Repeatedly he reorganised his men after they had been scattered by the concentrated fire of German machine guns. He also performed an excellent service in bringing in wounded.

It rained almost continuously throughout the night and it was intensely cold for October. The battalion was still in a position of great danger, enfilade fire being very troublesome. Nobody had much sleep.

The next day the combined efforts of all ranks in rescuing wounded were so effective that it would be impossible to apportion credit to the individuals concerned. Every stretcher case required the services of eight men, so thick was the mud. Even then progress was reduced to a speed of a mile an hour. In some cases the men were so exhausted that ten men were employed on a single stretcher. Officers, N.C.Os. and men shared equally in this humane task.

Throughout the battle the work of Sergeant Ernest H. Zelman and Sergeant Francis J. McEwan was conspicuous. They set an inspiring example and ran tremendous personal risks to help their men. By their courageous bearing they did much to keep up the spirit of those under their command.

All the original A.M.C. detail, except Private Hunter, took part under Captain Ivan Blaubaum in the approach-march to the Battle of Passchendaele. Corporal S. V. Heath voluntarily replaced Private Hunter, who was ill.

About 15 minutes before zero hour, the half-ruined house occupied by the detail received several direct hits from shells. All the stretcher-bearers except two were killed. Captain Blaubaum was partly buried; his batman, Private Richardson, was wounded in the leg; and Sergeant Ellis was deafened.

Covered with mud, blood, and brick dust, the doctor and his few remaining helpers dashed for safety to a position near the 37th Battalion Headquarters. During that run Richardson, the M.O.'s batman, was again wounded in the leg.

Although the A.M.C. detail had lost stores and dressings, casualties began to pour into the pill-box where the aid post was located.

Forced eventually to go back for dressings, the M.O. and his men reached the main dressing station about 4 p.m.

The C.O. of that unit ordered Captain Blaubaum to have a rest. By that time he was exhausted—and no wonder.

Later the M.O. and his men returned to duty. Fortunately there was then little to be done.

Whenever men of the 39th foregather, Captain Ivan Blaubaum and his gallant band of helpers are remembered with pride and gratitude.

At 9 p.m., on October 13, the battalion was relieved by the 11th Brigade. Owing to the bad ground and the damaged condition of the approach tracks, the relief took six hours to complete. The march back to Hussar Farm was a most trying experience for the exhausted men, and one which severely tested their morale and endurance. The duckboards of "K" track had been smashed by the shell fire, and the men were constantly slipping into the deep mud beside the track. The night was very dark and each gun flash and flame from a bursting shell revealed little groups of men pulling comrades out of the mire all along the route. The foremost men of the battalion arrived at Hussar Farm at 3.30 a.m. on the 14th, almost too weary to stand. A hot meal awaited them, after which they threw off their soaked garments and rolled themselves into their blankets to sleep. Stragglers who had fallen out during the march back continued to arrive throughout the day, and by nightfall, the battalion was complete —less its casualties.

It must be admitted that the Battle of Passchendaele was a distinct reverse. The 39th Battalion had, however, reached its first objective, and held it until its flanks became so exposed as to make the position untenable. Only then was a withdrawal decided upon by Captain A. T. Paterson, the senior officer in the line. The battalion had shown a maximum resistance compatible with human endurance. Those who survived the engagement may well feel proud of the part the 39th played during those terrible days.

The experiences which befell the 39th on the swampy flats beyond Ypres were the worst and most trying of the whole war. Throughout that awful nightmare—this Battle of Passchendaele may justly be so described—the men had lived up to the highest traditions of their country, and had borne the dreadful ordeal with patience and gallantry.

On the way out of the trenches after the battle, Captain A. T. Paterson was informed by the Brigade Major (Major Eric Connelly) that he had been promoted to the rank of Major, in recognition of his excellent work. He was also recommended for a Bar to his Military Cross.

By 10 a.m., on October 15, the battalion was on the move again en route for Vlamertinghe. The men were still tired, but the knowledge that they were leaving the war-scarred surroundings of Ypres for a period of peace and rest was sufficient to put them in good spirits, however far they might have to march. At 12.30 they left Vlamertinghe by motor bus for Zoteux, which was reached at 2 a.m. on October 16. They went straight to their old billets, and, although the arrival of the battalion was unexpected, the villagers turned out and quickly prepared hot coffee and brought clean straw.

These village people could not do enough for the war-weary "diggers." They threw their doors wide open in welcome, lit their stoves, and busied themselves cooking hot meals. This cordial reception by the peasant people of Zoteux is one of the 39th's most pleasant memories of the years spent in France.

Two days later the battalion marched to the town of Desvres where hot baths in the cement works were available. Having now abundant opportunity for regular rest, food and exercise, the men quickly recovered from their experiences in Belgium, and before many days had passed were quite themselves again, ready for action whenever the call might come.

Heavy fighting continued in the Ypres salient throughout October and the early part of November, but it was not until November 6 that the Passchendaele Ridge was captured by Canadian troops. The expanse of mud, so long as it lay between

Casualties on the Menin Road, Ypres

the jumping-off line and the objective had formed a barrier absolutely insuperable.

Since July 31, 1917, the British troops fighting in front of Ypres had taken 24,065 prisoners, 74 guns, 941 machine guns and 138 trench mortars. Seventy-eight German Divisions had been engaged, many of which were fresh from the Russian front.

The dominating feature of the Battle of Passchendaele was the magnificent endurance and courage of the troops engaged. Fighting under conditions which for utter horror and misery had never been equalled in war, they won the admiration and the gratitude of the whole of the Allied countries.

Sir Douglas Haig, in paying a highly-merited tribute to his Armies, wrote:—

"Throughout the northern operations our troops have been fighting over ground, every foot of which is sacred to the memory of those who, in the First and Second Battles of Ypres, fought and died to make possible the victories of the Armies which to-day are rolling back the tide stayed by their sacrifice. It is no disparagement of the gallant deeds performed on other fronts to say that, in the stubborn struggle for the line of hills which stretches from Wytschaete to Passchendaele, the great armies that to-day are shouldering the burdens of our Empire have shown themselves worthy of the regiments which in October and November of 1914 made Ypres take rank for ever amongst the most glorious of British Battles."

Map No. 6
BATTLE OF PASSCHENDAELE

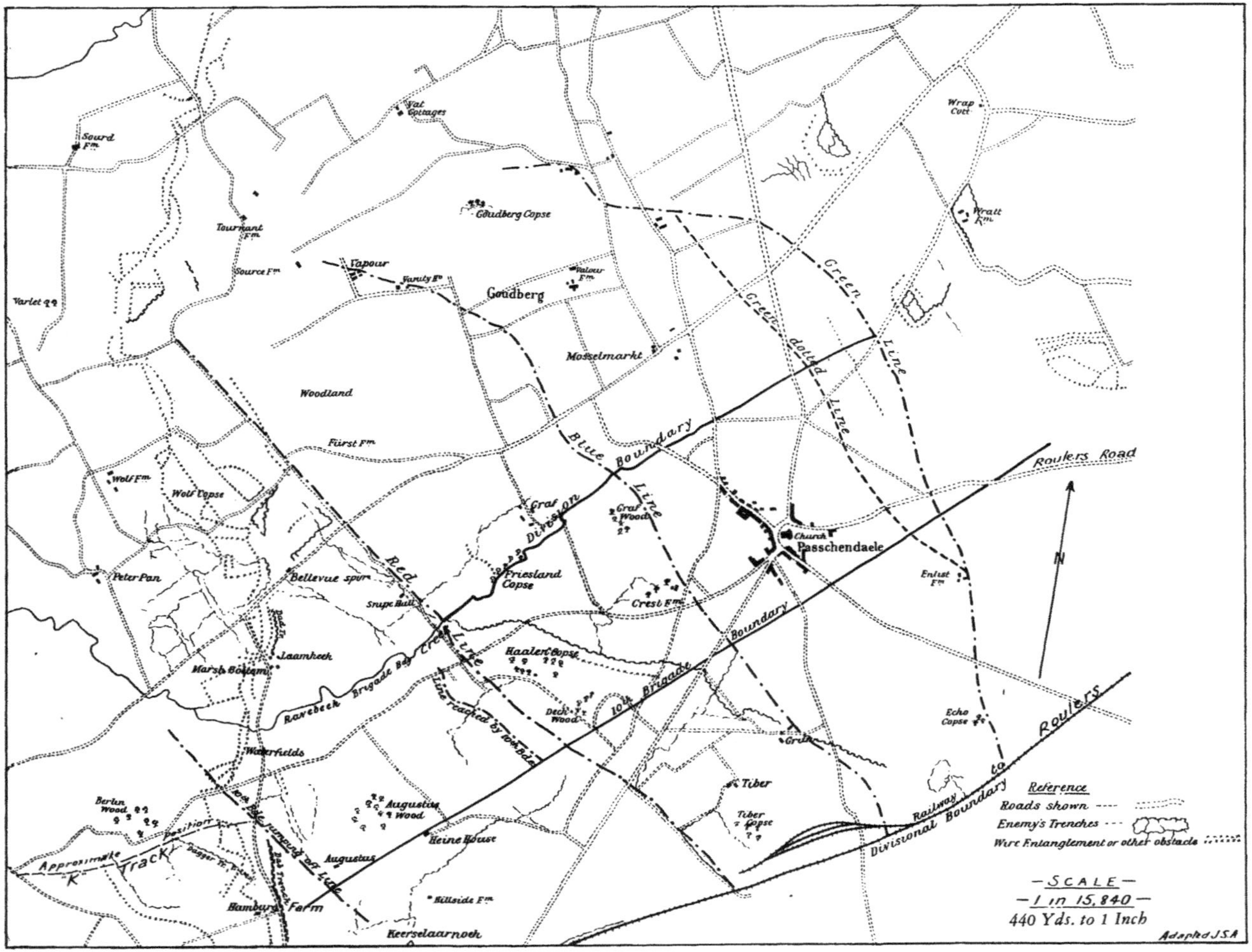

MAP No. 6

BATTLE OF PASSCHENDAELE

CHAPTER XI.

Holding the Line in Belgium

*"Harder must be the heart, bolder the spirit,
Greater must be our courage as our strength grows less."*
—Battle of Maldon.

DURING the three weeks following the Battles of Broodseinde (October 4) and Passchendaele (October 12) the battalion enjoyed a period of comparative rest at Zoteux.

Not only were the troops exhausted mentally and physically but the numerical strength of the unit was also diminished. If the battalion were to engage again successfully in battle, it was essential that every man should be fit. The battalion had been fighting almost continuously for twelve months, and the arduous experiences of the campaign were beginning to tell. The spirit and morale of the "diggers" had been magnificent, and had evoked the admiration of their leaders.

It is difficult for those at home to appreciate the outlook on life of a man at the front with its hardship, misery, and hopelessness. Every time he came out of the line he knew that, within a few days, he would be back again facing death—back again to line the parapet at dawn and at dusk; to watch through the dreary nights the forbidding shadows of No Man's Land; or to sit helpless while enemy shells rained down on the trenches. What a life! And so it went on, this cruel, hard fighting broken only by brief periods of relief.

Even when the men were not actually fighting they were working hard. Sometimes the very day after being relieved they worked strenuously for 14 or 16 hours under shell fire. A man lived only from day to day on the front. Few thought much about the uncertain future, and the past was too oddly incongruous to seem real. Life was just a gamble and Death held the cards. The war dragged on; the end seemed as far off as ever. Only the spirit which ruled on the shell-swept beaches of Anzac carried the "diggers" through in France. Cheerful under the appalling conditions which existed, they lived on through those dark days, brightening them by good comradeship, splendid courage, and whimsical humour.

Most of the time at Zoteux was spent in training and recreation. Every Wednesday and Saturday inter-company football matches were played. Sometimes the men visited the neighbouring town of Desvres, and occasionally a few men spent a day in Boulogne. Despite the indifferent weather the three weeks at Zoteux passed pleasantly, and the men regretted leaving this rural district of the Pas-de-Calais when marching orders came.

The 3rd Division was now to join the First Anzac Corps under General Birdwood, which was to include all the Australian divisions, with its title the "Australian Corps."

On November 9, the battalion's billeting party left for La Motte to arrange for billets for the battalion when it arrived.

The following day the 39th marched from Zoteux to Senlecques, where motor buses were waiting. After a short halt for lunch, the men boarded the buses and were conveyed to the village of La Motte, situated in the heart of the great forest of Nieppe. Only limited accommodation was available in the village, and the stables and barns in which the battalion spent the night provided very poor shelter.

At 11 a.m., on November 11, the 39th marched out of La Motte and reached the village of Vieux Berquin in a little over half an hour. Here slightly better billets were provided. During the afternoon and evening several of the men walked across to the village of Merris, where the battalion had billeted when it first arrived in France.

At 9.45 a.m., on November 12, Vieux Berquin was vacated and the march to Negate Farm begun. This camp was situated a few kilometres south-east of the town of Steenwerck. Nissen huts with arched roofs like elongated bee-hives were provided for accommodation. They were roomy, warm, and comfortable, and, as they were clean, excelled the ordinary farm-house billet.

On the morning of November 13, the battalion marched to Steenwerck railway station. Here the light railways up to the forward areas of the front had their starting point in a large engineering depot which stored materials used by the engineers in the construction of trenches, strong points, and dug-outs. Every day loads of this material were hauled to the front by small engines. At 2.45 p.m. the battalion entrained in open trucks on the light railway and was conveyed to a position known as Red Lodge on the slopes of Hill 63. During a halt at Hyde Park Corner soup was served to the men and gum boots were distributed.

At Red Lodge the 39th relieved a battalion of the 24th Brigade, 8th Imperial Division, and became battalion in support. The men lived in the subterranean passages cut by Australian tunnellers into Hill 63. Whilst here they were almost immune from enemy shell fire. The most dangerous feature of living in these artificial caves was from the gas which the Germans frequently used in the vicinity of Ploegsteert Wood and the adjacent sectors of the front. To guard against this, gas sentries were constantly on duty at the entrances to the underground passages to give warning and to release the gas-proof curtains.

While the battalion was in support at Red Lodge many working parties were supplied. The work consisted mainly of carrying engineering material and ammunition up to the line. Occasionally a wiring party erected or repaired barbed wire entanglements in front of the trenches. The working parties had to plough their way through deep mud and slush, and while the gum boots afforded some protection they were ineffective against the cold. Made of stout rubber, and reaching to the thighs, the boots were fastened to the men's belts. Most of the work was

St Yves Avenue. Ploegsteert.

done under cover of darkness, and the men had several strenuous and nerve-racking experiences during those dark, wet nights of November, 1917. Usually the working parties left Red Lodge at dusk and returned shortly after midnight. On their return they received a tot of rum and then turned in to snatch a short, well-earned sleep—often to be wakened in the early morning for the performance of another task. On account of the reduced strength of the battalion, it was not possible to give the men alternate spells of rest and work. Reinforcements were small in numbers and slow in coming. The entire battalion was therefore constantly employed.

After spending eight days in support at Red Lodge, the 39th relieved the 37th at 4.30 p.m., on November 21, in the St. Yves sector. The front line defences in this sector consisted of a number of isolated strong points about eighty yards apart and at varying distances from the most advanced line of trenches. These posts had no communication trenches connecting them with the main trench system so their garrisons could be relieved only at night. As these defences were only slimy, shallow excavations, the men who occupied them had to exercise great care to escape enemy observation.

Two companies of the battalion supplied the garrisons for this line of outposts, and the remaining two companies were quartered in dug-outs at Prowse Point and "The Crater." These two companies were employed in carrying rations and ammunition to those holding the strong points. The dug-outs in which they lived afforded no protection against heavy shell fire and only moderate security against splinters of big shells. Though over-run with rats, they were rain-proof—and that is the best that could be said of them. After four days, positions were exchanged, "C" and "D" companies taking over the forward lines and "A" and "B" the dug-outs. During this period the British artillery fired great numbers of gas shells on the enemy lines. While these bombardments were in progress, the two forward companies were withdrawn, re-occupying the strong posts in readiness for an enemy counter attack as soon as the fire ceased. Following an intensive gas bombardment by the British artillery, the enemy replied with heavy minenwerfer fire. So intense was the retaliation that the most advanced post held by No. 14 platoon was evacuated for the time. While this platoon was retiring a short distance, a messenger from No. 1 platoon arrived with the news that a minenwerfer shell had fallen on its post burying alive 12 men. Some of the men of No. 14 platoon returned with the messenger to the wrecked post and found Private R. N. Bucholz making strenuous efforts to rescue his unfortunate comrades in full view of the enemy. For his gallant conduct he was awarded the Belgian Croix de Guerre. Out of the 12 men buried, nine were rescued alive, the other three being dead when extricated.

The weather was extremely cold and the garrisons of the outposts suffered considerably. In one post the men stood knee-deep for two days in half-frozen mud and water, and out of 17 men who originally occupied the post only eight remained at the end of four days. The other nine had been evacuated to hospital—victims of that dreaded ailment, "trench feet."

On November 29, the battalion was relieved and marched out to Racine Dump in Ploegsteert Wood, from which the men were conveyed by light railway to Romarin Camp.

The ground was now so muddy that large-scale battles were impossible; but this did not mean a cessation of hostilities. There was no retiring into snug winter quarters as was the case in previous continental campaigns as far back as the Roman times. The men had to be fit enough to withstand the severity of the Winter, and they had to hold the line and fight when the opportunity was made for them.

Whilst the main body of the battalion had been holding the trenches, a special party had been training under Captain N. G. Booth for the purpose of conducting a raid on the enemy trenches.

The objects of the raid were to inflict losses on the enemy and identify the German Division holding the Warneton sector. The raiders were given different uniforms so that the Germans would gain no accurate information if any were killed or taken prisoner.

The operation was carried out on November 30 early in the evening so that the enemy S.O.S. barrage might slacken before another party from the 40th Battalion, which was to raid the same sector, came into the danger zone. The 39th party arrived at the front line without the enemy knowing what was about to happen. Suddenly the British barrage opened, and the raiders went over the top in good spirits. It was a wonderful barrage, and did much to maintain the infantryman's confidence in the artillery.

The German front line and the covering barbed wire were shattered, and the enemy seemed unnerved for a time by the artillery fire. What was left of the front line was easily taken, but as the raiders neared the defensive system the German opposition stiffened. At this stage Sergeant Albert Levy did splendid work in breaking down some strong resistance.

There was a sharp fight in the second line and the conduct of Lance-Corporal Leo Clark and Private P. C. Richards was conspicuously gallant.

So far everything had proceeded according to plan. The task was now to capture prisoners and bring them back safely to the British trenches. Two prisoners were quickly taken, and, as the time to return was approaching, the order was given to withdraw. German reinforcements began to arrive, and it was necessary to fight a rear-guard action, which was carried out in masterly style.

It is difficult to select the names of individuals whose work was exceptionally good because all did so well; but particular mention must be made of 2nd Lieutenant J. S. Beavis, who was leader of the left storming party. He led his men with splendid dash and excellent judgment, and was the first to enter the enemy trench and did not leave until the last of his party had withdrawn. Right through the operation he set a fine example to his men. On several occasions, prior to the raid, he rendered invaluable service, reconnoitring ground in front of the enemy sector to be raided; the information he supplied assisted materially in the success of the whole operation. He was awarded the Military Cross.

Private Edgar Victor, who was scout to the right storming party of raiders was instructed to find a gap in the enemy wire, and to return to act as guide to the raiders. He found the gap but before he could return, he was shot by an enemy rifle-man in the knee and was unable to move, and was lying in No Man's Land through the opening barrage. When the party advanced, he hailed them and directed them to the gap, refusing to be moved until he saw the party through. He was again wounded severely in the arm. The Distinguished Conduct Medal was awarded to Private Victor for his splendid courage and devotion.

Privates Andes V. Olson and George H. Donohue, also displayed great fighting spirit and materially contributed to the success of the raid.

This was the most successful raid carried out by the battalion. The objects had been achieved at a remarkably small cost—one officer and four other ranks being wounded. No one was killed. A large number of the enemy was killed by artillery fire and by the raiders. The unit attacked fared so badly that it had to be relieved that night. When the 40th Battalion went over a few hours later the relief was being carried out. This Tasmanian unit exploited to the greatest advantage the success gained by the 39th.

On December 3, the 3rd Divisional Pierrot Troupe, "The Coo-ees"—already making a name as entertainers—gave a performance to the men who carried out this raid.

At Romarin, on December 4, Lieutenant-General Sir W. R. Birdwood presented the medals gained in the battles of Ypres.

While billeted at Romarin the men were employed continuously on working parties. The light railways carried these parties to and from "Dead Horse Corner"—a terminus of the line on the northern edge of Ploegsteert Wood.

On December 6, the battalion relieved the 37th in the Catacombs. Four days were spent in support and four in the front line. During this period the enemy shelled the support position very heavily; but, as good cover was available there were very few casualties. On the whole the tour of duty passed very quietly, and, on December 15, the battalion was relieved by the 21st Battalion, and marched out to billets in the village of Neuve Eglise. The severity of the northern winter was making itself felt and the men suffered severely from the cold. Everything possible was done to add to their comfort by the administrative authorities of the Division and by their own officers. In the vicinity of the line soup stalls were established, where hot soup was given to the men any hour of the day or night. In the centre of Ploegsteert Wood there was a Red Cross staff who supplied cocoa and biscuits to men relieved from duty in the trenches. At that time it seemed as if life behind the line might have been much worse than it was. The necessity for the utmost economy in man power caused the authorities to give special attention to the care and comfort of troops both in and out of the line.

On December 18, mild excitement was caused by the taking of a poll for the Commonwealth Conscription Referendum. There was a great amount of controversy on this issue throughout the A.I.F. Generally, the opinion of the men was against the proposal. They had seen something of the conscript armies of the old world, and had had opportunities of weighing up the advantages and disadvantages of compulsory service. In a great many cases the spirit of freedom which holds pride of place in all true Australian hearts urged the men to reject the proposal. None will suggest that these men were actuated by any motive other than the highest patriotism. They themselves would be the sufferers if reinforcements were not forthcoming. Already they had suffered through a lack of men, and must have realized that, if the war continued and reinforcements did not arrive, their lives would be doubly endangered, their battalions split up, and the hardships of life increased immeasurably. Opinions, however, were much divided, and the monotony of life was broken by many keen arguments round the braziers in the huts.

The greater part of the work done by the battalion at Neuve Eglise consisted of the unloading of trucks of coal at the railhead. Fatigue parties for this work were detailed daily.

On December 20, camp was moved from Neuve Eglise to the hamlet of De Seule, near the Steenwerck railway station. Here the second Christmas was passed. Christmas dinner was served to the men in the De Seule Y.M.C.A. hut. With the battalion band in attendance, everything possible was done to create an atmosphere of festivity and good cheer. The Comforts Fund of the 10th Brigade sent £76 to the battalion, and this money was distributed to the men on the basis of two and a half francs each.

There was no slackening of activity on the front. Work proceeded as usual. In 1914, by common consent, an unofficial truce had been called on Christmas Day, and on some parts of the front the opposing forces laid down their arms and fraternised in No Man's Land. But things had changed since then. British and German troops could not meet at that time with feelings other than those of enmity. On Christmas morning a solitary Gotha came over the line and dropped a few bombs near Croix du Bac.

The weather was very cold, and on the night of Christmas Day a heavy snow storm swept over the area. On New Year's Eve the 39th moved back to Neuve Eglise, and during the following weeks enjoyed comparative rest from its recent hard work.

The days were spent in recreational training and in drilling. Equipment was cleaned and polished, and in a very short time the battalion had regained the smartness for which it had been known in Victoria and in England. At the foot of the Neuve Eglise Hill there was situated a large army baths establishment known as Palmer's Baths. The 39th was stationed close to these baths, and its men enjoyed the unaccustomed luxury of hot bathing and frequent changes of underclothing. At this time a large number of men from the battalion was sent for duty to the 184th Tunnelling Company, Royal Engineers. One party went to St. Eloi, and others to Wulverghem and Wytschaete. Their work was to assist the engineers in the construction of dugouts. On January 19 these detachments re-joined the battalion at Neuve Eglise.

On January 27, the 39th handed over its billets to the 24th Battalion, and, leaving Neuve Eglise at 10 a.m., marched once more up to the Catacombs in Hill 63. Here the men lived in the underground galleries for eight days. Once more the routine of nightly working parties began, and this time the work was more strenuous than usual owing to the slowly-dwindling numbers of the battalion and the hazardous nature of the tasks. The defences of the entire front were being strengthened against the heavy fighting which, it was anticipated, would commence with the advent of the spring weather. In the sectors adjacent to Ploegsteert Wood the 39th was employed mainly in improving the barbed wire defences. The greater part of the work had to be done in No Man's Land, and therefore headway could be made only in darkness. Little parties left the Catacombs soon after dusk, and, laden with coils of barbed wire and bundles of pickets, marched three or four miles to the front line trenches. The men were compelled to work as silently as possible, and every now and then had to stop and crouch low as a German Very light lit up the surroundings, followed sometimes by a burst of machine gun fire.

On February 4, the 39th relieved the 37th Battalion in the St. Yves sector. Two companies occupied the front line and the remainder of the battalion was located at Prowse Point and the

Crater. The dugouts formerly occupied by the battalion at those places were found to be completely wrecked—the result of enemy shelling. The troops had to live in hastily-constructed shelters, which were inadequate as protection against shell fire. At the end of four days the men in the line changed over with those in the dugouts, and, during this relief the enemy opened a bombardment which had disastrous effects on the dugouts at Prowse Point. Fortunately these had just been evacuated, otherwise casualties would certainly have been heavy. A few men were killed and wounded and the dugouts almost destroyed. A light trench railway leading to the 40th Battalion's position was badly damaged.

On February 10 a raid was carried out against enemy trenches near Warneton by a combined party from the 37th and 38th Battalions, while the 39th held the front line and support trenches. The Third Divisional Artillery fired a magnificent box barrage, enclosing the area of the operation. The raid was wholly successful. Over twenty prisoners were captured, and much valuable information was gained. The brunt of the enemy's counter bombardment fell upon the 39th. The German guns fired furiously for some time, and a hail of shell fell upon the battalion's trenches.

At 9 p.m., on February 12, the 37th relieved the 39th, and the battalion moved back and occupied a position near Red Lodge on the slopes of Hill 63. From this date until February 19, the men were engaged in searching the surrounding country for salvage. The urgent necessity for saving as much material as possible from damage or loss had been recognised, and a well-organised salvage corps had been raised and attached to each division on the front. Systematic propaganda brought to everybody a realization that large scale waste might have serious consequences. Large salvage dumps were established where great piles of military gear accumulated, to be sorted out and despatched to England—old uniforms to be re-woven, scrap iron to be re-smelted, worn and damaged arms and equipment to be patched or

General Sir W. R. Birdwood presenting Decorations to Members of the 3rd Division at Neuve Eglise, Belgium

repaired. For a week the men scoured the wilderness of trenches and shell holes, and collected every description of article left behind by troops. Rusted rifles, bundles of barbed wire, sheet iron bent and twisted by shell fire—everything was collected and brought in to a battalion salvage dump. Every man was expected to do his share; and all enjoyed the novelty and exercise provided by the new work.

While the battalion was at Red Lodge, General Birdwood inspected the Australian troops in the vicinity.

At 5 p.m., on February 19, the 39th again took over the defence of the front line from the 37th Battalion. The relief was completed under normal conditions by 9 p.m., and the men settled down to six days duty in the line. During this period a close watch was maintained on the enemy lines by fighting patrols in No Man's Land. These patrols were on duty every night from 6 p.m. to 6 a.m., a relief being arranged every four hours. Four Lewis gunners with their gun, and four riflemen armed with rifles, bayonets, and bombs, all under an officer, formed a patrol. Approaching close to the enemy wire, and selecting a position which afforded some cover, the men spread water-proof sheets on the mud and lay down to watch for enemy movement. The object of these patrols was to prevent the enemy's freedom of manoeuvre in No Man's Land.

On the night of February 21 the enemy batteries opened a heavy bombardment of the front and support lines of the battalion's sector. The fire which lasted from 7.30 p.m. until midnight caused several casualties, including one officer and one N.C.O. killed.

The following day six members of the House of Commons visited the line on a tour of inspection and were shown round the battalion frontage.

On February 25, the 33rd relieved the 39th, and the men entrained on the light railway at "Dead Horse Corner" at 11 p.m. A short journey brought the battalion to Kortepyp Camp, where the following week was spent. Working parties were attached temporarily to the Divisional Artillery, and were engaged in the construction of reserve gun positions, and also in building concrete observation posts on the top of Hill 63. As many of the men were working on a sky-line in the open, camouflage was employed to screen them from view. All heavy material was brought forward during the night.

As the winter was ending, the men at the front, in common with the whole civilized world, were wondering what change finer fighting weather would bring. No secret was made of the fact that the enemy contemplated and had prepared an offensive on a colossal scale. The German press boasted with arrogant confidence of the coming annihilation of the Allied Army. The British aeroplanes reported daily feverish activity behind the enemy lines—huge concentrations of troops and the construction on a titanic scale of railways, roads, and gun emplacements. At the end of February the atmosphere on the entire front was electric. At any time on any day the blow might fall, and everyone realized that the troops which had to meet it would be under a terrific ordeal. No one could say where Hindenburg would strike. The general opinion was that the Germans would attack in the neighbourhood of St. Quentin. The ground in Flanders was still too soft to permit the easy movement of guns and material. Defences were strengthened all along the front, and the men of the Allied Armies awaited the attack. They felt that it was the enemy's last desperate throw, that he was staking all his resources in one colossal effort to crush the French and British armies, and to capture Paris and the Channel ports. Thus the British troops waited while each day brought Spring nearer, and time moved on slowly to that fateful hour when the destiny of civilization would be in the balance.

On March 3, a billeting party left Steenwerck for the Lumbres area to arrange accommodation for the battalion. The following day, at 2 p.m., the remainder of the 39th entrained at

Steenwerck and was conveyed to the town of Lumbres in the Department Pas-de-Calais. Detraining at Lumbres at 4.30 p.m., the battalion moved off by road, and marched a few kilos. to its destination, the hamlet of Bayenghem-les-Seninghem. The following eighteen days were occupied in training, the afternoons being devoted to sport and physical drill. Motor bus trips to the old city of Lumbres were arranged, and as the weather was fine the men had a very pleasant time compared with their experiences of the past few months.

On March 16, a battalion sports meeting was held about a mile from the village. Various events were closely contested and the meeting was a complete success. During the night of March 21/22 the battalion received its marching orders and at 5 a.m. the following day a billeting party of one officer and five N.C.Os. left Bayenghem-les-Seninghem for Winnezeele.

Suddenly the news spread like wildfire—the German avalanche had fallen on the British lines in the Somme Valley, and already Haig's armies were reeling before the onset of a million Germans.

CHAPTER XII.

The German Offensive—1918

"Every position must be held to the last man: there must be no retirement. With our backs to the wall, and believing in the justice of our cause, each one of us must fight on to the end."
—FIELD-MARSHAL SIR DOUGLAS HAIG.

EARLY in the morning of March 23, 1918, the 39th Battalion paraded in the village street of Bayenghem-les-Seninghem, and after the roll had been called, marched in the direction of Lumbres. The railway station at Lumbres was reached at 9 a.m., and, according to arrangements, a train should have been awaiting the arrival of the troops. An abnormal demand having been made on railway facilities as a result of a sudden movement of troops towards the front, this train did not arrive till after midday. It departed at 1 p.m.

The first signs of the violence and extent of the German attack were seen soon after the train passed through Hazebrouck railway station. Although firing at very long range, the enemy had been so accurate that the majority of the shells had fallen within twenty yards of the rails. Craters each large enough to hide a horse and waggon had been formed. During the day immediately prior to the launching of the main attack on the Somme the enemy had demonstrated the power and accuracy of his long-range guns right along the front.

Presumably his object was to destroy or disorganise the centres and main arteries of the British lines of communication. The brunt of his long distance shelling fell upon such places as Hazebrouck, a railway centre of vital importance, and Aire, a link in the Army's chain of canal transport services. During the days to come the German artillery was to astonish the whole world by the tremendous range of its guns. A few days after the enemy offensive opened, the astounding news was circulated that the Germans were firing on Paris, more than seventy miles distant from the nearest point of the enemy line.

The battalion arrived at Caestre at 4.30 p.m., on March 23, only to find everything in a state of utter confusion. The situation in the south had suddenly become extremely grave, and the scanty official reports received were very alarming. The strategic plans of the enemy were to drive a wedge between the British and French armies, and, having taken Amiens, a city whose tactical importance was paramount, finally to separate the two armies and deal with them singly.

Reports on March 23 said that enemy forces had advanced twelve miles, and that Amiens was in imminent danger. Such was the position when the 39th Battalion arrived at Caestre.

The whole of the 10th Brigade was moving northwards to re-join the Fourth Army, but on the way it received orders to turn back to help in supplying the urgent need for reinforcements on the Somme. The 39th's new destination was Sercus, a village about four miles west of Hazebrouck. The billeting party was recalled from Winnezeele, and another sent on by motor transport to Sercus, which the battalion reached at 9 p.m. Here confusion and disorganisation prevailed. The billeting officer and his men had not had time to secure accommodation for the unit, and that available at the time was quite inadequate. Too tired to search far for the shelter of a roof, the men philosophically proceeded to bivouac in the village street. Some of the men found lodgings for the night in the village cemetery, and the pale light of early dawn showed quite a number of "diggers" slumbering peacefully on the flat-top tombs. The quartermaster's store stood roofless in the village street.

On March 23, the troops moved out about mid-day and marched to a spot near the village of Wallon Cappel where a convoy of motor buses was waiting. They boarded the vehicles and leaving Wallon Cappel at 1.30 p.m., were conveyed through Wardrecques to the small town of Heuringhen, where they billeted for the night.

The following day the G.O.C., 10th Infantry Brigade, visited the 39th, and explained to the officers the military situation on the Somme. He told them that the 39th, in company with other battalions of the A.I.F., was going into action in front of Amiens within the next few days, and that the responsibility of saving that city rested on the Australian troops. The men were by no means dismayed at the prospect of heavy fighting. They were keen to go into action under conditions of open warfare. Up to that time, war to them had meant endless days in muddy trenches, fighting an unseen enemy, with only an occasional raid to bring them into contact with the foe. Open warfare suggested more dash and glamour, something which would give Australians a better chance of showing their mettle and initiative than ever trench warfare had done. Hasty preparations were made for the coming days. All surplus stores were dumped at Heuringhen, and each man's kit was reduced to a bare minimum. At 1 a.m., on March 26, the men were roused from their billets, and, after breakfast, left Heuringhen at 3 a.m. for St. Omer. They reached the outskirts of the city about dawn, but on arrival at the railway station found that the train which should have been waiting for them was not there. It was learned later that one of the trains intended for the 10th Brigade had been commandeered by the authorities and sent up to the front as an ammunition train.

A departure was made from St. Omer shortly after 9 a.m., and Doullens was reached about mid-day. Then were the first tangible sings of the British retreat witnessed. The platform was crowded with troops and civilians amongst whom was a group of Y.M.C.A. workers from the evacuated area. They were awaiting trains to take them to safety. The wildest and most improbable rumours were in the air, and the military situation seemed obscure. Some said that Uhlan patrols had been seen on the outskirts of Doullens. Everybody seemed convinced that the German advance would be almost irresistible. All these stories were far from true, but they reflected the panic which had been caused in some circles by the rapidity and magnitude of the enemy onslaught. Nevertheless the situation was serious enough, and the refugees had good cause for alarm.

At 8 p.m., on March 26, the train conveying the battalion stopped at the small station of Monde-court-Pas and the unit detrained. Here further signs of the British retreat were encountered. The roads were crowded beyond their capacity with a jumbled stream of military and civilian traffic—columns of artillery and motor transport, carts and heavy farm waggons, cars "crawling" behind the slower moving vehicles. All passed in one long line, and, most significant of all, they were moving back. In addition hundreds of civilians were hurrying along on foot. They were a part of the thousands of refugees from the villages of the Somme Valley and from towns which lay in the path of the enemy's advance.

From Monde-court-Pas the battalion marched through the village of Pas to a small wood known as the Bois Laleau, near Authie. Here a halt was called, and preparations to bivouac for the night were made. Before the men turned in they were warned by their officers to be ready for action at a moment's notice. Orders were also issued to the effect that no commands were to be taken from any officer not belonging to the 10th Brigade. It was known that spies were in the vicinity, and cases had already occurred where some of them, taking advantage of the disorder behind the British lines, had masqueraded as staff officers, and had actually given orders to certain units to retire. About midnight the battalion settled down for a few hours' sleep. The men were fatigued by the strain of the last few days and by the excitement of that critical period. The night was bitterly cold. Every man had been ordered to leave a blanket behind at Heuringhen. Despite the cold conditions the weary "diggers" were soon sleep-

"C" Company, Bouillancourt, France

ing under the trees of the wood. Silence reigned over the camp except for a faint rumble of traffic and the far-off mutterings of guns. The troops were not to rest long. About 3 a.m. a bugler sounded the alarm. The men turned out quickly—half expecting the enemy to be within rifle shot of the camp. After a hurried meal the battalion fell in and marched to the neighbouring town of Thievres, where a halt was made until a convoy of buses arrived to take the men to the front. These vehicles were old London General Omnibus vehicles, refitted to carry about 30 men with their arms and equipment. They moved off immediately for Franvillers. As the journey proceeded, the white clouds from bursting shrapnel could be seen away on the horizon, and now and then a great column of dirty black smoke and earth shot into the air as a high explosive shell burst. The rumble of the guns grew closer and more incessant.

On reaching Franvillers the men realized for the first time the extent of the devastating onslaughts which the enemy was making against the Allies' territory. Most of the people had already left the village, and the few who remained were busily packing their most treasured possessions and placing them on hand-carts and barrows. These sombre, sad-eyed, dazed souls caught in the mesh of war worked silently as if bewildered by the sudden change of circumstance which was forcing them to abandon their homes for the ranks of the army of refugees.

The German batteries had been shelling the outskirts of Franvillers during the previous day, and therefore our troops took all precautions against enemy observation and formed up under cover of the houses. The battalion eventually moved off towards the front along the Heilly Road. This road ran down hill across a wide stretch of open country which was under direct observation from the advanced German positions. As the enemy gunners had already bombarded the valley with gas shells, orders were given that gas masks must be worn at the "Alert."

The Somme.
March 27th 1918.

On approaching the village of Heilly, the troops encountered a pitiable procession of refugees from the adjacent villages—old men hobbling along on sticks and crutches, women struggling along with crying children and heavy bundles, donkey carts laden to capacity with remnants of furniture making their way slowly along the up-hill road. Perhaps the most pathetic sight was that of an aged couple. The wife was ill and her husband, feeble and tottering, was wheeling her to safety in a hand-cart. Every few yards the old man halted to regain his breath, and to look back longingly at the village in which their lives had been spent. Such sights brought home to the men the real meaning of war, and they went forward to their grim tasks with greater determination than ever.

The unit halted in a deep gully on the outskirts of Heilly. The enemy was shelling the village and the roads leading to it, and no move was made until the fire slackened. While the troops rested, a few high velocity shells burst in the vicinity and some men were wounded by flying splinters. The fire of the German guns having died down considerably within an hour, the men entered the village in small parties. They found that the best houses and cellars had been requisitioned, and it was late in the afternoon before accommodation had been secured for everybody. Here were found traces of the hurried flight of the villagers. Everything was in utter disorder. Bedding and clothing were strewn on the floors of the rooms; drawers were pulled out and their contents lay scattered over chairs and tables; bookcases were up-ended; broken crockery and household utensils lying on kitchen floors added to the confusion. In some of the houses half-cooked food was still in saucepans, suggesting the hurried departures of the village folk. Fowls, cows, and pigs had been left behind. Battalion cooks were able to add some unexpected dishes to the evening meal. Champagne and other wines had been left in the village and these were served in limited quantities to the men with their meals.

Practically the whole of the 10th Brigade was billeted in Heilly. The men were advised to take every opportunity of resting during their stay in the village, as an early attack was anticipated. Guards were mounted to give warning of a surprise or gas attack by the enemy. Even now, six days after the opening of the German attack, the limits of the enemy's advance seemed to be unknown. The days when troops in the back areas were secure from attack had vanished. Under conditions of trench warfare, before the enemy could reach units behind the line, three or four lines of well-fortified defences had to be pierced. Now the fighting was all in the open, and gaps existed in the line through which small parties of the enemy might pass, executing swift, sudden raids on villages close to the fighting zone.

Just before midnight on March 27 the battalion was ordered by Brigade to send two companies to the village of Ribemont-sur-l'Ancre, about 1½ miles from Heilly, to take over an outpost line from the 9th Brigade, and to act as support to an English brigade fighting in the vicinity of the village. At midnight these two companies ("A" and "C") commanded by Major A. T. Paterson, M.C., set out on their new task. The approach to the front was made under fire. On arrival at Ribemont-sur-l'Ancre, the positions were taken over from the 33rd Battalion. The men again were forbidden to take orders from any source other than an officer of the 10th Brigade, and were told that in case of attack, the village was to be defended to the last. Hardly had the 33rd Battalion departed when a Brigadier-General from an English brigade entered the newly-established headquarters of the 39th companies and asked for an explanation of their presence in the village. He informed Major Paterson that he was commanding the remnants of an English Infantry Brigade, and that, as he did not wish other troops to occupy his area, the Australians would have to evacuate the village. A certain amount of suspicion was cast on this general, as many instances had been reported where bogus staff officers had given orders to troops. Eventually Major Paterson decided to withdraw one company at a time, and unknown to the English General, he decided to form a defensive line on the outskirts of the village, leaving scouts behind to report to him any movement of the troops in the village. Some of the men had a few hours' rest in a large barn which was filled with hay and straw.

About daybreak the enemy put down a heavy bombardment of 5.9 shells on the village and its approaches. To minimise the casualties the men were ordered to spread out. As it was thought that an enemy attack might follow the shelling, a close watch was kept on all roads leading from the village; but nothing happened. Returning from Brigade Headquarters when the shell fire was at its height, Major Paterson again took over the original positions. In the meantime the English Brigade had received instructions from its Division that it would be relieved by an Australian Brigade. Fortunately no casualties were caused amongst the 39th. Many cows grazing in fields adjoining the village were hit by shells, and some of the men shot those which were wounded. In daylight it appeared that Ribemont-sur-l'Ancre had been a prosperous little village before enemy shell fire brought desolation to its quiet streets. At one end of it was a mill which had been hurriedly vacated by the workers. Early in the following month the wool at the mill was salvaged by Australian troops.

Strong barricades had been thrown across the village streets of Ribemont-sur-l'Ancre, and carts and hay waggons had been pulled across the roads.

The remainder of the morning of March 28 passed without event, and shortly before mid-day the two companies of the 39th were ordered to withdraw from the outposts, and re-join the battalion at Heilly. About 12.30 p.m., the men marched into Heilly, and just as they had thrown off their equipment and settled down for a sleep they were roused and told to prepare for action. The 39th had received orders to carry out an attack against the enemy from positions held by the 38th Battalion.

Maps were closely scanned, and a rapid reconnaissance of the approach-march route was made by officers and N.C.Os. At 4.30 p.m., the battalion left Heilly, and, marching through Mericourt l'Abbe, assembled in a valley in front of that village.

Prior to the arrival of the 3rd Australian Division on the Somme front, an isolated cavalry patrol had been holding the enemy in check in this sector. The assembly of the attacking troops was carried out without any interruption by the enemy. The Quartermaster's store and transport had been left at Heilly; but field cookers had been brought up as far as Mericourt l'Abbe. The movement towards the front had been screened from the enemy by natural features.

Fronting the battalion was a gentle slope up which the advance was to be made. Beyond the crest of this rise lay the enemy positions.

At 7.40 p.m., when the valley was almost in darkness, Lieut.-Colonel R. O. Henderson, D.S.O., sounded the three shrill whistle blasts which were the signal to advance. Immediately the men moved towards the enemy. It was different from the old trench-warfare days of Flanders, for no artillery barrage helped them. Only four light field guns covered the 10th Brigade frontage. Admirable covering fire was supplied by the battalion's Lewis gunners. The 39th and 40th Battalions attacked simultaneously, the 40th on the right. Although the men came under heavy machine gun fire from enemy posts on the ridge, all objectives were taken, and consolidation was carried out on a line about 200 yards east of Marett Wood. Enemy machine guns placed on the fringe of the wood provided the greatest opposition. Eventually the German guns were silenced and the crews killed. Lance-Corporal Michael Sheridan greatly distinguished himself by the manner in which he led his section against overwhelming numbers of the enemy, and by his conduct and leadership enabled his section to overcome a critical situation. Throughout the operation, the bravery and initiative of this N.C.O. were of great value to the battalion.

The company attacking in the centre met with little opposition, so it was moved to the left flank where the fighting was hardest. Consequently when consolidation was completed there was a gap of some hundreds of yards in the line. On the right the battalion was in touch with the 40th, and, on the left, with an Imperial Brigade. The flanks were well protected.

The 39th's first task was the closing up of the gap in the line. While this was in progress patrols were pushed out to protect the men from interruption. Doing excellent work, these patrols penetrated enemy territory for a considerable distance. One of them, from "D" company, reached the outskirts of the next village up the valley, Ville-sur-Ancre, which was in the hands of the Germans.

Two wounded officers were the battalion's total casualties. As the advance was made under heavy fire our good fortune during this engagement was extraordinary. Three prisoners were taken, and the enemy dead numbered thirty-five. It is likely that a large number of Germans was wounded; throughout the night their groans could be heard. The first light of dawn revealed the slaughter effected by the Lewis guns, but most of the German wounded had been recovered by that time by stretcher-bearers.

During the night of March 28/29 two runners attached to Battalion Headquarters had been sent out to locate the exact positions of the two companies and bring back reports of the progress of the attack. Owing to darkness and the gap in the line they proceeded further than they had intended. Suddenly they heard the snapping of twigs. They stopped to listen. Soon they could faintly discern five enemy figures. One of the men took aim and pulled the trigger. Nothing happened as he had forgotten to push forward the safety catch of his rifle. He took aim again, but missed. The strangers were an enemy patrol, which, probably thinking that they had met superior resistance, retreated hurriedly, firing as they went.

During the morning of March 29, Lieutenant-Colonel R. O. Henderson, D.S.O., was wounded in the hand by a piece of falling shrapnel fired by our own anti-aircraft batteries, necessitating his evacuation to hospital. Major A. T. Paterson, M.C., was appointed to the command of the battalion, and on the following day was promoted to the rank of Temporary Lieutenant-Colonel.

Numbers of enemy soldiers were observed walking carelessly about in the open, during the early part of the morning. Evidently they imagined that only a small party of Australians was opposing them and that it was unnecessary to observe ordinary precautions. They were quickly undeceived, for they tumbled over one after another as the bullets of the Australian snipers found their marks.

On the right flank an enemy machine gun post was causing a lot of trouble and hampered the work of the carrying parties. A fighting patrol of one N.C.O. and 15 men moved out from the front line to reconnoitre the ridge in front of the battalion's position and to put the German gun out of action. When the patrol had advanced about 200 yards, it was caught in a hail of rifle and machine gun bullets. The work of Lance-Corporal Rupert Duggan was conspicuously gallant. He exposed himself to great danger by bringing in several of the patrol who were wounded. He was quite fearless in the face of heavy machine gun fire, and his coolness and initiative were instrumental in extricating the patrol from a difficult situation. The N.C.O. in charge, Sergeant A. Levy, was wounded in the leg by a bullet. Stretcher-bearers went out and picked him up. While being carried back to the 39th's lines he attempted to sit up on the stretcher and was killed instantly through being hit in the head by an enemy sniper's bullet.

As darkness approached, the work of consolidating the positions proceeded, and scouts were sent out to give warning of any

Battalion Headquarters, Marett Wood, France

surprise move by the enemy. The erection of barbed wire entanglements was begun before morning.

During the day of March 29, and the following night, there was great activity behind the British lines. Batteries of artillery were arriving in ever-increasing numbers along the front, and the guns were being placed in position to cover the defensive lines. Supplies of rations, material, and ammunition were being rushed up to the front with all possible speed, and every preparation made to resist to the last any further advance by the enemy.

The positions held by the 39th were of great tactical importance. The line lay between the Somme and Ancre rivers, and any further advance by the enemy would have imperilled the city of Amiens. The men of the battalion had no misgivings, but were in high spirit—ready to resist strenuously.

An unusual stillness prevailed on the front at dawn, March 30. Not a shot from the German lines broke the silence of that spring morning. The enemy might have been many miles away instead of just a few hundred yards. A sharp look-out was kept; for long experience had taught the "diggers" that the Germans were most dangerous when they showed the least activity.

Suddenly, at 11 a.m., a heavy artillery barrage fell upon the positions held by the 11th Brigade on the right flank of the 39th Battalion, and shortly afterwards the enemy launched a vigorous attack upon the whole brigade front. The German waves came over in their traditional massed formation, and the Lewis guns of the defenders were responsible for great slaughter amongst the dense ranks of the enemy. The attack was completely repulsed, and the Germans retired, leaving their dead strewn thickly over No Man's Land. Shortly after 1 p.m. everything was quiet again.

The positions of the 39th Battalion were so exposed that very little could be done towards their improvement in daylight, and all extensions and additions to the defences were made under cover of darkness.

At 8 p.m., on March 30, the right company of the battalion pushed forward about 800 yards in order to conform to the line of the adjoining battalion on the right flank. Prior to this advance No Man's Land had been over one thousand yards wide, and the new line afforded excellent observation of Ville-sur-Ancre. During this operation no opposition was encountered, and before morning the new line had been consolidated.

The following day, March 31, passed very quietly in the trenches. Immediately behind the line a storm of shell fire swept over the country during the day. A considerable number of British guns had been hauled into position, and on the same day commenced to range on enemy targets. German transport on the roads near the front came under heavy fire, and more than one enemy motor lorry were hit and reduced to a mass of smoking debris.

At dusk the advance parties of the relieving 38th Battalion came up, and by 10.30 p.m. the relief had been completed. The 39th moved out to support trenches in front of Mericourt village. Three companies occupied the trenches, and the remaining company was kept in reserve in the village. Battalion headquarters was established in the Mericourt Chateau. Many of the undamaged houses in the village made ideal billets. Some of the troops were fortunate enough to be sleeping on beds, and as there was a good supply of food in the cupboards and plenty of fuel to burn in the stoves the men of the company were extremely comfortable.

Although the three companies in the trenches could not fare so well, they were supplied with straw and timber from the village.

The 39th occupied this position for three days, during which little of importance occurred. On April 3 the battalion left Mericourt, and during the evening relieved the 37th which was holding the line at the village of Treux, in the Buire-Treux sector. The positions taken over were situated along the main Amiens-

Albert railway, with battalion headquarters in an old farm house near the railway crossing over the River Ancre. During the following day the front was quiet. Scouts reconnoitred the country towards Ville-sur-Ancre without encountering any enemy.

At 7 o'clock on the morning of April 5 a violent enemy bombardment fell upon the whole front held by Australians, and continued without slackening for twelve hours, and the enemy who, on the 4th, had attacked Villers Bretonneux, a few miles to our right, now attacked to our left.

The main enemy thrust was developed against the 4th Australian Division at Dernancourt, on the left flank of the 39th. Although this assault was eventually repulsed, the position of the 39th was at times anxious. It was essential that information of the progress made by the enemy be reported to battalion headquarters at frequent intervals.

The barrage was so heavy that communication by telephone was frequently interrupted. Signaller Leslie R. G. Smith on one outwards journey effected nine repairs to one line, and on returning, he had to mend the same line in five different places.

The conduct of this linesman in doing this work under heavy shell fire was meritorious. This, and other experiences, convinced company commanders that they would have to rely on the runners, but efforts were still made by the linesmen to keep up a telephone service. Signaller Frederick A. Orders succeeded in maintaining for some hours quite a good service. Signaller Charles A. Mann also mended breaks under constant shell fire.

Although the main attack was on the left flank, a strong party of the enemy made a determined assault upon the bridgehead near Ville-sur-Ancre. The attack was checked by accurate fire by Lewis and machine guns. Privates Albert J. Marner and William C. Jenkins, whilst holding an isolated strong point, did good work in carrying back their section leader who was severely wounded. They had to go overland for 400 yards in full view of the enemy and run the gauntlet of shells, machine gun fire and the deliberate aim of snipers.

The enemy did not press the attack against the battalion, but there was still danger that, if the 4th Division were forced to yield ground the position of the 39th might become untenable.

The work of the runners was deserving of much credit. Signaller Archibald Scrivener kept on carrying messages back from the front line through heavy barrages, and although exhausted, refused to allow anybody to take his place. Private Albert Cunningham continuously carried messages from his company backwards and forwards from Battalion Headquarters, along a track selected by the enemy artillery as a special target.

Everyone recognised that special efforts were required to check the great German offensive. The situation was so desperate that wounded men insisted on fighting until withdrawn by the command of the Medical Officer (Captain L. T. Allsop). The example of Driver Russell S. Gull was typical. This Driver, when bringing up rations, was severely wounded in the head by a fragment of a shell which burst nearby. Though suffering greatly he quietened his team, and drove on and delivered the food whilst it was still hot. He then had his wounds dressed and had to be ordered to cease duty.

Though unknown at the time, this attack ended the enemy's thrust against Amiens.

The following day, April 6, was marked by artillery activity on both sides. At 8.30 p.m. the battalion sent out a patrol with the object of establishing the identity of the opposing troops. The patrol forded the Ancre and found the body of a German belonging to the Jaeger Regiment. At 10.30 that night the 39th Battalion on being relieved by the 38th moved back to billets at Ribemont.

During the following three weeks the battalion spent alternate periods in the line or in billets at Ribemont or Mericourt, the 38th and 39th relieving each other in the Marett Wood sector.

"Ici" returned to his owner at Ribemont, France

THE GERMAN OFFENSIVE—1918

While at Ribemont the 39th became possessed of a dog which was adopted by the battalion, and eventually was regarded as its mascot. When the battalion was first at Ribemont the village was being continually shelled. In the centre of the village stood an abandoned butcher's shop. While searching for billets, the officers discovered a large dog locked in the yard at the back of the shop. Half-mad with fright, he was rescued, taken back to billets, and fed. At first savage, he gradually became friendly, and later could always be seen running behind the "diggers." As his name was unknown, he was called "Ici." He accompanied the 39th Battalion wherever it went in France until after the Armistice, when he was restored to his surprised and grateful owner at Ribemont by the C.O. (Colonel Paterson).

On April 22 the battalion took up a new support position covering the whole of the Brigade front. These trenches were situated on the slopes of a hill near Buire and were much exposed to enemy observation. The sub-soil here was very chalky, and the white parapets showed up in bold relief against the dark background of the surrounding country. Early in the morning of April 24 the enemy commenced to shell the British lines (and the country immediately in rear) with gas and high explosive shells. The bombardment was spread over the whole front held by the Australians, and covered an attack on Villers Bretonneux, south of the Somme.

Poison fumes drenched the villages of Ribemont, Heilly, Buire, Treux, Mericourt, and the surrounding country. Gas shells poured into these places continuously for three hours. But thanks to the steady gas-discipline maintained in the battalion the gas casualties were kept down to six persons. On one occasion a gas shell exploded on a roof, and its liquid contents poured down on to sleeping men. The 10th Brigade had 23 casualties, but the 9th and 11th were not as fortunate and incurred more than two thousand gas cases.

The Sunken Road, Mareth Wood, Mericourt.

The small number of gas casualties of the 10th Brigade reflected great credit on the anti-Gas N.C.Os. Theirs were the tasks of seeing that all ranks had efficient gas masks, that by careful training the masks could be adjusted within five seconds, that loud sounding gas alarms were placed near all sleeping men, and that the gas sentries did their work efficiently.

When troops were under heavy gas shelling, movement was cut down to a minimum; the men had to endure patiently the inconvenience caused by the wearing of tight fitting rubber-lined masks; the masks became hot and clammy, and the temptation to tear them off was great. However, in the attack just mentioned nearly every man who was not in a gas-proof dug-out resisted this temptation.

The transport section was caught in this severe bombardment whilst bringing up rations and three times it was forced off the route it was taking. Lance-Corporal Daniel F. Coffey did effective work in getting the section safely through without casualties. After some hours the horses were so exhausted that he had to go back for fresh ones. He eventually reached his destination after struggling for six and a half hours.

No account of operations within a battalion or brigade sector can convey the gravity of the situation on the Western Front at this time. Field-Marshal Sir Douglas Haig issued the following memorable order.

"TO ALL RANKS OF THE BRITISH FORCES IN FRANCE:—

"Three weeks ago to-day the Enemy began his terrific attacks against us on a 50 mile front. His objects are to separate us from the French, to take the Channel ports and destroy the British Army.

"In spite of throwing already 106 Divisions into the battle and enduring the most reckless sacrifice of human life, he has as yet made little progress towards his goals.

"We owe this to the determined fighting and self-sacrifice of our troops. Words fail me to express the admiration which I feel for the splendid resistance offered by all ranks of our Army under most trying circumstances.

"Many amongst us now feel tired. To those I would say that Victory will belong to the side which holds out the longest. The French Army is moving rapidly and in great force to our support.

"There is no other course open to us but to fight it out. Every position must be held to the last man; there must be no retirement. With our backs to the wall, and believing in the justice of our cause, each one of us must fight on to the end. The safety of our Homes and the Freedom of mankind alike depend upon the conduct of each of us at this critical moment."

The following day, April 25, was the third anniversary of the Gallipoli landing. The 39th again relieved the 37th in the Marett Wood sector where the battalion then held the line for four days, returning to the support positions on April 29.

On May 4, after five days as battalion in support, the 39th marched up to take over the Marett Wood positions for the last time. Previous tours of trench duty in this sector had passed more or less quietly, but the final period was extremely eventful. At 11.45 on the night of the 5/6th the 9th Brigade, which was on the right flank of the 39th, successfully attacked the German positions on a front of 1,500 yards.

To conform to the new line thus established, two Lewis gun sections of the 39th, under the command of Lieutenant Herbert Frederick Miles, were sent out to establish two posts in advance of the battalion's trenches. This party achieved its objectives and returned later without loss. Heavy rain and extreme darkness frustrated an attempt to push out further outposts the following evening.

On the night of the 7/8th, with the assistance of artillery co-operation, four strongposts were established by two large fighting patrols from the battalion. These patrols moved out from

A Parcel from Home

THE GERMAN OFFENSIVE—1918

"C" company's trenches and with little difficulty accomplished their object. The new posts (which gave excellent observation of the village of Morlancourt) were heavily shelled by the enemy very soon after their establishment, and Lieutenant Miles, who was in command of one of the 39th parties, was killed. The other casualties sustained by the battalion during the operation consisted of one officer and two men wounded.

On May 8, a hundred rounds were fired by six-inch Newton trench mortars on to a sunken road, south of Ville-sur-Ancre, which was occupied by the enemy. The projectiles fired by these mortars were particularly severe, and on this occasion were very effective. This fact was established by the story of three German soldiers who came over to the Australian lines during the night and surrendered. According to them many casualties had been inflicted on the enemy's troops.

At 9.30 on the night of May 8/9, two fighting patrols, each twenty strong, commanded respectively by Lieutenants J. W. Gration and R. H. Overton, were sent out. Their task was to work in conjunction with patrols from the 40th Battalion with the object of pushing through the village of Ville-sur-Ancre and establishing a line east of it. Moving carefully and taking advantage of cover the patrols reached a point within a hundred yards of Ville-sur-Ancre. At this stage they heard the 40th Battalion patrols attacking an enemy strong-post on the left. The patrols of the Tasmanian battalion had evidently encountered strong opposition, for they were repulsed with casualties. The 39th parties were held up by heavy machine gun fire from the village, and Colonel Paterson knowing that it would be folly to attempt an attack, informed brigade headquarters that he was withdrawing his men. The signalling officer of the 40th Battalion, who was in telephone communication, was also informed. Valuable information of the positions of enemy posts was obtained, and the 39th patrols reached their own line without a casualty.

At 2 a.m., on May 19, the village was attacked and captured by the 6th Australian Infantry Brigade. The total number of prisoners taken exceeded 300.

During the night of May 9/10 the 39th was relieved by the 22nd Battalion. Heavy shelling was encountered during the progress of the relief, and there was a considerable number of casualties. The relief was completed at 3 a.m., on May 10, and the battalion marched out through Mericourt and Heilly to Franvillers, where a halt was made to enable the weary men to get a few hours' sleep. At 9 a.m. this march was resumed via Allonville to the village of Cardonnette, which was reached at two o'clock in the afternoon.

The 39th enjoyed a well-earned rest at Cardonnette during the following three weeks. The men had been holding the trenches for forty-three days, during which time the Australian Divisions in front of Amiens had successfully opposed the German advance. Although further enemy attacks had to be anticipated the "diggers" had beyond doubt saved the city from capture. The Australians during the most critical stages of the fighting had no division in reserve, and had the Germans attacked with anything like the violence which had marked the opening of their offensive, nothing could have stemmed the tide. As it was, the splendid fighting qualities of the Australian Divisions completely deceived the enemy, and while he delayed the attack, the line was consolidated and the British positions in front of Amiens made secure.

The following message of appreciation was promulgated to all ranks of the battalion:—

11th May, 1918.

To THE OFFICERS, N.C.OS. AND MEN
OF THE 39TH BATTALION, A.I.F.

I desire to convey to the Officers, N.C.Os. and men of the battalion my highest appreciation of the excellent manner in which all ranks have behaved during the past six weeks, when we have been helping to prevent the advance of the enemy on Amiens.

General Birdwood asked us to "take the strain," and we know it has been a strain, but all ranks have answered his wish nobly.

In our minor operations you have gained all the objectives you were asked to take, and instead of being pushed back, you have advanced our line, on three occasions, aggregating considerably over 2,000 yards.

The enemy's counter-bombardment was heavy, especially when he tried to advance on Buire and Treux. His artillery caused many casualties among our brave men but not as many as you caused on him.

The manner in which you have carried out reliefs has been splendid.

On your work of consolidating the objectives you gained, and also on the second defensive system, I cannot comment too highly.

The spirit and energy in which you have carried out all that has been asked makes one feel that everyone has realised his responsibilities, and that should occasion again arise you will still further "take the strain."

A. T. PATERSON, Lieut.-Colonel,
C.O. 39th Battalion, A.I.F.

On May 12, the battalion marched from Cardonnette to Allonville where a church parade was held in the aerodrome. Bishop Long conducted the service, and at its conclusion General Sir W. R. Birdwood presented decorations won during recent fighting.

On May 17, the 39th again marched to the Allonville aerodrome where, after a rehearsal in the morning, the 10th Australian Brigade was reviewed by the Commander-in-Chief, Field-Marshal Sir Douglas Haig. Three days later an advance party of the 39th left Cardonnette for Blangy Tronville. On arrival at the latter village the billets occupied by the 16th Battalion were inspected and arrangements made by the 39th for taking them over.

On May 22, the battalion left Cardonnette at 9.30 a.m., and, marching through Allonville, Lamotte-Brebiere and Glisy, arrived at Blangy Tronville at 3 p.m. The billets of the 16th Battalion, about half a mile east of the village, were taken over and the men rapidly settled down in their new quarters. The Somme flowed close to the village, and, the weather being pleasantly warm, the men spent the afternoon swimming in the lagoons of the river. During the day the 39th officers made a reconnaissance of a sector held by the 9th Brigade just north of Villers-Bretonneux.

From Blangy Tronville the village of Villers-Bretonneux could be seen, and the heavy shell fire which fell on it bore witness to its tactical importance, and the desire of the enemy to capture it from the Australians. The twelve days which the battalion spent at Blangy Tronville passed pleasantly. The weather continued fine and warm, and the men could bathe in the river to their hearts' content.

The Somme was full of fish, and a favourite practice of the "diggers" was to throw bombs into it, the explosion killing the fish and bringing them to the surface. Large numbers of fish were caught in this way and made a welcome variation in the diet of the battalion.

At Lamotte-Brebiere, on May 27, General Sir W. R. Birdwood presented ribbons to those who had distinguished themselves in the recent fighting. This was General Birdwood's last official appearance as Commander of the Australian Corps. A few days later he took command of the Fifth Army and was succeeded by Major-General Sir John Monash, K.C.B., V.D. Brigadier-General John Gellibrand (afterwards Major-General Sir John Gellibrand, K.C.B., D.S.O.) took over command of the Third Division in place of General Monash.

MAP NO. 7
THE SOMME—MORLANCOURT

THE SOMME — MORLANCOURT MAP No. 7

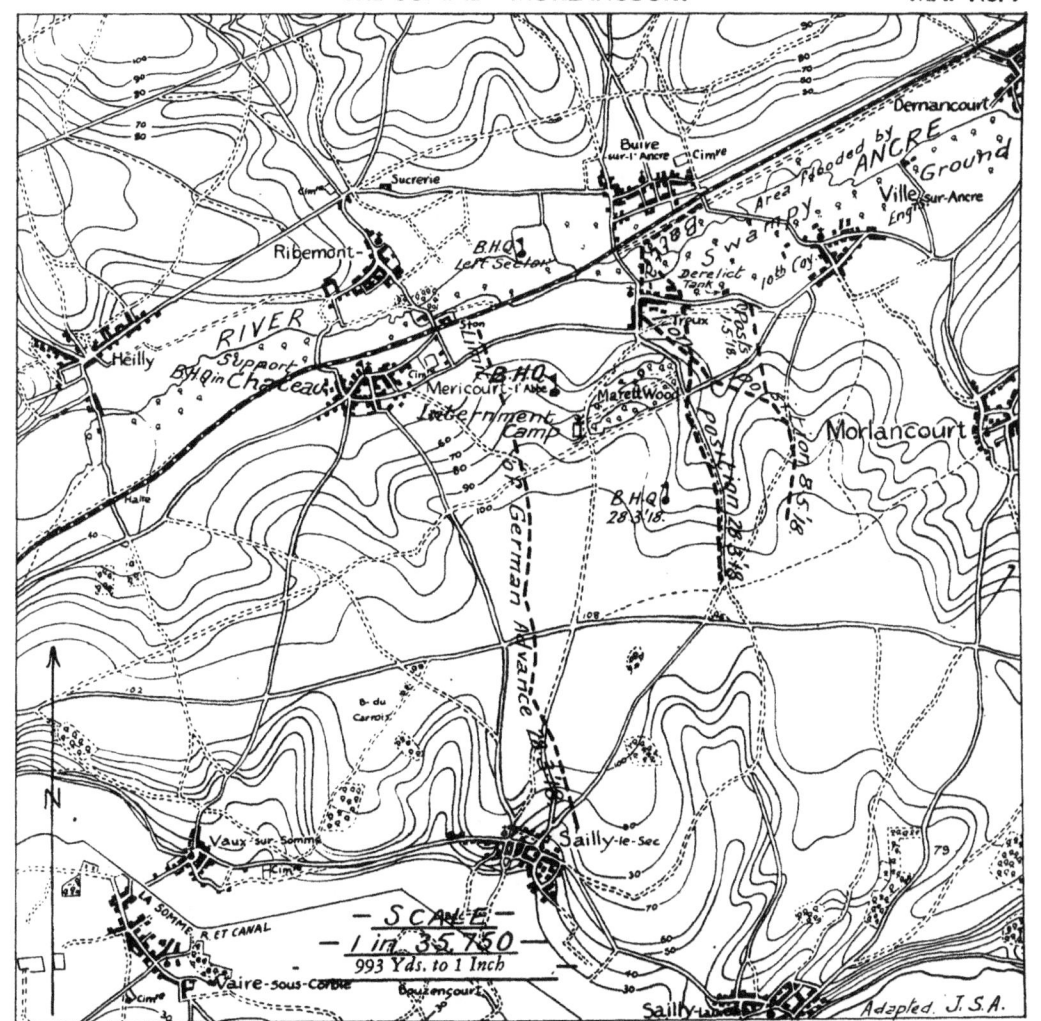

CHAPTER XIII.

The Allies Advance

"Then came the attack in the Amiens sector on August 8. That went well, too. The moment had arrived. I ordered General Humbert to attack in his turn. 'No reserves.' No matter. Allez-y (Get on with it). I tell Marshal Haig to attack, too. He's short of men also. Attack all the same. There we are advancing everywhere—the whole line! En avant! Hup!"
—MARSHAL FOCH.

DURING the evening of June 3 the 39th moved out of Blangy Tronville and relieved the 41st Battalion in the support trenches of the Villers-Bretonneux sector. These trenches lay a few hundred yards to the right of the village. Battalion headquarters was established in the White Chateau, which was built on a hill in the Bois l'Abbe, overlooking the valley of the Somme.

The support trenches taken over by the battalion were on the extreme right flank of the British front in France. On the right flank of the 39th the line was held by the 3rd Regiment of Zouaves, which formed the extreme left of the French Army. This was the first occasion on which the battalion had junctioned with the French, and very soon both officers and men of the two Armies fraternised on exceedingly good terms.

The 39th remained in support for a week, during which period working parties were engaged in the construction of trench mortar positions and dug-outs. On June 10, the 39th relieved the 37th Battalion in the front line at Villers-Bretonneux. Thus the 39th held the right sector of the Brigade front and linked up with the French Army by establishing what were known as International posts. These were in the front, support and reserve lines at points where the British and French trenches met. In the front line the post consisted of an equal number of French and Australians under the command of an Australian officer. In the support line a French officer commanded. The French troops in these posts did duty on the British side of the dividing point and the Australians on the French side, thus facilitating liaison between the two armies in case of attack.

On the slopes of the hills the poppies made vivid patches of crimson among the corn; the woods that crowned the ridges were beautiful in their luxuriance of leaf and branch; and the country stretched in a sweep of verdant loveliness back to the ancient spires of Amiens. But seldom were the guns silent for long. British air squadrons were constantly passing and re-passing above the men in the line. In the evenings, when the shadows began to lengthen, swift planes wheeled and banked and glistened golden as they turned in the last rays of the setting sun. Eventually the squadrons returned homeward, and with many daring evolutions, went skimming over the tree-tops towards their aerodromes.

The order, "Stand To," would come soon after the planes had departed, and the men lined the parapet in the twilight, listening to the intermittent rat-tat-tat-tat of the machine guns and watching the luminous arcs of the enemy Very lights against the darkening sky.

At night British bombing squadrons passed over, and from the German lines long searchlight beams swept across the sky, and the rattle of anti-aircraft machine guns sounded on every side. Patrols and wiring parties went out and returned. From time to time officers visited the posts. When, about dawn, the order to "Stand To," was repeated, the men once again lined the parapet ready to repel the waves of grey-clad enemy which might at any moment emerge from the mists of No Man's Land.

On June 14, Lieut.-Colonel Henderson, D.S.O., returned from hospital and again took over command of the battalion from Lieut.-Colonel Paterson, M.C., who had been in command

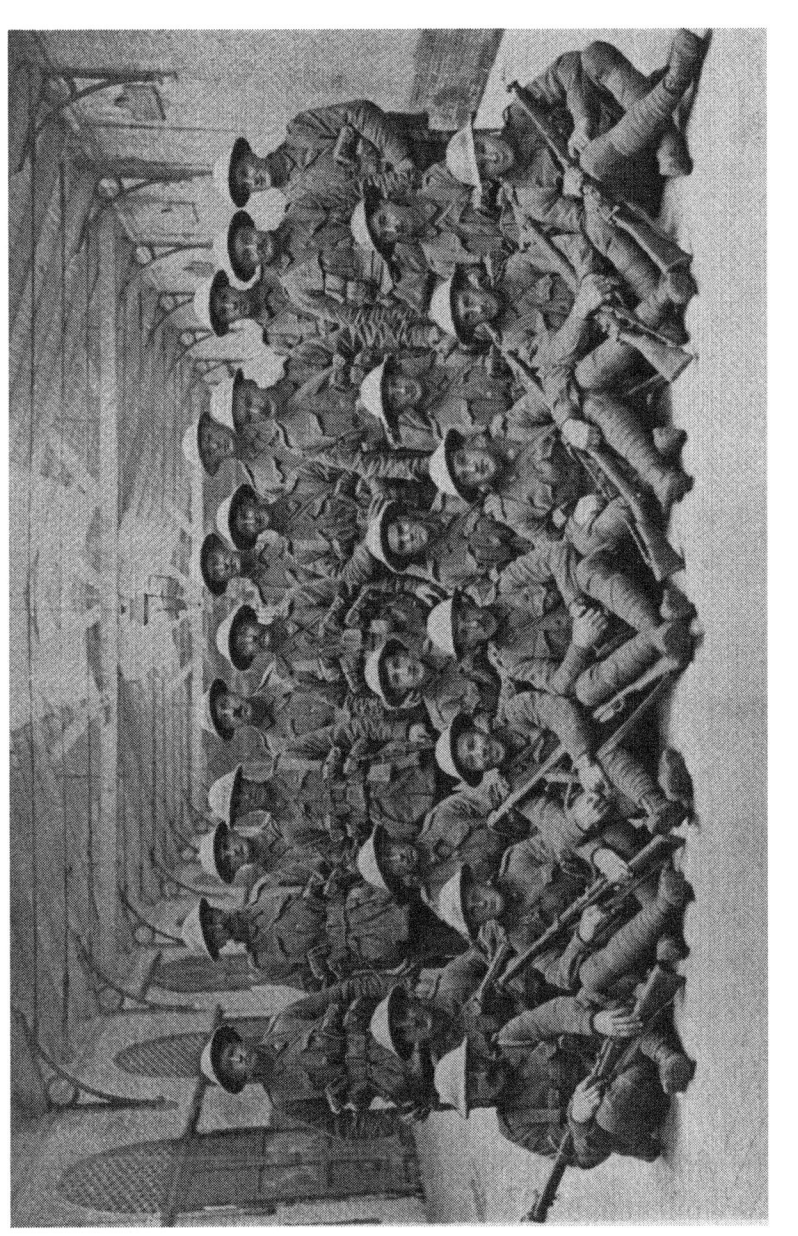

N.C.Os. of "B" Company, Armentières, France

for three months. Two days later a raid against the enemy trenches was attempted, the 39th working in conjunction with the French. Lieutenant A. E. Guyett commanded the party from the battalion. A barrage from the trench mortar batteries assisted the operation. The raid was unsuccessful owing to the deep barbed wire entanglements in front of the German trenches. The 39th casualties were one killed and two wounded.

On June 17 the 39th was relieved in the front line by the 37th Battalion and returned to the trenches in front of Bois l'Abbe, thus becoming Brigade support. Immediately after the relief the enemy attempted a raid on the right of the 37th's sector. This raid was preceded by a heavy barrage which rested on the front line for five minutes and then lifted on to the support trenches. The enemy raiders reached the barbed wire entanglements in front of the Australian trenches, but failed to enter the line.

On June 22 the 39th Battalion was relieved by the 43rd in the Villers-Bretonneux support trenches and moved back to take up a position in a wood about a mile south of Blangy Tronville. During the following morning three stray eight-inch high explosive shells fell on "B" company's position, killing four and wounding six men. While the battalion remained near Blangy Tronville for three days, a number of men was engaged in laying cables near Villers-Bretonneux under the supervision of the Divisional Engineers. As the ground was very hard the task of burying the cables to protect them from shell fire proved laborious. The first night in which the men were engaged in this work the party came under shell fire—both high explosive and gas. Ten men were wounded and many others slightly gassed.

At 8.30 a.m. on June 26 the position was handed over to the 26th Battalion and the 39th marched to Cardonnette. After passing through the village of Glisy, a halt was made alongside the river. As the day was hot and the roads dusty, many men

Towards Bois l'Abbé from Villers Bretonneux.

had a hasty dip in the Somme. The battalion reached Cardonnette about 5 p.m. and billeted in the village for two days.

On June 28 the 39th left Cardonnette at 9 a.m., and marched to a position near the small town of Querrieu, where the camping ground was taken over from the 24th Battalion. Querrieu was a straggling, drab little place, situated in the valley of the River L' Hallue, a tributary of the Ancre, and without a special feature except a large chateau in beautiful grounds. Many lagoons in the low-lying ground near the river provided excellent swimming facilities. During the following days sports meetings and swimming contests were held at Querrieu.

On July 6 a Brigade sports meeting was held near Querrieu at which the Corps Commander, Lieut.-General Sir John Monash, K.C.B., was present. The fancy dress competitions caused much amusement and were excellently carried out.

On July 8 the battalion officers made a reconnaissance of the Vaire Wood sector. Situated near Hamel, north of Villers-Bretonneux, this sector was to be taken over by the 39th the following week. At 8 p.m. on July 8 the Fourth Army ordered a general "Stand to Arms" on the whole of the Army front. Everything was prepared for action; and for five hours the men awaited further orders while rain poured down. The anticipated enemy attack did not eventuate, and, at 1 a.m., came the welcome order "To Stand Down."

At 2 p.m. on July 9 the battalion left Querrieu and marched to the village of Camon, which is situated on the banks of the Somme, about three miles south-east of Amiens. It arrived at 4.30 p.m. and bivouacked in shelters made of tarpaulins slung over ridge poles. At 8.30 on the following morning the unit marched nine miles to St. Vast, where contact work with tanks was practised, both with and without artillery co-operation. The camp at Camon was reached again at 7.30 p.m. Half an hour later the 39th advance parties left Camon by motor lorrry to commence the relief of the 16th Battalion in the Vaire Wood sector.

Reveille sounded at 3 a.m. on July 11 and the men moved off at 6.45 and marched along the banks of the Somme to a position south of Vecquemont, where they rested until nightfall. At 9 p.m. the approach-march to the front was commenced and shortly after midnight the relief of the 16th Battalion in the Vaire Wood sector had been completed. During the night the line was advanced about 300 yards to conform with that held by the 20th Battalion on the right flank of the 39th. While this operation was in progress, Lieutenants H. J. Ware and J. S. Beavis were wounded, and the following day Lieutenant Beavis died.

In front of the 39th trenches the ground sloped upwards to form a ridge beyond which lay the enemy positions. In order to secure observation of the German trenches, a party of men under the command of Lieutenant J. S. August was sent out from the battalion during the evening of July 14 to construct outpost positions on the crest of the high ground. Two posts were dug in front of the left flank of the battalion's sector, one slightly in advance of the other. Daylight intervened before barbed wire defences could be thrown out; but notwithstanding this the posts were manned with Lewis gun sections.

The more advanced post was situated about 300 yards forward from the front line, in a clearing between two belts of tall ripening crop which stood high on each flank. It was a dangerous post and was manned by two Lewis gun crews under the command of Sergeant Francis J. McEwan. At 10.30 on the morning of July 15 enemy patrols made their way through each crop, unobserved until they opened fire with machine guns and rifle grenades.

The German patrol on the right came into action first. The Lewis guns were immediately directed against this patrol. Private James E. Johnston, as No. 1 of a gun, did wonderful work in holding the enemy in check. It was his efficient handling of the gun that prevented the enemy from overwhelming the post. His courage and devotion inspired the remainder of the men, and they needed inspiration. Without warning, the post was now attacked from the left flank, and grenades put one gun out of action, killed one man and severely wounded several others.

It was a critical situation which called for leadership.

Sergeant McEwan wisely decided on a withdrawal. While he remained in the post to keep the enemy at bay, he ordered the remainder of his men to make their way back to the front line.

The raiders seeing that they had for the moment only one man to deal with attempted to rush the post. Single-handed, Sergeant McEwan encountered four and put the others to flight. Observing that his men had made good their withdrawal, Sergeant McEwan then picked up the Lewis gun and, firing as he walked, retired to the front line.

His skill in handling the situation enabled the garrison to hold the post until the last possible moment; his competent leadership, coupled with coolness and great courage saved a critical situation, and extricated his men from almost overwhelming odds with a minimum of casualties. Only one was killed, one badly wounded and taken prisoner, and two were wounded. The enemy casualties numbered three killed, and several wounded.

At 3.30 p.m. the 39th launched a counter-attack against the enemy troops who had occupied the captured post. The Germans were driven out by rifle grenades and trench mortar bombardment, and the post recaptured without a casualty. Barbed wire entanglements were erected during the night of July 15, and the posts strengthened against further enemy attacks.

The following day was uneventful except for the capturing of a prisoner who wandered into the 39th's trenches. This man belonged to the 13th German Infantry Regiment.

On July 17 the 38th Battalion relieved the 39th. It is probable that the enemy knew in some way that a relief was in progress, because both battalions suffered many casualties from an enemy bombardment. The relief was completed at 2 a.m. on July 18, and the 39th moved out to a line of support trenches about a mile west of Vaire Wood.

On July 21 two officers and six non-commissioned officers from the 39th Battalion were sent to the 131st Regiment of the United States Army as instructors to the American units which had arrived for the first time on the Somme front.

At dusk on July 22 the gas sentry on duty in the battalion lines reported that enemy gas shells were falling thickly between the 39th's position and Villers-Bretonneux. The shells were easily recognised by their sound during flight and their characteristic "pop." After dark a change in the direction of the wind brought the gas towards the positions of the 39th. It was identified by its odour as mustard gas, and precautions were taken to protect the men sleeping in dug-outs. Gas-proof curtains were placed over the entrances, and the men ordered to remain behind these protective screens. Two hours after the opening of the bombardment a gas cloud of great density was hanging over the battalion's trenches. Then the enemy shelling ceased abruptly, and the gas slowly dispersed. At midnight the "All Clear" signal was given, and the men, who had been sweltering in air-tight dug-outs, came out into the open air. Owing to the precautions taken there were no casualties in the battalion.

On July 25 the 39th left the support positions, and, moving up to the front line, relieved the 38th Battalion. In order to gain experience in the trenches, detachments from the 129th American Regiment went into the line with the 39th Battalion. During the time spent in the line the situation on the front remained normal. In the Morlancourt sector on July 28 the 5th Australian Division launched a successful attack. This position lay to the left of the Vaire Wood sector occupied by the battalion.

At 3 p.m. on July 30 two enemy soldiers attempted to crawl up to No. 9 post on the battalion's left flank. They were probably enemy scouts seeking information. Sentries observed their approach, opened fire, killed one, and wounded the other. The wounded man reached his own lines, but the body of the dead soldier was brought in after dark, and he was identified as having belonged to the 13th Regiment.

On August 2 the 39th was again relieved by the 38th Battalion. Heavy enemy shelling occurred while the relief was in progress and several casualties resulted. On being relieved, the battalion moved out to the Villers line of trenches, situated about 1,000 yards west of Vaire Wood. About noon on the following day, August 3, information was received that the battalion would relieve the 42nd in the sector between the River Somme and the village of Hamel. An attack against the enemy on a large scale was to be launched on August 8, and amidst active preparations for battle, the relief of the 42nd by the 39th was carried out on August 4 without incident. From this date great activity prevailed on the front.

On August 6 two platoons of "A" company, under the respective commands of Lieutenants Oswald R. Brown and Cecil M. Cobden, were temporarily attached to the 42nd Battalion to work in liaison between the 42nd Battalion and an English Division on its left. As the 10th Brigade was to be in reserve during the battle, these two platoons would be the only part of the 39th in the attack. On August 7, the final preparations were completed. Officers from the 39th Battalion reported to the Headquarters of the 10th and 11th Brigades, and also to the English Brigade on the left flank for liaison work during the battle.

At midnight on the night of August 7/8 the 11th Brigade took over the patrolling of the front from the 39th Battalion, so as to cut gaps in the wire for the attacking troops. At 3 a.m. on August 8, the 42nd and 44th Battalions relieved the 39th in the front line.

The scheme for the impending battle was that the 3rd Australian Division—with the 11th Brigade on the left flank, the 9th Brigade on the right, and the 10th Brigade in reserve—should attack simultaneously with the 2nd Australian Division. This attack was to be part of a large operation by English, Canadian and Australian Divisions in front of Amiens. At the commencement of the battle the 3rd Australian Division occupied a line extending from the south bank of the Somme to a road about 3,000 yards south-west of Accroche Wood. The 58th British Division was to attack on the left flank, on the north bank of the Somme, and the 2nd Australian Division was to move forward on the right of the 3rd Australian Division.

Lieut.-General Sir John Monash issued the following message, which was promulgated to all the troops on the forenoon of the day before the battle.

AUSTRALIAN CORPS.

Corps Headquarters,
August 7, 1918.

To the Soldiers of the Australian Army Corps,

For the first time in the history of this Corps all five Australian Divisions will to-morrow engage in the largest and most important battle operation ever undertaken by the Corps.

They will be supported by an exceptionally powerful Artillery and by Tanks and Aeroplanes on a scale never previously attempted. The full resources of our sister Dominion, the Canadian Corps, will also operate on our right, while two British Divisions will guard our left flank.

The many successful offensives which the Brigades and Battalions of this Corps have so brilliantly executed during the past four months have been but the prelude to, and preparation for, this greatest and culminating effort.

Because of the completeness of our plans and dispositions, of the magnitude of the operations, of the number of troops employed, and of the depth to which we intend to over-run the enemy's positions, this battle will be one of the most memorable of the whole war; and there can be no doubt that, by capturing our objectives, we shall inflict blows

The Scouts of the Battalion, Bouillancourt, France

upon the enemy which will make him stagger, and will bring the end appreciably nearer.

I entertain no sort of doubt that every Australian soldier will worthily rise to so great an occasion, and that every man, imbued with the spirit of victory, will, in spite of every difficulty that may confront him, be animated by no other resolve than a grim determination to see through to a clean finish whatever his task may be.

The work to be done to-morrow will perhaps make heavy demands upon the endurance and staying powers of many of you; but I am confident that, in spite of excitement, fatigue, and physical strain, every man will carry on to the utmost of his powers until his goal is won, for the sake of Australia, the Empire, and our cause.

I earnestly wish every soldier of the Corps the best of good fortune, and a glorious and decisive victory, the story of which will re-echo throughout the world, and will live for ever in the history of our home land.

JOHN MONASH,
Lieut.-General,
Commanding Australian Corps.

At zero hour, 4.20 a.m. on August 8, a thick mist, mixed with smoke from artillery fire, hung over the country. Through this haze, waves of attacking troops steadily advanced. Many of the troops and some of the tanks engaged in the action lost their direction in the mist. Meeting very little opposition, the 3rd Division reached and captured the first and second objectives well ahead of the time-table for the battle.

About 10 a.m., the progress of the attack having exceeded the most optimistic expectations, the 39th Battalion received orders to move to newly-captured enemy trenches on the eastern edge of Arquaire Wood. Here the 39th remained in the trenches until 2.45 p.m., when, acting under further orders, it moved to Hazel Wood, about a mile N.E. of the village of Warfusee-

Abancourt. In this position it bivouacked and settled down to await orders.

Meanwhile the two platoons of "A" company attached to the 42nd Battalion had taken part most successfully in the operations. When these platoons (Nos. 3 and 4) left the battalion on the morning of August 6 they marched to Corbie, reporting to the 42nd Battalion at 11 a.m. After comfortable billets had been found, the remainder of the day was spent in preparing for the attack on the enemy. On August 7 the two platoon commanders (Lieutenants Brown and Cobden), accompanied by their sergeants, reconnoitred the ground over which the advance was to be made. They returned to Corbie about 4 p.m., and explained to their men the part they would have to play. These platoons were to act as a link between the Australian left flank and the British right flank, and to work along the marshy ground beside the river, clearing it of the enemy as they advanced.

A few hours before the battle the men held high carnival in Corbie. Fancy costumes had been found in one of the houses. They "dressed up" and sang appropriate songs until it was time to march to the assembly point. Shortly after 11 p.m., the platoons marched out of Corbie.

It was a fine moonlight night as they marched along the tree-lined road beside the canal. Further on, the road led through a valley where a faint smell of gas lingered in the air. As the party neared the assembly point the enemy commenced to shell the road, but the platoons of the 39th reached their destination without casualties.

At zero hour a heavy fog overhung the valley. When the barrage opened it was impossible to see more than thirty yards in any direction. Lieut. Cobden's platoon (No. 3) advanced along the tow-path on the north of the Somme River, and Lieut. Brown's platoon (No. 4) traversed the swamp also on the north side. Moving through the swamp in extended order No. 4 platoon struck opposition only from desultory enemy machine gun fire, and an occasional shell which dropped short from our own guns.

Thick belts of barbed wire, half-hidden in the grass and reeds, retarded the progress of the advance. Wire-cutters carried by the men were ineffective and the wire had to be beaten down by rifle butts. The enemy was first seen while the platoon was negotiating these entanglements. German machine gunners, carrying their gun, hurriedly retreated through the fog, and shots fired at them missed. Eventually the platoon found itself on the outskirts of the town of Sailly-Laurette. Only one man had been wounded.

On entering Sailly-Laurette, Lieut. Brown found that a number of enemy machine gun posts lay in the way of his advance. On catching sight of the Australians, the Germans left their guns and took refuge in a cellar which was surrounded by No. 4 platoon. When called upon to surrender they did so. Lieut. Brown led his platoon, with the captured guns and prisoners, back towards the starting point.

Meanwhile Lieut. Cobden's platoon had pushed along the tow-path beside the river, and had encountered obstruction from the enemy's wire entanglements. This platoon also captured a German machine gun post and Lieut. Cobden decided to escort the prisoners and guns to the rear. Nos. 3 and 4 platoons met each other. Forty prisoners with eight machine guns were placed under a small escort, and the two platoons moved forward again to their objectives. They had successfully completed their task by 6.30 a.m. and had lost only one man.

While waiting at the objective, the men searched the enemy dug-outs for such trophies as revolvers and compasses. At 9 a.m. the fog suddenly lifted and they were able to see the progress that troops had made on their right flank. The attacking waves of the Fourth Australian Division were just passing through the 11th Brigade, cheering as they advanced. Battalion and Company Commanders were riding at the head of their men, who were moving in perfect formation. Tanks were creeping steadily forward, and behind the troops, guns and ammunition limbers were advancing in the open. Even the field cookers were coming forward. Smoke was issuing from their chimneys as dinners were being cooked in their ovens. The 39th platoons remained in position during the day, and about midnight received orders to rejoin their battalion at Hazel Wood. By 3 a.m. on August 9 they had returned. Congratulations were showered upon them for the success of their enterprise. The G.O.C., 10th Brigade, sent a special message expressing his satisfaction at the results achieved.

On August 10, orders were received that the 39th Battalion would take part in an operation which had for its object the capturing of a village and the encircling of considerable enemy forces. The idea was very daring, and had been attempted previously at Villers-Bretonneux.

It was proposed that the 10th Brigade should march along the Peronne Road through the enemy positions, while the 15th Brigade followed a parallel route along the Bray Road. The two brigades were then to turn inwards and meet behind the village of Proyart, thus cutting off the enemy's retreat. The 9th Brigade was to launch a direct attack on the village. Surprise was the essence of success. The night of August 10/11 was selected for carrying out this movement.

At 7 p.m., on August 10, the storming party marched out of Hazel Wood in broad daylight and in full view of German observation balloons. During two hours of daylight good progress was made and the battalion reached the assembly point on the main road south-east of the village of Morcourt before the tanks arrived. The function of the tanks was to form a spearhead and penetrate the organised defences, leaving the way comparatively clear for the infantry to follow through.

Meanwhile a number of hostile bombing planes came over, bombed the waiting troops, and caused many casualties and much confusion. Picking up the range from the bursting bombs, the German artillery put down a barrage on the storming party. The tanks now arrived and proceeded along the metalled road, thus announcing the approach of the infantry, with the result that the enemy machine gunners directed their fire on to the road.

The combined effect of the artillery, bombs and machine guns temporarily disorganised the storming party. Sergeant Charles J. Hewland, of the Orderly Room, did very good work as a guide, directing scattered troops and maintaining communication with the left flank, which was in danger. His coolness and disregard for personal safety did much to inspire confidence. Company Sergeant Major John W. Burn found a platoon without a commander, so re-organised it under heavy shell fire and led it into action. Throughout the whole operation he displayed the utmost gallantry.

After his officers had been killed, Sergeant Duncan B. Cowan took charge of another platoon, re-organised it, and led it to a position where he established a strong post within the enemy's territory. He then arranged for the evacuation of the wounded.

Meanwhile the enemy fire increased, and in the darkness the men experienced much difficulty in keeping touch and finding their way. They were in unfamiliar territory which a few days before had been miles behind the front line trench systems. The whole party had to rely on the technical skill of Lieutenant Frank M. Shaw who acted as guide. As in previous battles this gallant officer was largely responsible for maintaining direction over broken ground. With great coolness he placed himself in prominent positions from which he could best serve his battalion.

The enemy mixed gas shells with shrapnel and high explosives, and this necessitated the wearing of gas masks. In a short time the eye pieces became blurred with the condensation of the vapour, and with the noise of the barrage it was impossible to be heard at a distance of a few feet.

Lieutenant Stanley Le Fevre borrowed a horse and rode up and down the road through a hail of machine gun bullets and did most valuable work in keeping the battalion together. He used his voice and soon became gassed, but he refused to be evacuated and carried on to the end, thereby setting a fine example to the men.

Despite all the difficulties, the storming party made some progress. It seemed that as the advance proceeded the enemy fire became hotter; and, as casualties were being caused every minute, it was decided to dig in and form a series of strong posts.

Sergeant Richard J. Matthews was an inspiration to his whole company. He went overland from post to post and thus was able to establish communication and convert a series of isolated posts into a formidable defensive system.

Lieutenant John M. Prentice did the same kind of work. He started from Battalion Headquarters and visited every post of the battalion and the nearer ones of adjoining units. On returning he was able to give valuable information. He went out again with the Brigade Intelligence Officer and established a communication system.

Meanwhile the stretcher-bearers were busy. Thanks to their own resource and the splendid example of the Medical Officer, Captain L. T. Allsop, they did everything possible to alleviate the suffering of the wounded men. Undaunted by the bombs, artillery and machine gun fire, Captain Allsop established his aid post well forward and carried out his work with much skill under most trying conditions.

The stretcher-bearers had to travel along the shell-swept road. The work of Privates Joseph W. Bollow and Albury Neal was outstanding, whilst Private Louis J. Andrews in addition to going twice up and down the main road especially distinguished himself by volunteering to carry out dangerous evacuations.

The tactical situation now became hopeless. The whole attack depended on surprise, but this was lost when the troops had to make a considerable portion of the approach-march in daylight. In addition, the noise of the tanks on the metalled roads made every German in the sector alert. Once again the battalion had to rely on Lieutenant F. M. Shaw, and he rose to the occasion. He established a system of guides to direct each company to the new line it was to occupy, and the fact that this withdrawal was made with a minimum of loss and confusion was directly due to the work of this gallant officer.

The new line, which was known as the Amiens Defence Line, was situated immediately south of the main road near La Flaque. The withdrawal was completed just before daylight on August 11. The enemy appeared to suspect what was happening for he put down a heavy machine gun barrage.

Meanwhile the 38th and 40th Battalions consolidated a position on the northern side of the road, their line running roughly from the old British front line to a point 750 yards east of La Flaque. The 39th remained in position during August 11 and 12, coming under heavy machine gun fire from enemy posts in the villages of Proyart, Framerville and Rainecourt. At 12.30 p.m. on August 12 the remainder of the 10th Brigade attacked and captured Proyart, taking up positions along the line which had been the objective of the previous night's attack.

On the night of August 12 the 39th was relieved by a Dorsetshire battalion of the 50th British Brigade. During the relief enemy squadrons came over the line and dropped bombs. The English troops moving up to the front suffered most heavily, and the relief was delayed on that account.

One of the relieving companies lost all its officers and became disorganised. Private Donald G. Coutts, of the 39th, took charge. He organised stretcher-bearers and personally supervised the evacuation of the wounded. Displaying high qualities of leadership, he directed this English company to its new positions, and by disregarding his own safety he heartened the relieving troops throughout the night. During the change over, one officer and four men belonging to the 39th Battalion were wounded.

In the unsuccessful attempt to surround Proyart, Lieutenant C. M. Cobden, who had done such good work a little earlier, was killed, and thirty-nine others were wounded or gassed.

The 39th Battalion moved back to its old position in Hazel Wood, which was reached at 2 a.m. on August 13.

On August 12 a platoon of 25 men, under the command of Lieutenant O. R. Brown, was sent from the 39th Battalion to represent the 10th Brigade at the ceremony of conferring a Knighthood upon Lieut.-General Sir John Monash by His Majesty the King. The platoon left the battalion shortly after mid-day and marched to Warfusee-Abancourt, where a motor bus conveyed the men to Coisy. There a hot bath and a change of clothes and comfortable billets were provided. The ceremony in which they took part was held the next day, August 13, on the terrace of a large chateau near Coisy. Every Division of the Australian Corps was represented. The privilege of supplying the Guard of Honour fell to the 1st Australian Division. The assembled troops were inspected by the King accompanied by Generals Rawlinson and Monash. His Majesty remarked on the smart appearance of the men.

The following day the platoon rejoined the battalion. In camp at Hazel Wood, the 39th spent a period of eight days in well-deserved rest. The companies and platoons were re-organised, equipment and arms cleaned, and light tactical training carried out. Inter-company cricket matches were arranged, such features as shell holes in the pitch added unexpected variety and interest to the games. Warm weather enhanced the pleasure of this open air camp.

Plans to renew the British offensive were now well advanced. The Australian Divisions were to attack towards Bayonvillers, east of Villers-Bretonneux. Two of the Divisions had already moved south when plans were suddenly altered. The 3rd Division

"D" Company (with "Ici"), Bouillancourt, France

was ordered to attack on the north of the Somme while the remaining four Divisions of the Australian Corps operated on the opposite side of the river.

On August 21 orders were issued for the 10th Brigade to move across the river to support the 9th Brigade, which was already in action. At 6.30 p.m. the 39th Battalion moved off from Hazel Wood, crossed the Somme, and occupied a line of trenches adjacent to the shattered town of Sailly-le-Sec.

The following day was hot and the men enjoyed bathing in the river. Considerable activity prevailed along the front. Further north the British attack was in full swing, and on the Somme the Australian Divisions were playing a leading part. On the 22nd, north of the river, the 9th Brigade attacked the enemy at Bray. On the 23rd, on the south bank of the river the 1st Division carried out a successful operation and hundreds of enemy prisoners were escorted to the rear.

After an early breakfast on August 23 the battalion moved forward at 5 a.m. to a donga near the ruined town of Sailly Laurette, where the remainder of the day was spent. Early in the morning the British observation balloons were advanced beyond the 39th's position, which suggested that the main attack was progressing satisfactorily. Several large parties of German prisoners taken by the 9th Brigade came down from the front during the day. The weather was again hot and sultry, and the "diggers" sought relief in the Somme. Desultory enemy shelling occurred during the day, but no casualties resulted. Not very far from the battalion's position were the remains of some horse lines which the enemy had "strafed" either with shells or bombs. Flies swarmed in black clouds over the bodies of dead horses.

At 9 p.m. the battalion set out along the main road parallel to the course of the Somme. The night was close and the dust rose in choking clouds as the men tramped on. After a time the column left the main road and marched across country past Gressaire Wood, through Tailles Wood. There was a faint smell of gas in the depressions, and the men had their masks ready in case heavier fumes were encountered. About midnight the battalion reached a position a mile north-west of Bray-sur-Somme where the 33rd Battalion was holding the new front line. The headquarters of the 39th was established in a quarry on the main road about two miles from Bray, and the battalion moved forward and relieved the 33rd in the trenches.

The position now occupied by the 39th was tactically interesting. It might have proved very hazardous if an enterprising enemy had been encountered. Two days previously the 9th Brigade had advanced, a British Division being on the left. Although the English troops successfully took their objectives, they subsequently retreated several hundred yards in order to take advantage of the protection of a water-course, known as Happy Valley. The left flank of the 33rd Battalion was therefore left unprotected until several posts had been thrown out to the left to connect with the English troops.

The 39th Battalion took over these positions about midnight on August 23/24. About 1 a.m. on August 24 the English troops advanced under cover of their own artillery, and, after stiff fighting, re-established the line. The enemy batteries strenuously opposed the British advance, and the 39th's trenches came under heavy artillery fire. The bombardment continued throughout the day. Despite such heavy fire, casualties were light. Lieut. A. E. Guyett was severely wounded by a sniper early in the day, and several men were killed whilst traversing Happy Valley. Ration parties were obliged to pass through that dangerous area when going to and from the line.

The 39th Battalion was to take part in an assault upon the town of Bray in the early morning of August 25, and therefore, shortly after midnight on August 24/25 the line held by the battalion was handed over to the 38th, and the 39th moved off to the assembly point.

Map No. 8
AMIENS TO GRESSAIRE WOOD

MAP No. 8

AMIENS TO GRESSAIRE WOOD

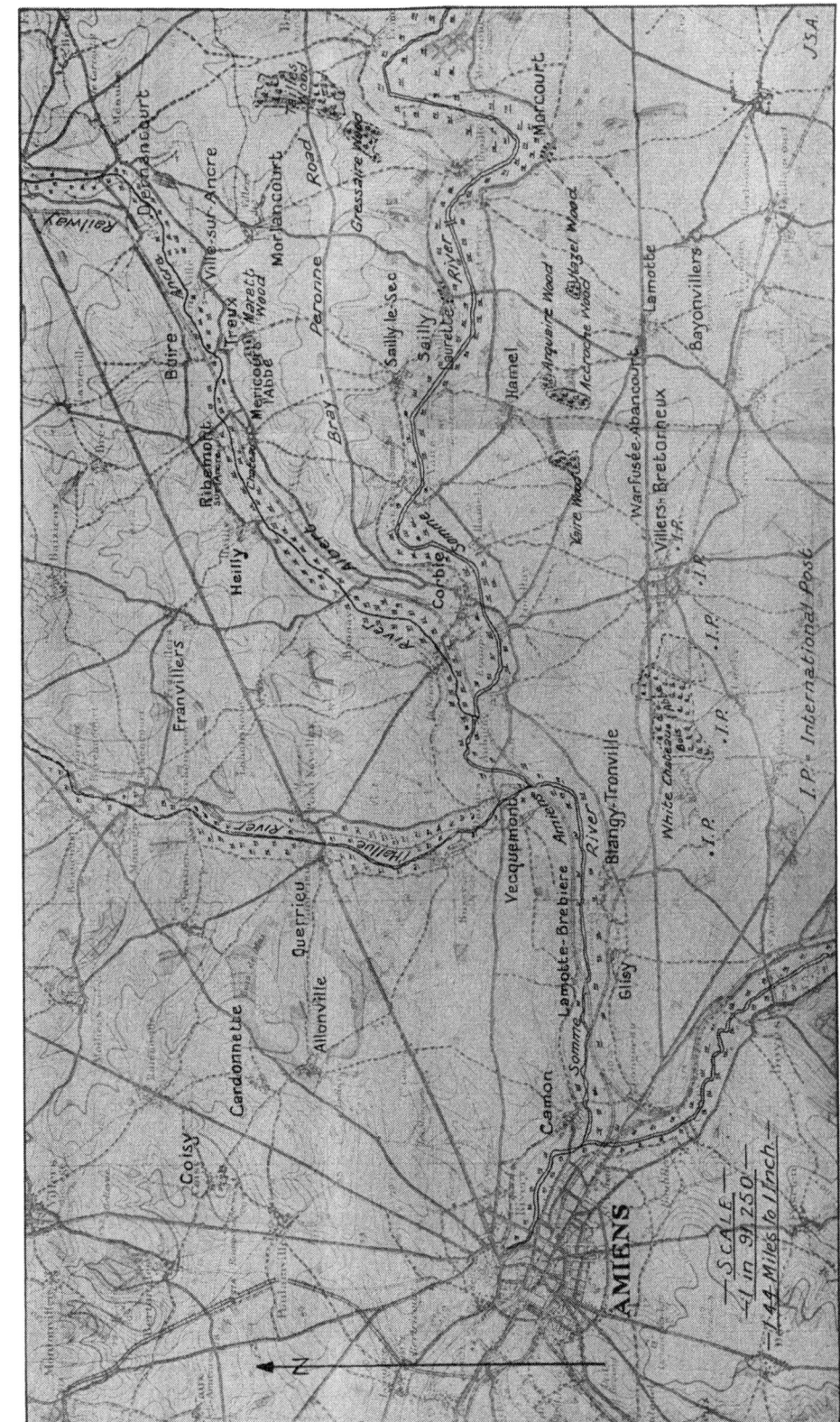

CHAPTER XIV.

Still Advancing

"I am going on to the Rhine. If you oppose me, so much the worse for you, but whether you sign an armistice or not, I do not stop until I reach the Rhine."
—MARSHAL FOCH, *to the Germans who came to ask for an armistice.*

THE assembly point to which the 39th moved on the night of August 24/25 was near the railway yards at Bray. Heavy shelling was encountered on the approach-march, and, whilst casualties were few, the wearing of masks caused considerable inconvenience. The attack was timed to commence at 2.30 a.m. Prior to the opening of the barrage there was a trying period of inactivity when few guns on either side were firing. This was a good omen as it implied that the enemy was unaware of the impending advance.

Suddenly there was a tumultuous explosion as the British guns for miles around opened fire. It was a magnificent barrage and fell directly on the opposing organised defences and obliterated them, leaving only a few machine gun posts to be overcome by the infantry.

Two German gunners displayed much courage. They sought shelter from the creeping barrage, and, immediately it had passed beyond them, came out and opened fire at a range of less than 25 yards. Sergeant F. T. A. Edwards promptly ordered a Lewis gun to retaliate. Private Arthur D. McLinden jumped into a ditch, brought his gun into action very speedily, and silenced the guns. By the resource of these two men an ugly situation was averted.

The enemy artillery, apparently in doubt as to the depth of the opposing advance, would not risk hitting its own men. Shells were therefore passing over the heads of the 39th, which was able to advance steadily, with few casualties. The runners and signallers were less fortunate. Their task was to maintain communication between Battalion and Brigade Headquarters. Though slightly gassed, Corporal Victor P. Coe went out again and again to repair the broken lines, and, by his example, inspired his men to follow his lead. Privates John J. Reeves and D. M. W. Marsh repeatedly carried messages successfully and returned with answers, despite the risk they ran in passing through heavily shelled areas.

Having reached a hill overlooking the village of Suzanne before daylight, the battalion immediately proceeded to consolidate its position against possible re-capture. At daybreak, a heavy fog in the valley limited visibility to a few yards. This added to the battalion's dangers. Patrols reconnoitred, and reported that the enemy had retreated. Lance-Corporal Percy A. Bishop, while under machine gun and rifle fire, did some excellent sniping, which put two machine guns and their crews out of action. The crew of a troublesome "whizz-bang" gun was disposed of by Private Thomas T. Mitchell.

A message was received from the 37th Battalion that its advance was held up by machine gun fire from Murray Wood. Lieutenant S. Le Fevre handed over the work of consolidation and went forward with Sergeant Cornelius Loxton and a runner to investigate. They proceeded along a trench until Lieutenant Le Fevre decided to leave and dash for the wood. Just as he reached its fringe enemy soldiers were encountered. The officer, supported by the revolvers of Sergeant Loxton and the runner, charged with fixed bayonet, and put the enemy to flight. Lieutenant Le Fevre and Sergeant Loxton held the position while the runner went back for a Lewis gun crew. When they arrived the wood was cleared, the enemy retiring to a strong post a short distance away.

When the Lewis gun had been placed in a flanking position Lieutenant Le Fevre and Sergeant Loxton bravely charged this post, killed the gun crew, and captured the gun. The gallant conduct of this small party enabled the 37th to proceed with the advance. Without loss of life additional territory was won by the 39th. The company now came up and occupied the wood.

About 8 o'clock the fog lifted, and, from the elevated position held by the 39th, a splendid view of the Somme was obtained. On the far bank a high bare bluff overlooked the river, and from the battalion position Ceylon and Chateau Woods extended along the valley to the village of Suzanne. Small bodies of troops and enemy transport could be seen moving in the woods 1,000 yards behind Suzanne. Enemy observation was also good, for his first shells arrived almost with the first rays of the sun. Fire from the enemy's batteries continued during the day.

During the afternoon the 39th watched with interest the advance of the 1st Australian Division on the southern side of the river. At that time the 3rd Division had advanced slightly ahead of the troops on its flanks, and shelling from enemy positions on the other side of the Somme had caused some trouble. It was therefore hoped that the 1st Division's advance would cause the enemy to withdraw his guns on the south of the river. Orders were received that Suzanne was to be taken during the afternoon, but a change of plan postponed the attack until nightfall.

The 11th Brigade had advanced on the left and the 10th Brigade had to move forward to conform to the line.

As the troops were assembling about 9 p.m. on August 25 the sultry weather of the previous day culminated in violent thunder storms. The rain splashed down and vivid flashes of lightning lit the sky every few seconds. While the storm was at its height enemy batteries opened fire, which, fortunately, caused only two casualties to the 39th. On the left the gloomy Chateau stood high above the marching columns. On the right, low-lying swamps extended to the river's edge. The outskirts of Suzanne were reached without loss. Excitement was caused when an enemy machine gun hidden in the wood opened fire on the leading platoon. Two of the platoon's Lewis guns were immediately brought into action, and the enemy gun was silenced. Its crew retreated through the wood. On reaching Suzanne a line of posts was established. The right flank of the 39th rested on the river and the company on the left was in touch with the 44th Battalion. By 5 a.m. on the 26th the new line had been consolidated and some patrols sent out to reconnoitre the village. At 9 a.m. the battalion advanced with the object of capturing Suzanne and clearing the village of the enemy.

Heavy machine gun fire from German posts in the village was experienced as the men advanced, but this opposition was rapidly overcome by the prompt action of Private David M. O'Brien who took his Lewis gun team forward, and with much skill put two enemy machine guns out of action. Corporal Charles A. Holmes, a section commander, displayed fine leadership in the fight for the village and his work materially contributed to its capture.

Several critical local situations developed through the tenacity of the German gunners, who refused to abandon their guns. In this battle and those which followed, the enemy machine gunners behaved magnificently.

Exposing himself to great personal danger, Private Thomas P. Roberts rendered invaluable service in carrying messages from his platoon to company headquarters. Eventually a position beyond the village was occupied and consolidated.

The 39th Battalion Headquarters had been established in Suzanne church, but the heavy enemy fire on the village compelled a withdrawal to Chateau Wood, west of Suzanne. Several

Officers, Battalion Headquarters, Bouillancourt, France

direct hits were obtained on the church during the day by enemy batteries.

At mid-day on August 27 the 39th handed the positions over to the 37th Battalion, and withdrew to an old German Prisoner of War compound near Bray. As the battalion was passing through Suzanne, the G.O.C. 10th Brigade met the column and congratulated the men on their achievements. On arriving at their destination the troops were quartered in old German dug-outs which were fitted with bunks. The operations around Bray had been very strenuous, and the men took every advantage of peaceful sleep during the thirty-six hours spent in the dug-outs.

The transport section of the 39th had worked splendidly under severe conditions. Roads were bad, and shelling was heavy. In spite of the hardships to be faced by the men on transport duty, the troops never had to do without their daily rations. Driving limbers through shell-swept areas, along almost impassable tracks was a difficult and nerve-racking task, and high praise for their skill and courage is due to Lieutenant William B. Crayford, Lance-Corporal D. F. Coffey, and the men of the 39th's transport.

On August 29 the 39th Battalion received orders to move forward. Lieutenant-Colonel Henderson, D.S.O., who had been sick for some days, was unable to march. Major L. H. Payne, D.S.O., of the 40th Battalion, therefore took command temporarily. During the morning the battalion marched along the river, passed through Suzanne and halted for the mid-day meal in Vaux Wood, from which the enemy had been driven. Through the wood and down a steep hillside, the march was continued during the afternoon. Bridges destroyed by the retreating enemy had just been repaired by the 10th Australian Field Company Engineers. After crossing the Somme the battalion halted for a brief rest in the ruined village of Curlu. Here, for the first time during the day, it came under shell fire. Enemy guns were firing at long range. As the march progressed the shell fire became heavier, and two A.M.C. orderlies attached to the battalion were killed. About a mile south-east of Curlu, the 39th took up its position in what became known as "Discomforture Trench."

Until now the enemy resistance to our advance had not been strong. Curlu, however, was within sight of the high ground rising to Mont St. Quentin, the key to Peronne.

Peronne was the furthest point from which the enemy could effectively dispute the holding of the Somme in that locality. It seemed certain that the Germans would offer the most stubborn resistance to any further advance by our troops. Throughout the night of August 29/30, our guns and howitzers were being thickly concentrated in front of Curlu.

After breakfast the battalion moved forward by way of Hem railway station towards Clery-sur-Somme, which had been taken the previous day. The 39th took up a position in some recently evacuated enemy trenches about a mile N.W. of Clery. German dead lay unburied on all sides. At 2.30 p.m. the battalion moved forward again to a donga near Clery where the 10th Brigade established its headquarters. Here a short halt was made.

Meanwhile the other battalions of the brigade were heavily engaged in a stiff fight to the left of Clery and beyond. The enemy was in a difficult position. Peronne was threatened on one flank by the British advance, and on the other by the 3rd Australian Division.

The 2nd Australian Division had completed its work in front of Clery, and during the night of the 29/30 had achieved a difficult crossing of the Somme under heavy fire. The 2nd Division's objective was now Mont St. Quentin. The 3rd Division was to co-operate by taking the ridge to the left.

After a short rest, the 39th Battalion moved in extended order to take up its position in support of the 37th. As the enemy had clear observation of the ground to be crossed, the battalion came under heavy fire during the advance. Whilst reconnoitring the positions Major Payne was wounded and had to be evacuated.

Although still far from being well, Lieut.-Colonel Henderson again assumed command of the battalion.

The men found several deep dugouts in the chalky banks of the sunken road. These were dry, and seemed quite safe. "A" company established its headquarters in one of them. No sooner had the dugout been occupied than a shell burst at its entrance. The walls collapsed and the occupants were buried alive. A rescue party worked feverishly to recover the buried men, but the entrance to the dugout was so narrow that only one man could dig effectively at a time. After an hour's efforts the men were reached. Three, including Lieutenant Le Fevre, the acting O.C. of "A" company, were dead, and six had been severely wounded. Five of the six wounded men died later.

Heavy shelling of the position continued during the night of August 30/31. In conjunction with other battalions, the 39th was ordered to launch an attack the next morning. This was to be made in an easterly direction from the trenches occupied by the 37th Battalion, the 33rd Battalion being on the left and the 38th on the right of the 39th Battalion. At 3 a.m. on August 31 the relief of the 37th Battalion was commenced, but during its progress orders were received to clear the line to allow heavy artillery to deal with enemy trenches in the vicinity. The 39th withdrew to its former position, and at 5.10 a.m., in compliance with further orders, moved to St. Goud trench just beyond Clery-sur-Somme and there took up positions for the attack.

At 6.10 a.m. the British barrage opened; and in face of a hail of bullets from enemy machine guns situated in the village of Bouchavesnes, the 39th commenced to advance. The men moved forward in short rushes. Many fell. Despite its difficult task, the 39th overcame the opposition, took its objectives, and consolidated the captured positions. Consolidation was completed by 8 a.m. on August 31.

In this action Sergeant Edgar E. Walter distinguished himself. He was subsequently awarded the Distinguished Conduct

Medal. There is no better way of describing his bravery than by quoting in full the recommendation forwarded to headquarters:

"Near Clery-sur-Somme on 31st August, 1918, for most conspicuous gallantry in action.

"During the advance his company was held up by strong machine gun fire and this N.C.O. called out his section and led it against the opposition. He out-distanced his men and joined by a N.C.O. from the 38th Battalion rushed the position and succeeded by bombing and rifle fire in silencing eight enemy guns and in putting the teams to flight. The guns were all captured.

"Afterwards in a communication trench they encountered a number of machine guns—again this N.C.O. was equal to the occasion and the crews not killed were captured.

"Still later in a storming party Sergeant Walter was once more doing splendidly with Corporal Grinton, of the 38th Battalion. This time these intrepid N.C.Os. captured three high velocity enemy guns. These incidents were carried out with the utmost coolness and utter disregard of personal danger and had a very inspiring effect on the company which advanced successfully to the final objective."

Casualties were heavy. One officer (Lieutenant C. E. Garrard) and twelve other ranks were killed, and three officers and 30 men were wounded. During the attack the 39th captured six field guns, one trench mortar, and a large number of machine guns.

At 9 a.m. the battalion was ordered to move forward and take up a line along the Rancourt Road with the 40th Battalion on the right flank. This advance was carried out without mishap, and the battalion spent the remainder of the day and the following night in this position. At 4 a.m. on September 1 the 11th Brigade moved forward through the 39th, to continue the advance. The battalion moved back to a quarry about half a mile N.W. of the village of Hem. The barrage for the 11th Brigade's attack was timed to open at 5 a.m. and the last company of the 39th had barely passed the positions of the field batteries when the guns opened fire. The field cookers had a hot breakfast in their ovens awaiting the men's arrival, and seldom had a meal been more appreciated.

During the remainder of the day the troops rested and built rough shelters for themselves with waterproof sheets and tarpaulins. Just at sunset, on September 2, the officers and men of the battalion who had been killed in the recent fighting were buried in the civilian cemetery at Curlu. The sad but impressive ceremony was attended by the whole battalion.

The following three days were spent in resting and in cleaning arms and equipment. As the weather was still warm, some of the "diggers" swam, while others sought diversion in bombing fish along the river. During this period the 2nd Division attacked and took the heights of Mont St. Quentin—an operation facilitated by the recent successes of the 3rd Division in front of Clery. Peronne, attacked on all sides, had fallen, and the enemy was retreating towards the Hindenburg Line with the English and Australian troops in hot pursuit.

At 5 p.m. on September 5 the battalion set out for a position which it had formerly occupied about a mile N.E. of Clery. The roads were crowded with transport and the men had to march in single file through heavy rain. The trenches were reached at 8 p.m. Some of the troops found shelter in dugouts while others, less fortunate, protected themselves with water-proof sheets. The following day officers and N.C.Os. reconnoitred in the direction of Mont St. Quentin. During the evening fires were observed behind the enemy lines. It was assumed that the enemy was destroying stores preparatory to a further retreat.

At 9 a.m. on September 8 the battalion, under the command of Major Charles R. Hutton, moved via Mont St. Quentin to Ronces Wood. During the afternoon several of the officers reconnoitred the line held by the 38th Battalion, west of the village of

Hervilly, with a view to advancing during the evening to a position east of Hervilly Wood. At 8 p.m. the 39th formed up in the hollow below Ronces Wood and moved off, accompanied by the cookers and the transport. The route followed led through Tincourt and Hamelet to a quarry about half a mile south of the village of Roisel.

There a halt was made so that the men might have a hot meal before going into action. The enemy put down a barrage of 5.9's. Three men were killed and several wounded. Captain Chris. L. Giles minimised the danger by personally supervising the distributing of the men under cover. He ran a big personal risk, but his action saved many lives. The horses harnessed to the cookers and Lewis gun limbers were terrified by the bursting shells and several of them bolted. Thanks to the prompt action of the drivers and the excellent work done by the acting Transport Officer, Lieutenant H. N. R. McDonald, and his sergeant (Sergeant D. F. Coffey), the threatened stampede was checked without any damage having been done.

At 1.30 a.m. on September 9, the advance was continued by way of Hervilly Village and Hervilly Wood. The objective was reached without opposition. A line was taken upon the eastern edge of the Wood, the 37th being on the right and the 40th Battalion on the left. By daybreak the new position had been consolidated. In the early morning a prisoner belonging to the 18th German Fusilier Regiment was captured by "B" company. During the day the enemy heavily shelled Hervilly Village.

On September 10 parties from the 2nd and 4th Battalions reached the position held by the 39th. During the evening these platoons pushed forward to capture the enemy's outpost line. Heavy machine gun fire made their attempt unsuccessful. Later in the evening the remainder of the 2nd and 4th came up to relieve the 39th, and the relief was completed at 10 p.m. The battalion then commenced the return march to Ronces Wood moving by companies marching at intervals. One of the companies halted beside a Y.M.C.A. post in Hamelet Wood for some hot cocoa. Several enemy bombing 'planes were in the vicinity and one machine dropped its deadly cargo in the wood. Several of the bombs fell close to the men at the Y.M.C.A. depot, and eleven men were killed and twenty wounded. Although himself wounded in the back, Private John Davidson did not acquaint anybody of the fact until he was on the point of collapsing through loss of blood. In the meantime he had rendered all possible assistance to men who appeared to be more seriously wounded than he.

At 2 a.m. on September 11 the battalion reached Ronces Wood, and the men speedily turned in to snatch a little sleep. Some found reasonable shelter, while others lay under bushes or trees. At mid-day a move was made to Handel Copse, about a mile south-east of Bussu, where the troops erected shelters and bivouacked. During the day Lieut.-Colonel Henderson, who for some time had been prevented by sickness from taking an active part in the affairs of the battalion, resumed command.

The 39th remained in Handel Copse until September 27. During this period re-fitting and re-organisation were carried out, and the men were given every opportunity for recreation and sport. Cricket matches were arranged, and musketry practices carried out with captured German rifles and machine guns. At the end of a fortnight the troops had recovered sufficiently from months of fighting to enable them to go into action again. Nor had they long to wait. The German Armies facing the British Forces had been driven back by repeated blows on a wide front, and they were now holding their last strong defences, the Hindenburg Line.

During the morning of September 27 Lieut.-Colonel Henderson visited Brigade Headquarters to attend a conference which discussed the launching of an attack on that line near Bony. On his return the battalion prepared to move the same evening. During the afternoon a reconnaissance of the route to St. Emilie was carried out, and, at 6.45 p.m. the 39th struck camp at Handel Copse and moved off. The roads were congested with traffic moving towards the front. American troops were to carry out the first stage of the coming attack; some were already in the line and others were marching forward. Moving by way of Longavesnes and the ruined village of Villers Faucon, the 39th reached the bivouac area near St. Emilie about 11.30 p.m. Here the men took possession of some old dugouts and settled down for the night. This temporary camp was surrounded by artillery of every description, which suggested that the operation impending was a very big one.

During the following day, September 28, active preparations were made for battle. Supplies of ammunition, grenades, flares, and other fighting equipment were issued, and the plan of action was explained to the troops. In the evening scouts reconnoitred the battalion's line of approach.

The 27th American Division was first to attack from a frontage known as "the Brown Line," which ran practically north and south through the ruins of Gillemont Farm, about 2,000 yards west of the village of Bony and the trenches of the Hindenburg Line. The Americans were to fight their way forward to their objective, "the Green Line," which ran east of the towns of Le Catelet and Bony.

They were to attack at 5.40 a.m., and at 9 a.m. the 3rd Australian Division, accompanied by tanks, light horse and artillery, was to be in position in "the Brown Line."

As soon as the American troops had taken their objective, the 3rd Australian Division was to advance, pass through the Americans on "the Green Line" and continue to advance to Prospect Hill and Guizancourt Farm, N.E. of Bony.

It will therefore be seen that the successful progress of the 3rd Australian Division depended on the successful functioning of the American plan.

At 5.40 a.m. on September 29 the barrage opened for the advance of the Americans, and at 9 a.m. the 39th moved off in artillery formation via Ronssoy. The battalion passed through several lines of artillery, and finally marched across country following the tracks of some tanks. At one stage of the march gas was encountered, compelling the men to wear their masks. Arriving at Duncan's Post on the road leading to Gillemont Farm, the 39th came under heavy machine gun fire. This came as a complete surprise as the 39th was still 1,000 yards west of the supposed starting point of the American attack. Afterwards it was found that the Americans had had to start their attack 800 yards short of that position—but this was unknown to most Australian troops at the time. Officers went forward to investigate. Hostile machine gun fire was too intense to allow an advance to "the Brown Line." The 39th therefore proceeded under heavy fire from Duncan's Post to a trench known as Dog Trench, south-west of Gillemont Farm. Here orders were given to form a defensive line.

It now became evident that the American attack had failed. The trenches were full of American soldiers without officers, and a state of complete chaos and disorganisation prevailed. The situation on the front remained obscure and there was no course open to the battalion other than to maintain its position in Dog Trench and await events.

At 11 a.m. Lieut.-Colonel R. O. Henderson, D.S.O., who had gone forward towards Gillemont Farm ruins, was shot through the head by an enemy sniper and killed instantly. Captain C. L. Giles took command of the battalion temporarily.

Shortly after mid-day the 39th received orders from 10th Brigade Headquarters to send patrols forward to try and link up with the Americans who were supposed to be ahead. These patrols advanced under a hail of machine gun bullets towards the ruins of Gillemont Farm and gained much valuable information.

It was found that the farm ruins and the sunken road leading to Bony were strongly held by enemy machine guns.

Sergeant Victor R. Haines, while commanding one of the patrols, did most useful work which enabled his company to advance 400 yards. Two days later he performed another valuable service. A comprehensive recommendation covering Sergeant Haines's part in these operations resulted in his being awarded the Distinguished Conduct Medal. The recommendation concluded with:—"On night 1st/2nd October, he located two members of his company who were wounded whilst on patrol that morning. He recovered the two men, both of whom had died, and conveyed them under fire back to the company lines. His excellent work, initiative and courage displayed, as well as the example which he set to his men throughout the whole of the operations September 29th/October 2nd, 1918, were of the greatest assistance to his battalion."

Before the patrols returned, the battalion attempted to advance but was held up by intense enemy fire. During the evening, however, the 39th pushed forward, and, though still under very heavy fire, occupied Gillemont trench running due south of Gillemont Farm. The day had been disastrous as the main American attack had failed with very heavy casualties. The 39th had lost one officer and seven other ranks, and forty had been wounded; for it the worst calamity of all was the death of the Commanding Officer, Colonel Henderson.

Formerly an officer of the 38th Battalion, Lieut.-Colonel R. O. Henderson, D.S.O., had been given command of the 39th early in February, 1917. He had quickly gained the confidence and esteem of every officer and man who served under him. He enjoyed universal popularity from first to last. As a commanding officer he possessed many admirable qualities. All had the greatest faith in his leadership and judgment. He was cool and courageous in action. During the hard fighting of August and September, he had remained in the forward area and had led his

Lieut.-Colonel R. O. Henderson, D.S.O.

battalion. His death on September 29 was the cause of sincere and deep regret throughout the 39th Battalion.

Sir John Monash wrote:—

"During practically the whole of its fighting career, the battalion was led by Lieut.-Colonel Henderson, D.S.O., and his death in action during what was practically the last operation in which it was engaged, meant for the battalion the loss of a gallant leader, beloved by all his men, and for me the loss of an old friend, who had, before the war, devoted long years to fitting himself for the crowning achievement of his life—to direct the efforts of this fine body of Australia's sons in the saving of Australia from foreign aggression."

At 11 a.m. on September 30, in order to conform to the line of the 38th and 40th Battalions, the 39th moved, without meeting opposition, to Gillemont Crescent in front of the ruins of Gillemont Farm. Nothing of importance occurred until 10 p.m. when a report was received stating that the patrols of the 11th Brigade were in Bony. Sending out patrols immediately to investigate the position, the 39th discovered that the report was unfounded.

Capt. L. T. Allsop established his Regimental Aid Post in close proximity to Gillemont Farm ruins, and regardless of the heavy machine gun and artillery fire, continued to dress and evacuate the wounded of whom the most were Americans.

For 48 hours he was continuously at work organising stretcher-bearer parties and dealing with wounded, many of whom had not received treatment for 36 hours. It was owing to his untiring energy and disregard for personal fatigue and danger that many lives were saved. This earned for him the respect and admiration of all who came under him. His resolute but cheerful spirit greatly helped to relieve congestion during a most trying time.

At daybreak on October 1, there were signs that the enemy had evacuated Bony, and the 39th again sent out a patrol from "D" company, under Lieutenant R. A. Johnston. The patrol left Gillemont Crescent about 9.30 a.m., advancing in extended order towards Bony. The patrol passed round the western side of the village, and then entered it, and, bombing a few cellars on the way, proceeded to a ridge 500 yards north of the village. Having eventually reached the canal tunnel, the patrol sent back a message to report progress. Continuing the advance towards Le Catelet, the patrol was then divided, the right patrol under Sergeant S. J. Folkes came under heavy enemy machine gun fire from the east of that town. Two men were killed. The remainder took cover in shell holes, afterwards making their way back to the battalion as best they could.

Meanwhile the 39th had advanced and occupied the line of the canal at 11 a.m. with the 38th Battalion on the right flank, and the 40th on the left. Despite enemy artillery fire, consolidation of the position proceeded.

Major A. T. Paterson, M.C., who had attended the Senior Officers' School, Aldershot, re-joined his unit, and was appointed to the command of the battalion, and promoted to the rank of Lieutenant-Colonel.

At 6 p.m. on October 2, guides from the 39th picked up two companies of the 1st Battalion, King's Own Yorkshire Light Infantry, and led them up to the front line. The relief was completed at 9.15 a.m., and the battalion moved back to the bivouac area near St. Emilie. Here hot soup and cocoa were awaiting the men, and a comfortable night was passed.

For the 39th Battalion, the attack on the Hindenburg Line was over. Although the battalion did not realize it at the time, its fighting career had ended too. The fighting around Bony had not been as successful as had been anticipated, due largely to the failure of the American attack on September 29. The Americans had gone into action keen and full of spirit, but the arrangements for the start of the attack were seriously defective and in the resulting difficulties the battalions were very short of officers to lead the inexperienced men. Communications had broken down early in the battle, and complete disorder resulted.

The relief of the 39th on October 2, 1918, brought to a close the period during which the battalion had participated in the British advance on the Somme. Since August 8 the battalion had experienced hard fighting, and had been constantly moving. The men had behaved splendidly throughout, and the various units of the 39th had functioned with marked efficiency.

Special credit is due to Lieutenant Herbert J. James, the Signalling Officer, who kept up communication with flanking units and Brigade Headquarters, day and night, whether the battalion was in action, on the march, or at rest. His work was a material contribution to the success of the battalion during those difficult days.

The battalion quartermaster, Lieutenant William Lindsay, carried out his arduous duties with great ability. The problem of feeding, clothing, and equipping the men was an ever-pressing one. Lieutenant Lindsay threw himself into his work wholeheartedly, and, with his genial disposition, he was truly regarded as a real friend by all the "diggers."

At various times throughout the battalion's life on active service the sick and wounded were attended by three Regimental Medical Officers, Captain Alfred E. Deravin, Major Ivan Blaubaum, and Captain Leslie T. Allsop, M.C. Each of these officers endeared himself to the men who passed through his hands. The battalion was indeed fortunate to find that each R.M.O. so happily blended professional skill and human sympathy.

Since May, 1917, Captain Leonard L. Beauchamp, M.C., had been Adjutant to the 39th Battalion. For him and his staff no praise seems too high. In no small degree the battalion's high efficiency was traceable to the many splendid qualities of its

Adjutant. It might almost be said that he was the main-spring of the battalion mechanism.

On October 3 the 39th boarded a light railway train en route for Peronne. Later it travelled by train to the village of Pont Remy, near Abbeville, arriving there at 4 a.m. on October 6. At 5 a.m. the men proceeded to Hocquincourt, which they reached in about two hours. Although the "diggers" quickly settled themselves and looked forward to a protracted stay, time seemed to fly. The villagers were very kind; military training was varied by recreation; and the news from the front was most encouraging. The enemy was trying to arrange an armistice.

Members of the 39th Battalion will recall with pride their association with two such fine men as Padres J. Best and W. A. Moore—who patiently endured the hardships of the front line.

While the battalion was at Hocquincourt news was received that Brigadier-General C. H. Jess, C.M.G., C.B.E., D.S.O., had taken over command of the 10th Brigade from Brigadier-General W. R. McNicoll, C.B., C.M.G., D.S.O., V.D.

On October 12 a company of the 37th Battalion, which had been disbanded, was transferred to the 39th, and became "C" company of the battalion.

Time quickly passed to November 11. When the momentous news was received that the armistice had been signed there was a singular lack of the enthusiasm which might have been expected from the 'diggers.' Their feeling was rather one of immense relief from the tremendous strain which had told so much upon all.

It meant more to these men than could be realized in a moment. The gloomy shadow of war which had been cast over them for nearly three years had been lifted as if by magic. The days of suffering, horror, and death were over for most of them. Soon—for the first time for years—they began to speculate about the future; life seemed worth while again.

The great objective had been reached at last—peace for the world and the prospect of future happiness.

Map No. 9
BRAY-SUR-SOMME TO ROISEL

MAP No. 9

BRAY-SUR-SOMME TO ROISEL

MAP No. 10
ROISEL TO HINDENBURG LINE

MAP No. 10

ROISEL TO HINDENBURG LINE

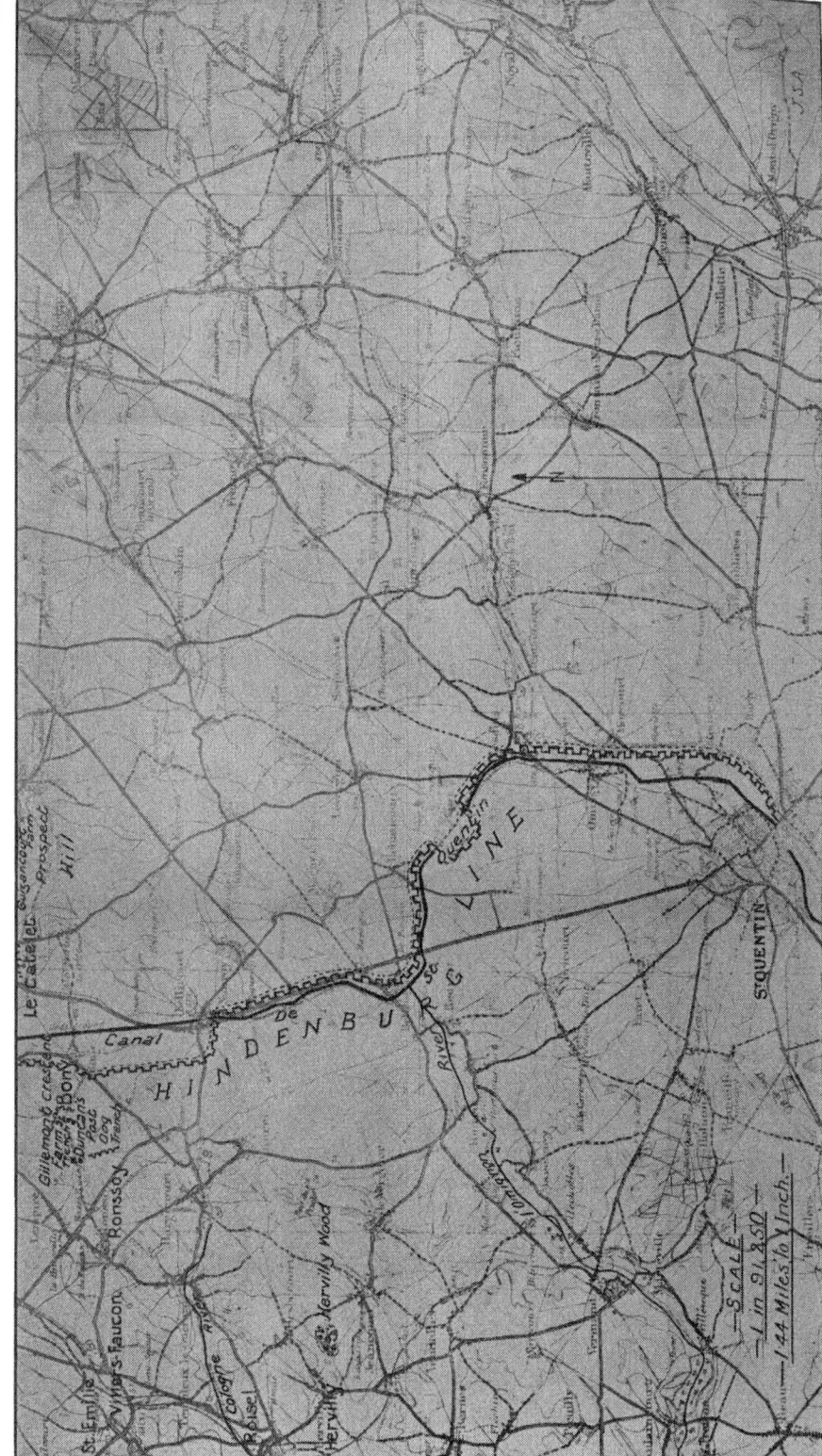

CHAPTER XV.

Peace

*"Buried was the bloody hatchet;
Buried was the dreadful war club;
Buried were all warlike weapons,
And the war-cry was forgotten.
Then was peace among the nations."*
—LONGFELLOW.

EARLY in November the 39th Battalion moved from Hocquincourt to the village of Bouillancourt-en-Sery, situated on the edge of the Foret d'Eu, and about six kilos. from the town of Blangy-sur-Bresle.

Bouillancourt was a quiet little village, and, until the arrival of soldiers, it slumbered in unbroken peace from year to year. In the centre of the village near the church stood the chateau. Stretching from the foot of the chateau's terrace to the Valley of the Bresle, a long avenue of stately trees lent beauty to the surroundings. The panorama across the valley was magnificent. Wooded hillsides sloped steeply down to the river. In the distance, hidden by a protruding spur, the little town of Blangy was snugly and picturesquely situated. Here and there along both banks of the river clustered small villages.

Although in Spring and Summer the floor of the forest around Bouillancourt would be carpeted with wild violets and lily-of-the-valley, when the 39th arrived in the village the countryside was held in the icy grip of the northern Winter. Trees and hedges were stark and bare; skies were grey and gloomy.

Game abounded in the woods, and before the war the district was renowned throughout Northern France as a home of the wild boar. Many fine heads in the lodge and hall of the chateau were reminders of the good sport to be had in the forest.

The battlements and keeps of many ancient chateaux stood among the woods. Chief perhaps among these was the feudal stronghold of Rambures, the seat of the Marquis de Rambures. This fine old castle has defied the ravages of Time for centuries and is famous as a relic of mediaeval days.

The 39th quickly settled down to life in billets at Bouillancourt, and very soon the men had made themselves comfortable. Due to the severity of the weather, each billet possessed a brazier and the "diggers" usually succeeded in keeping a good fire burning. Although fuel was sometimes difficult to obtain, the battalion received considerable supplies from Major Miles, the officer in command of English troops at Blangy saw mills.

Shortly after the signing of the Armistice, the A.I.F. Education Service commenced operations and military work gave place to educational training. Most of the battalion classes were held in a large Y.M.C.A. hut erected in the centre of the village. The local school master (Mons. F. Postel) rendered great assistance by allowing his schoolroom to be used for evening lectures. Classes for shorthand, book-keeping, mathematics, mechanics, agriculture, English and French were soon formed.

Most of the instructors were recruited from the battalion, and, in addition, Brigade and Divisional lecturers travelled round the Divisional area delivering lectures at various centres.

When Christmas came the men were able for the first time for three years to befittingly celebrate the occasion. The Quartermaster was extraordinarily busy beforehand scouting the country for all the extras that would be required to supplement the plain fare of an army ration.

On Christmas Day each company dined as a unit. At 12.30 p.m. the men sat down to a dinner which would have done credit to any chef in the prosperous times of peace. When dinner was over, every man received a Christmas box from the Brigade Comforts Fund. The officers had their Christmas dinner in the school hall which had been kindly placed at their disposal by the school master.

The battalion officers donated a sum of money to provide a Christmas treat for the children of the villages of Bouillancourt and Busmenard, and a Christmas tree was placed in a large marquee. Numbers of happy kiddies in high glee and full of excitement were present. Lieutenant C. T. Mason made an excellent "Father Christmas" and distributed toys from the tree. Effectively disguised as a buccaneer, Lieutenant O. R. Brown caused much fun. Appropriate band selections contributed to the pleasure of both adults and children.

After the children had received their toys they were given cocoa, cake, and chocolates. Finally they reluctantly left for their homes to tell their mothers and fathers all that Christmas had meant to them. Before leaving the school master delivered the following address:—

"COLONEL PATERSON AND OFFICERS OF THE 39TH BATTALION.

"The parents and the children of the villages thank you very much for your kindness and wish you a happy New Year. We will keep for years to come the worthiest recollection of your generosity. For myself I thank you very much, and pray you to accept my most hearty wishes for the New Year.

"It is a tradition in Australia to dress a tree each Christmas within the family for the pleasure of the children, and to present them with toys and sweets. Colonel Paterson and the officers of the 39th Battalion are deprived of the pleasure of being with their families on this festive occasion. To-day they desire to adopt the children of the battalion's billets and offer them presents. We are very proud of their intention, and it forms for us a very agreeable satisfaction. To-day everyone will have the pleasure of smiling, and the privileged ones will receive the toys their child hearts covet. As equality is a trait of Australian character each and all shall receive his or her share. I am very glad to tell you this. In Australia it is not a practice to make distinctions between the children of the rich and the children of the poor because distinction is made by the hand of Chance or Fortune. This remark I wish you to remember. The Australian officers are always good to their men, and, for this reason, we know them as a courageous army. They have supported the noble aims of the war rigorously and with animation, which will go down in history. In my address my children and you who are older, I ask you to endeavour to comprehend me. I ask you to keep this fete ever-green in your memory. Later, when you are older, and you re-unite to speak of the war, it will be a great pleasure to recount the kindness of the Colonel and the officers of the Australian Army whose battalion rested in the villages of Bouillancourt and Busmenard during Christmas and New Year, 1918 and 1919. Through the medium of the armistice you are gathered here to receive a gift. All the recognition I demand of your young age is to keep always the remembrance of the friends of France who left their parents, homes, wives and children without regret to succour us in our time of trouble and adversity. Just think! 5,000 leagues and more separate their country from ours. I will be very pleased to convey to the Colonel and his officers the sentiments of recognition you all express. With very great joy I join my thanks to yours in recognition of untold pleasure."

Happy was the thought which prompted the 39th Battalion to brighten the drab lives of the French children by giving them a Christmas party.

The Battalion's Last Parade, Bouillancourt, France

In February, 1919, the demobilization of the Third Division commenced, and the 10th Brigade was notified to send an embarkation quota of 1,000 men.

The 39th was to furnish one company of this quota and during the succeeding days the Orderly Room Staff of the battalion was busily occupied in making out rolls of those men who had first claim on demobilization.

The quota left the railway station at Blangy en route for Le Havre. The 39th's company, under the command of Captain L. L. Beauchamp, M.C., left Bouillancourt early in the morning and marched to Blangy. Each man was well supplied with cigarettes, biscuits and tinned fruit bought out of Regimental Funds.

The battalion band played the 39th's company down to Blangy and most of the men who were staying behind went down to the station to say good-bye to their comrades.

When the Australian troops first appeared on the Western Front the Germans boasted that only two ships would be required to take the A.I.F. home—one for survivors and the other for identity discs. It was, therefore, with some satisfaction that the battalion's first quota should return to the coast in railway trucks surrendered by the Germans under the terms of the Armistice. The enemy also supplied some of the ships used later to carry our men home.

Life at Bouillancourt was not so bright for the men who remained. Many gaps existed in the battalion and old friends were greatly missed. Everything possible was done to make the time of waiting pass pleasantly for the men. Excellent entertainments were given in the hut both by visiting concert parties and by vocalists and musicians belonging to the battalion. The band always contributed generously to the programmes.

Although discipline was relaxed and training practically abolished, the men enjoyed their new-found freedom without abusing their privileges.

The second batch of men from the 39th Battalion joined an embarkation quota at Gamaches. Though diminished in numbers, the battalion settled down to a six weeks' waiting. During this period the men of the other battalions of the 10th Brigade assembled at Bouillancourt, forming the 10th Demobilization Regiment under Colonel Paterson.

On April 24 the last company of the 39th Battalion left Bouillancourt for Gamaches to join the 45th Quota. The battalion was demobilized, its stores handed in and its records completed. On May 3 the quota left Gamaches railway station for Le Havre.

The history of the battalion would be incomplete without a brief personal sketch of the Battalion Commander, Colonel Alex. T. Paterson, D.S.O., M.C., V.D. Joining the battalion on its formation he left Australia as a junior officer. Colonel Paterson's interest in his men never flagged from first to last. In action, in the front line, or in billets he inspired his men by his personal example. He was their friend and the champion of their causes. "Pat," as he was affectionately called, was one of the youngest battalion commanders in the A.I.F. His keen sense of justice was always blended with a kindly sympathy which produced almost automatically a standard of discipline based more on personal loyalty than on the injunctions of military text books. One illustration will suffice. A sergeant approached Colonel Paterson and asked to be reduced to the ranks because he was too "jumpy" in the front line. The C.O. declined to grant the request and sent the N.C.O. for a rest out of the line. Returning later, with his full rank, this N.C.O. eventually won a decoration for conspicuous bravery in battle.

Countless considerations shown to his men gained and retained for Colonel Paterson the confidence and affection of the whole battalion. Since the war he has done everything possible to help members of his old unit; and has not spared himself in the production of this history, thereby perpetuating the memory of the 39th Battalion, Australian Imperial Force.

When recommending Colonel Paterson for the Distinguished Service Order, the G.O.C., 3rd Division (Major-General Sir John Gellibrand, K.C.B., D.S.O.) paid a fitting tribute to the qualities of the C.O.—a tribute which will be appreciated by every member of the battalion:—

"For consistent bravery and devotion to duty during the whole time his battalion has been in France. His work has always been of a very high order, and he has taken part in all operations of his unit till August, 1918, when he was absent at Senior Officers' School, Aldershot.

"Early in March, 1918, owing to his C.O. being wounded, he was appointed to command the battalion during the difficult period when the enemy was held in check near Buire and Treux. For almost three months he continued to command, and set an example of courage, fortitude and cheerfulness under anxious and dangerous conditions, which was an object lesson and an inspiration to the whole battalion. His leadership and ceaseless labour in the preservation and care of his men contributed very largely to the successful carrying out of the many minor operations of the unit while under his command.

"He again took command of the battalion in October last, on the death of the late C.O. and he has displayed under peace conditions all of the many fine qualities that he did under more active warfare, and has raised the battalion to a very high state of efficiency."

At last the 39th ended its days of active service and left France for home. The men were sad and glad in leaving France —sad for the comrades left behind for ever; glad for the family re-unions to follow.

That splendid young British poet, Rupert Brooke, who gave his life in his country's service on Gallipoli, wrote:—

> "If I should die, think only this of me:
> That there's some corner of a foreign field
> That is for ever England."

Many an unmarked spot in France must be for ever Australia. The youth and flower of Australia's manhood died valiantly fighting for their country and, by their sacrifices, laid the foundations of a Nation.

"LEST WE FORGET."

MAP No. 11
COMPREHENSIVE MAP OF THE BATTALION'S ACTIVITIES

MAP No. 11
COMPREHENSIVE MAP OF THE BATTALION'S ACTIVITIES

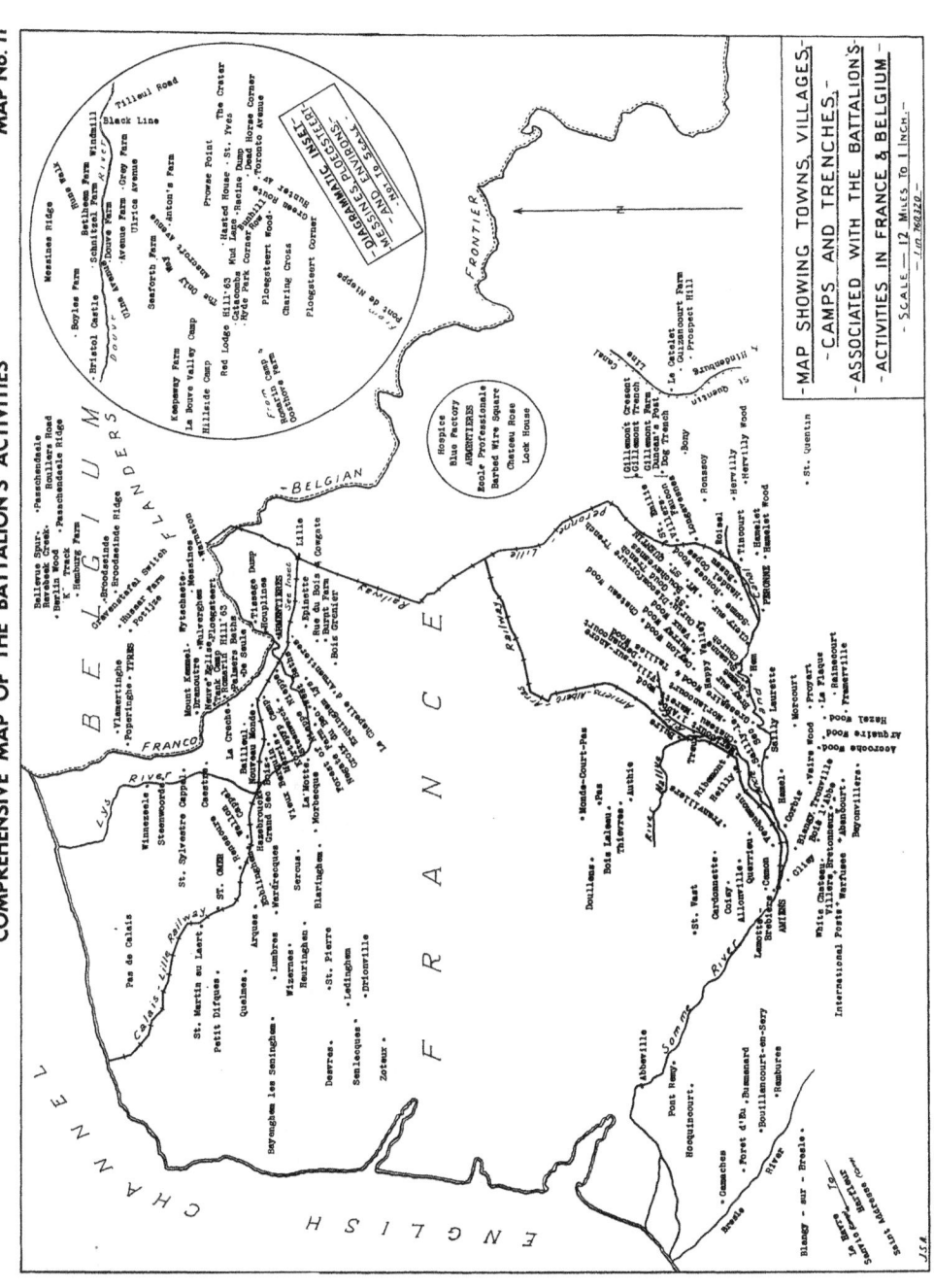

LEST WE FORGET

"Greater Love hath no man than this..."

Lest We Forget

Reg'tal No.	Rank	Name
1785	Private	ALLAN, F. J.
817	L/Corporal	ALLARS, W. S.
1206	Private	ALLIN, F. G.
5967	Private	ALLISON, W.
9	Private	ANDERSON, F. P.
2774	Private	ANDERSON, R. F.
3016	L/Corporal	ANDERSON, W. N.
13	Private	AUSTERBERRY, A.
14	Corporal	BACKWAY, A. J.
2044	Private	BAILEY, G.
400	Sergeant	BAILLE, J. McD.
823	Private	BAIN, F. A.
5972	L/Corporal	BAKER, L. F.
795	Corporal	BAKER, W. F.
5973	Private	BANCELL, H. R.
411	Private	BANKS, R.
796	Corporal	BARCLAY, W.
18	Private	BARKER, H.
2781	Private	BARNES, W. P.
1226	Private	BARR, G. H.
802	Sergeant	BARRETT, W. H.
2788	Private	BARTLETT, F. S. K.
1218	Corporal	BATTERSBY, H. D.
1239	Private	BAUGH, E. A.
2283	Private	BEATON, W. T.
	Lieutenant	BEAVIS, J. S.
1238	Private	BEECHAM, G. J. L.
2036	Private	BELL, J.
3030	Private	BELLCHAMBERS, H. A.
2531	Private	BENNETT, A. R.
2031	Private	BENNETT, L. G.
1229	L/Corporal	BIBBY, T. E.
1235	Private	BLACK, G. A.
1236	Private	BLACKNEY, J. A.
1224	Private	BLAIR, J. A.
3021	Private	BLUME, C. H.
3110	Private	BLYTHMAN, G. J.

Reg'tal No.	Rank	Name
1801	Private	BOLITHO, J.
3422	Private	BOLTON, J. E.
4675	L/Corporal	BOLTON, R. H.
3008	Private	BOND, J. R.
3257	Private	BOOTH, A. L.
1222	Private	BOSLEY, J. A. V.
406	L/Corporal	BOWDEN, A. T.
259	Corporal	BOWEN, J. A.
1216	Private	BOWTELL, V. B.
2041	Private	BOYD, J. C.
1212	Private	BRACHER, J. E.
2280	Private	BRADSHAW, S. G.
396	Sergeant	BRADY, E.
669A	Private	BRAGG, T. J. H.
2688	Private	BRAY, F. J.
35	Private	BREMNER, D. A.
2284	Private	BREW, J.
1796	Private	BROCK, D. P.
39	Corporal	BROCKWELL, C. H.
1799	Private	BROWN, J. A.
	Lieutenant	BRUCE, A. E.
1231	Private	BUCKLE, R. G.
1993	Private	BULL, R. R.
1187	Corporal	BURBIDGE, C. C.
398	Sergeant	BUSH, H. F.
839	Private	BUTLER, P.
1616	Sergeant	BUZOLICH, H.
2403	Private	BYRNE, D. J.
53	Private	BYRNE, H.
2435	Private	BYRNE, J.
	Lieutenant	CAHILL, T. K.
1631	Private	CAMERON, C.
1633	Private	CAMERON, H. R.
2057	Private	CARMICHAEL, A. N. L.
414	Sergeant	CARTER, C. H.
2544	Private	CARTER, G. S. R.
3041	Private	CASSIDY, G. H.
842	L/Corporal	CASSIDY, P. L.
424	L/Corporal	CHAPLIN, H.

Reg'tal No.	Rank	Name
	Lieutenant	CHRISTENSEN, C. P.
1032	Private	CHRISTIE, A.
1242	L/Corporal	CLARK, A.
423	Private	CLARK, W.
2796	Private	CLARKE, E. A.
69	T/Corporal	CLAYTON, E. F.
	2nd Lieutenant	COBDEN, C. M.
5992	Private	COCKLE, W. C.
2540	Private	COLTMAN, C. G.
2790	Private	COLWILL, W. J.
643	Private	CONBOY, G. F.
4997	Private	CONNELLY, W. F.
3044	Private	CONNER, G. A.
4525	Private	CONNOLE, W. F.
1254	Corporal	COOMBES, H.
421	Private	COSTELLO, J. L. R.
2800	L/Corporal	COTTRILL, F. E.
4523	Private	COUCH, W. J.
849	Private	COUTTS, R. H.
5991A	Private	COX, F. B.
2056	Corporal	COX, G. H.
803	L/Corporal	COX, W.
2801	Private	CUNNINGHAM, J. H.
856	Corporal	CUNNINGHAM, T.
857	Private	CUPIT, G.
642	Private	DALE, J. J.
2060	Private	DALTON, C.
2066	Corporal	DARLING, R. G.
2185	Private	DASHPER, W. J.
	Lieutenant	DAVIDSON, F. B.
96	Private	DAVIS, P.
93	L/Corporal	DAVIS, W. H.
6009	Private	DELAHOY, H. J.
2347	Private	DELANEY, J. J.
2301	Private	DOBLIE, L.
868	Private	DOUPE, H. F.
1264	Corporal	DOWN, L. J.
6132	Private	DRISCOLL, A. E.
4530	Corporal	DUGGAN, R.

Reg'tal No.	Rank	Name
4529	Private	DUNCAN, L. L.
2304	Private	DUNSTER, A. J.
99	Private	EADE, D. W.
2811	Private	EDWARDS, F. B.
1649	L/Sergeant	EDWARDS, F. T. A.
444	Private	EDWARDS, H. R.
1817	Private	ELLEN, J. A.
441	Private	ELLIOTT, P. S.
440	L/Corporal	ELLSWORTH, G. W.
740	Private	ELSON, R.
873	A/Corporal	EMMETT, A. R.
3058	Private	EMONSON, P. S.
3057	Private	EVANS, G. J.
6007	Private	EVANS, J. G.
5072	Private	FACEY, D. R.
425A	Private	FINLAY, G.
108	Corporal	FISHER, F. H.
1825	Private	FISK, G. J.
1287	Sergeant	FOLKES, S. J.
1827	Private	FOUND, L. D.
5689	L/Corporal	FOUND, N.
109	Private	FOWELL, W. J.
6025	Private	FRAMPTON, G.
448	L/Corporal	FRANKLIN, L. R.
1284	Private	FREELAND, W. H.
2813	Private	FULLER, G. A.
885	Private	GALLAGER, N.
1297	Private	GARDNER, H. B.
	Lieutenant	GARRARD, C. E.
3070	Private	GEORGE, J. S.
1836	Private	GERDTS, R. A.
2499	Private	GERRING, A. S.
2080	Private	GIBSON, C.
676A	Private	GILBERT, S. H.
1947	Private	GILLESPIE, N. J.
6028	Private	GITSHAM, C. F.
891	Private	GLOVER, P.
116	Private	GLOVER, T.
3072	Private	GOODE, W.

Reg'tal No.	Rank	Name
2273	Private	GOOLEY, C. J.
1294	Private	GORDON, C. R.
1837	Private	GOULD, F. R.
	Lieutenant	GRANT, L. E.
894	Private	GRAY, H.
1298	Private	GREENBANK, J. L.
3387	Private	GREENWOOD, J. T.
896	Private	GREENWOOD, S. J.
4543	Private	GRIFFITHS, H.
2558	Private	GRUNDY, L. J. C.
898	Corporal	GUINEA, J. L.
4555	Private	HALE, H. E.
1321	Private	HALL, W. T.
668A	Private	HAMMOND, C. W.
2841	Private	HANKS, A. C.
123	Sergeant	HARBECK, A. R.
2410	Private	HARBOURNE, M. J.
2832	Private	HARDWICK, J. R. G.
477	Private	HARPER, J. H.
1310	Private	HARPER, R. H.
1839	Private	HARRIS, L. D.
6123	Private	HARVEY, A. J.
1322	Corporal	HEATH, S. V.
3164	Private	HEFFERNAN, L. A.
	Lieut.-Colonel	HENDERSON, R. O.
909	L/Corporal	HEWITT, F. B.
2083	Private	HEWITT, W. B.
1313	Corporal	HICKFORD, J. C.
3076	Private	HILBURN, A.
1666A	Private	HIRD, W. B.
2835	Private	HODDER, M. H.
2564	Private	HOSKINS, R. M.
474	Private	HOWELL, E. J.
1847	Private	HUGHES, T.
1849	Private	HUNTER, W. R.
2767	Private	HURST, C. P.
4063	Private	INGLIS, F. N.
2575	Private	IRVINE, H.
6045	Private	JAMIESON, J. A.

Reg'tal No.	Rank	Name
1330	L/Corporal	JENKINS, W. C.
	Lieutenant	JEWKES, W. G.
1332	Private	JOHNSON, L. J.
921	Private	JONES, P.
137	Private	JONES, W. J.
1327	L/Corporal	JULIAN, L.
2582	Private	KABLE, P. G.
923	Private	KARLLSTROM, G.
144	Private	KEATING, J. P. A.
498	Private	KEEGAN, R. J.
1854	L/Corporal	KELLY, J.
6052	Private	KENT, A. A.
925	Private	KILKELLY, J. P.
579	Private	KING, R.
4150	Corporal	KIRKPATRICK, G. A.
145	Corporal	KISLER, W. J.
1202	Sergeant	KYLE, L. G. C.
2594	Private	LAIRD, C.
3092	Private	LAMB, C. H.
2105	Private	LANDY, A. R.
501	Private	LANIGAN, R. E.
500	Private	LAURENT, A. E.
2831A	Private	LAWRENCE, W. C.
	Lieutenant	LE FEVRE, S.
509	Private	LEIGH, V. L.
505	Sergeant	LEVY, A.
4567	Private	LEWIS, C. W.
2329	Private	LIERSCH, G. A.
2107	Private	LIPPIATT, C. M.
1021	Private	LLOYD, J.
6059	Private	LOOKER, E. A.
154	Sergeant	LORENSINI, W. R.
2108	Private	LUMSDEN, J.
2700	Private	LYNCH, J. J.
155	Sergeant	LYNCH, P. J.
1874	Private	MABBITT, N. B.
	Lieutenant	MACKAY, D. G.
1867	Private	MAGUIRE, P. T.
2109	Corporal	MALIN, L. J.

Reg'tal No.	Rank	Name
2765	L/Corporal	MANSON, W. N. E.
2116	Private	MARNER, A. J.
521	Private	MARSHALL, G.
179	Private	MARTIN, G.
1683	Private	MARTIN, T. W.
1950	Private	MARTIN, T. W.
4136	Sergeant	MATTHEWS, R. J.
160	Private	MATTHEWS, W. J.
948	Private	MAXWELL, L. A.
2332	Private	MEAGHER, J. P.
6067	Private	MELLISH, E. J.
162	Private	MERIFIELD, W.
518	L/Corporal	MILDREN, A. A.
2861	Private	MILES, F. T.
	Lieutenant	MILES, H. F.
164	Private	MILLER, A. F.
6068	Private	MITCHELL, R. E. H.
2414	Private	MITCHELL, W. E.
168	L/Sergeant	MOLLOY, W. L.
789	C.S.M.	MOORE, A. R.
267	Private	MOORE, H. W. G.
2333	Private	MOORE, W. H.
2330	Private	MORRIS, J. R.
173	Private	MORTON, L.
1962	Private	MOSELY, H.
962	Private	MOY, A. W.
2127A	Private	MUIR, G. F.
2401	Private	MULLANE, L.
4572	Private	MULVAHIL, J. A.
2118	Private	MUNRO, D.
1360	Driver	MURPHY, J. P.
3099	Private	MURRELL, H. E.
2336	Private	McADAM, C. L. H.
2682	Private	McALISTER, D.
1366	Sergeant	McANALLY, G. F.
536	Corporal	McCALLUM, A. J.
534	Private	McCOLL, A. J.
933	Private	McCONACHY, S. L.
2120	Corporal	McDONALD, I.

Reg'tal No.	Rank	Name
2121	Private	McHARG, A. G.
2122	Private	McIVER, C. G.
2611	Private	McKAY, D. L.
4587	Private	McKENNA, T. J.
2859	Private	McKENZIE, A.
2914	Private	McKENZIE, A. A.
532	Private	McKENZIE, D. D.
1362	L/Corporal	McKENZIE, R. G.
1877	Private	McLAINE, D. J.
182	Private	McLAREN, J.
1689	Private	McLEAN, N. L.
2338	Private	McLEAN, R. N.
1364	Private	McMULLIN, G.
2340	Driver	McNAMARA, T. J.
938	Private	McNISH, J.
391	L/Corporal	NAYLOR, J. J.
1884	Private	NAYLOR, W. T.
3121	Private	NEVILL, W. J.
2125	Private	NEWELL, E. R.
1700	Private	NEWTON, C. H.
	Lieutenant	NICHOLES, W. P.
3119	Private	NIELSEN, V. L. W.
199	Private	O'BRIEN, J.
551	Sergeant	OLIN, A. A.
	Lieutenant	OLIVER, J. D.
2619	Private	O'NEALE, L.
1887	Private	ORME, G.
2933	Private	OSBORN, G. S.
6109	Private	OWENS, B.
4592	Corporal	OWINS, T. G.
639	Private	PATERSON, G.
638	Private	PATRICK, R. A. H.
2624	Private	PERRY, L.
2202	Private	PHILLIPS, C.
1896	Private	PHILLIPS, W. G.
6081	Private	PICKFORD, A.
977	Private	PICKFORD, L. J.
1897	Private	POLLOCK, W. G.
3127	Private	PORTER, V. A.

Reg'tal No.	Rank	Name
979	Private	PREECE, H. P.
3131	Private	PRICE, J.
4350	Private	PRITCHARD, C. R. W.
5891	Private	PUGH, J. W.
4601	Private	QUICK, R.
2348	Private	QUIN, W. C.
2706	Private	QUINTON, H. A.
2705	Private	QUINTON, W. J.
	Lieutenant	RAMSAY, C. J. A.
212	Private	RATHGEBER, J. H.
2135	Private	RHOOK, H. J. W.
2890	Private	RICHARDS, E. W.
572	R.S.M.	RICHARDS, J. T.
2425	Private	RICHARDS, P. C.
2633	Private	RICKETTS, C. F.
561A	L/Corporal	RIDGWELL, J. E.
	Captain	ROBERTS, L.
580	L/Corporal	ROBERTS, O.
6088	Private	ROBERTSON, P. L.
3006	Private	ROBINSON, A. B.
216	Private	ROSS, E.
1390	Private	ROSS, M. J.
6569	Private	ROUSE, G. R.
7365	Private	ROWATT, L. A.
2352	Private	RUSSELL, H. E.
220	L/Corporal	RYMER, J.
596	L/Corporal	SALONEN, U. L.
589	Private	SAMUELS, S.
1405	Private	SARGENTSON, C. E.
4594	Private	SCOTT, G. R.
2144	Private	SHARP, S.
2637	Private	SHARPE, C. E.
602	L/Corporal	SHARROCK, C.
2145A	Private	SHAW, A.
2636	Private	SHEATHER, E. L.
1400	Sergeant	SIMPSON, E. J.
1716	Private	SLATER, H. A.
2151	Private	SMITH, L. J.
600	L/Corporal	SMITH, N. W.

Reg'tal No.	Rank	Name
	Captain	SMITH, P. L.
995	Private	SMITH, W. L.
228	Private	SMITH, W. T.
2892	Private	SMYTH, R.
1393	Private	SMYTHE, J. H.
2640	Private	SOMMER, S. W. P.
	Captain	SOUTHBY, H.
	Lieutenant	SPEERING, K. D.
14497	Private	SPENCER, A.
19826	Private	SPENCER, E.
6099	Private	STACEY, S.
3148	Private	STAIT, C. H.
1910	Corporal	STANDEN, J. V.
2367	Private	STEPHENS, J. B.
1711	Private	STEVENS, L. T.
1719	Sergeant	STEVENSON, A. J.
2155A	Private	STEVENSON, E. R.
1399	Private	STEWART, A. A.
232	Private	STEWART, A. E.
2894	Private	STEWART, H. J.
1398	Private	STEWART, T.
997	Corporal	STORER, L. J.
235	Private	STRANGE, W. H.
6085	Private	STREET, R.
2031	Private	SUMMERS, G. A.
2901	Private	TATE, N. W.
1921	Private	TAYLOR, A. W.
2159	Private	TELFER, A.
2160	Private	THACKER, S. F. C.
610	Private	THOMAS, N. H.
614	Private	THOMAS, S. J.
1411	Private	THOMPSON, J. H.
2161	L/Corporal	THORNTON, R. S.
2902	Private	TICHBORN, E.
2652	Private	TOMS, E. W.
	Lieutenant	TRANGMAR, A. J.
1723	Corporal	TRENGOVE, J. H.
241	Private	TURNBULL, J. C. McN.
2191	Private	TURNER, F.

Reg'tal No.	Rank	Name
1924	Private	TURNER, W. F.
4629	Private	TUTTLE, J.
6106	Private	TWATT, J.
1005	L/Corporal	VAUGHAN, R. D.
617	Private	VICTOR, E.
2198	L/Corporal	WADDINGHAM, G. E.
15521	Private	WALL, T.
2656	Private	WALLACE, A. B.
2660	Private	WALLACE, H.
2165	Private	WALTERS, F.
2166	L/Corporal	WARD, J.
2393	T/Sergeant	WATERS, L.
2170	Private	WATSON, T.
4146	Private	WATT, W.
248	Private	WEARMOUTH, J. W.
3160	L/Corporal	WEBB, F. H.
1011	Private	WEBSTER, F. T.
	Lieutenant	WHITE, B.
2391	Private	WHITE, E. J.
6113A	Private	WHITE, J. D.
1421	Private	WHITE, W. G.
1016	Private	WILLIAMS, E. A.
1934	Private	WILLIAMS, L. H. C.
2174	Private	WILLIAMSON, J.
2664	Private	WILSON, S. C.
1419	Private	WINSALL, A. V. E.
2905	Private	WINTERHALTER, G. A.
2666	Private	WOODLEY, W. R.
1728	Private	WOODWARD, E. S.
2426	Private	WRIGHT, W.
1935	Private	WYNNE, R.
1019	Private	YATES, W. J.
2179	Private	YOUNG, J.

DECORATIONS AND RECOMMENDATIONS

Decorations Awarded

Companion of the Distinguished Service Order
AND
Military Cross
Lieut.-Colonel A. T. PATERSON

Companion of the Distinguished Service Order
Lieut.-Colonel R. O. HENDERSON

The Most Excellent Order of the British Empire
Member
Captain W. R. BINGLE
Captain J. F. W. WEGENER

Military Cross

Captain	L. T. ALLSOP
Captain	L. L. BEAUCHAMP
Lieutenant	J. S. BEAVIS
Captain	N. G. BOOTH
Lieutenant	G. S. BROWNE
Captain	G. H. CROWTHER
Lieutenant	E. FLEITER
Lieutenant	H. J. JAMES
Lieutenant	R. A. JOHNSTON
Captain	R. LAMBLE
Lieutenant	S. Le FEVRE
Captain	D. F. MIDDLETON
Captain	A. J. MURRAY
Lieutenant	W. PALSTRA
Captain	P. L. SMITH

Distinguished Conduct Medal and Military Medal

553	Sergeant	J. J. OLIVER

Distinguished Conduct Medal

1198	C.S.M.	J. W BURN
88	Sergeant	D. B. COWAN
	Lieutenant	D. B. CROSS
	Lieutenant	J. W. GRATION
	Lieutenant	R. F. GRAY
1312	Sergeant	V. R. HAINES
809	Sergeant	J. H. HAMILTON
2574	Sergeant	H. C. IRONMONGER
504	Sergeant	O. J. LOONEY
154	Sergeant	W. R. LORENSINI
	Lieutenant	W. B. LOWE
506	Sergeant	J. LYONS
617	Private	E. VICTOR
1007	Sergeant	E. E. WALTER
1008	Private	F. W. WARING
1010	Sergeant	G. E. WATKINS

Military Medal and Bar

462	C.S.M.	R. GEDDES
	Lieutenant	F. J. McEWAN
2271	Corporal	H. R. WARD

Military Medal

10	Private	E. E. ANDERSON
4493	Private	L. J. ANDREWS
2043	Private	J. W. BARNES
256	Corporal	E. W. BATES
1237	L/Corporal	P. A. BISHOP
1234	L/Corporal	G. C. BLACK
4505	Private	J. W. BOLLOW
2222	Corporal	A. E. BOYD
396	Sergeant	E. BRADY

DECORATIONS AND RECOMMENDATIONS

𝕸𝖎𝖑𝖎𝖙𝖆𝖗𝖞 𝕸𝖊𝖉𝖆𝖑 *(Continued)*

673	L/Corporal	J. J. BRADY
42	Private	A. BROWN
416	Sergeant	S. O. CHAMBERS
390	Corporal	L. CLARK
7341	L/Corporal	J. W. CLINGAN
2056A	Corporal	T. CODY
845	Corporal	W. M. COGHLAN
413	Private	A. COLAHAN
1254	Corporal	H. COOMBES
89	Private	C. COX
91	Corporal	B. E. CROCKFORD
804	Sergeant	B. R. DAVIES
2300	Corporal	J. DEAN
4028	Private	G. H. DONOHUE
2694	Private	T. DUFFY
4530	Corporal	R. DUGGAN
1642	Private	L. V. DUNN
1649	L/Sergeant	F. T. A. EDWARDS
	2nd Lieutenant	A. R ELLIS
1287	Sergeant	S. J. FOLKES
1196	Sergeant	C. R. FRENCHAM
2078	Sergeant	I. W. GARDINER
1836	Private	R. A. GERDTS
2028	Private	F. J. GREEN
464	L/Corporal	R. S. GULL
	Lieutenant	A. E. GUYETT
900	Private	M. J. HANNIGAN
797	Corporal	W. HARRISON
2087	Corporal	E. W. HOGAN
914	Sergeant	W. J. HUME
482	Corporal	J. R. IRWIN
915	Private	C. A. JONES
4150	Corporal	G. A. KIRKPATRICK
505	Sergeant	A. LEVY
2181	Sergeant	C. LOXTON
155	Sergeant	P. J. LYNCH
940	Private	E. E. MAIN
1357	Private	C. A. MANN
2116	Private	A. J. MARNER

𝔐ilitary 𝔐edal *(Continued)*

729	Private	D. M. W. MARSH
6067	Private	E. J. MELLISH
519	Private	C. J. MILDREN
6055	L/Corporal	J. J. McMAHON
1881	Private	D. McMASTER
1885	Private	A. NEAL
551	Sergeant	A. A. OLIN
2618	Corporal	A. V. OLSON
3007	Private	F. A. ORDERS
969	Private	P. OVERALL
2189	Sergeant	E. A. PAGELS
2703	L/Corporal	A. E. PARRISH
4595	Private	W. PARTRIDGE
2887	Corporal	A. S. PHILLIPS
	Lieutenant	W. R. POWELL
2425	Private	P. C. RICHARDS
2441	Private	T. P ROBERTS
2138	Sergeant	D. A. ROSS
2142	L/Corporal	W. J. SCOTT
270	Private	A. SCRIVENER
2366	L/Corporal	G. N. SHARPIN
2368	Private	J. SHEEHAN
1394	Sergeant	M. SHERIDAN
1402	Private	R. G. H. SLOAN
1026	L/Corporal	L. R. G. SMITH
994	Sergeant	W. SMITH
233	Sergeant	G. H. STODDART
1199	Sergeant	C. W. STRAFORD
999	Private	J. SYPOTT
1726	Corporal	J. N. TYERS
246	Private	J. A. WATSON
6111	Corporal	J. A. WEIR
622	Corporal	T. D. WHITE
6124	Private	V. H. WHITFORD
	Lieutenant	E. H. ZELMAN

DECORATIONS and RECOMMENDATIONS

Meritorious Service Medal

1195	Sergeant	A. BROOKSBANK
454	ER/WO.1	W. E. GRIFFITHS
1683	Private	T. W. MARTIN
586	C.Q.M.S.	J. C. ROBINSON
996	C.Q.M.S.	W. H. SPARNON
1203	C.Q.M.S.	F. H. WILSON
1020	R.Q.M.S.	G. YOUNG

Mentioned in Despatches

	Lieutenant	J. S. AUGUST
	Captain	W. R. BINGLE
260	Corporal	V. P. COE
428	Sergeant	D. F. COFFEY
76	L/Corporal	A. L. COLYER
3043	Private	A. H. CONNER
80	Sergeant	A. C. COOK
	Lieutenant	W. B. CRAYFORD
3068	Corporal	A. F. GILES
	Captain	C. L. GILES
	Lieut.-Colonel	R. O. HENDERSON
	Lieutenant	R. HEPBURN
177A	Sergeant	C. J. HEWLAND
1859	Private	E. W. LAMBERT
	Captain	R. LAMBLE
	Captain	D. F. MIDDLETON
	Captain	A. J. MURRAY
	Lieutenant	H. N. R. McDONALD
	Lieut.-Colonel	A. T. PATERSON
	Lieutenant	J. M. PRENTICE
585	L/Corporal	J. RIDDOCH
586	C.Q.M.S.	J. C. ROBINSON
	Lieutenant	F. M. SHAW
	Lieutenant	E. H. ZELMAN

Congratulatory by Army Corps Commander

1198	C.S.M.	J. W. BURN
428	Sergeant	D. F. COFFEY
	Lieutenant	A. D. McARTHUR

FRANCE

Croix de Guerre

2278 Private H. BOLAND

BELGIUM

Chevalier l'Ordre de la Couronne

Lieutenant J. M. PRENTICE

Croix de Guerre

1225	L/Corporal	R. N. BUCHOLZ
	Captain	W. R. CUMMING
1683	Private	T. W. MARTIN
	Lieutenant	J. M. PRENTICE
6124	Private	V. H. WHITFORD
2388	Corporal	R. J. WORTHINGTON

Officers, N.C.Os. and Men who were also recommended for Decorations, or recommended to be Mentioned in Despatches

1784	L/Sergeant	H. T. S. ALDRED
2524	Private	L. BARDEN
828	Sergeant	G. A. BAXTER
2397	Private	E. B. BOEHM
	Lieutenant	O. R. BROWN
2405	Private	S. CARLYON
843	Private	R. CHAPPELL
1172	C.Q.M.S.	T. H. CHAPPELL
67	L/Corporal	C. G. CLAYTON
68	Private	C. C. COCKERILL
2792A	Private	R. COLLING
848	Private	D. G. COUTTS
1245	Private	A. CUNNINGHAM
435	Private	J. DAVIDSON

Officers, N.C.Os. and Men recommended, etc. *(Continued)*

1273	Private	W. H. DIWELL
1814	L/Corporal	A. DUFF
871	Corporal	J. DYSON
2552	Corporal	J. A. EASTWOOD
874	Sergeant	E. ENGBRIGTSEN
453	Sergeant	J. M. FORD
460	Corporal	S. L. GORDON
122	Private	W. J. GUPPY
3074	Private	W. HALLS
910	Sergeant	F. G. HILL
133	Sergeant	A. H. HOBBA
469	C.S.M.	L. F. HODGETTS
478	Corporal	C. A. HOLMES
1697	Private	H. G. HOLWELL
	Major	C. R. HUTTON
1330	L/Corporal	W. C. JENKINS
486	Private	J. E. JOHNSTON
	Hon. Lieutenant	W. LINDSAY
151	Private	D. L. LOGAN
2934	Sergeant	J. S. LOW
159	Private	L. W. MATTHEWS
4136	Sergeant	R. J. MATTHEWS
951	Corporal	E. J. L. B. MILES
955	Private	T. T. MITCHELL
173	Private	L. MORTON
524	L/Corporal	B. A. MOYLAN
7351	Private	G. J. McALLISTER
535	Sergeant	W. T. McGREGOR
3207	Sergeant	P. J. McINTYRE
4583	Private	A. D. McLINDEN
655A	L/Corporal	D. M. O'BRIEN
976	Corporal	F. I. PHILLIPS
6087	Private	J. J. REEVES
585	L/Corporal	J. RIDDOCH
1266	Sergeant	W. T. RISELEY
217	Private	H. W. ROSSER
	Lieutenant	F. M. SHAW
224	Sergeant	R. H. SIMMONS

Officers, N.C.Os. and Men recommended, etc. (Continued)

2377	Private	G. W. SMEDLEY
591	Corporal	G. D. SMITH
1955	Private	G. A. E. SPICER
1719	Sergeant	A. J. STEVENSON
5797	Private	V. W. STRAFORD
4625	Private	J. W. THOM
1200	Corporal	J. THOMLINSON
	Lieutenant	H. VAN ASSCHE
243	Corporal	T. H. VAUGHAN
3159	Private	S. B. WHINFIELD
3415	Private	H. B. YELLAND

NOMINAL ROLL

Nominal Roll

Reg'tal No.	Rank	Name	Casualty
	Lieutenant	AARONS, T. H.	
392	Private	ABBOTT, C. A.	Wounded
814	Private	ABBOTT, W.	
1021	Private	ABOLIN, P.	
815	Private	ABRAM, E.	Wounded
2	Private	ABSOLOM, A.	
395	Private	ACCOLA, T.	
2027	Private	ADAMS, H.	Wounded
3	Private	ADAMS, J.	
2274	Private	ADAMS, J.	
2778	Private	ADAMS, W.	Wounded
1208	Private	AISBETT, H. E.	Wounded
51531	Private	AITCHISON, H.	
4	Corporal	ALBERT, A. A. E.	Wounded
8	Corporal	ALDRED, A. B. C.	
1784	L/Sergeant	ALDRED, H. T. S.	
1209	Private	ALDRIDGE, H. H.	
51529	Private	ALEXANDER, A. C.	
2416	Private	ALEXANDER, R. B.	Wounded
1785	Private	ALLAN, F. J.	Died of Wounds
	Lieutenant	ALLAN, P. V.	
394	Private	ALLAN, T. B.	Wounded
391	Private	ALLAN, W. H.	
816	Corporal	ALLARS, S. G.	Wounded
817	L/Corporal	ALLARS, W. S.	Died of Wounds
51532	Private	ALLEN, A. R.	
5292	Private	ALLEN, A. V.	
2517	Private	ALLEN, E. T.	
2516	Private	ALLEN, F.	
	Lieutenant	ALLEN, H. S.	
2327	Private	ALLEN, J. E.	
2897	Private	ALLEN, L.	Wounded
5	Sergeant	ALLEN, R. B.	
1611	Private	ALLEN, W. J.	
	Captain	ALLEN, W. L.	
1206	Private	ALLIN, F. G.	Killed in Action
3254	Private	ALLINSON, A. D.	

[277]

Reg'tal No.	Rank	Name	Casualty
5967	Private	ALLISON, W.	Killed in Action
	Captain	ALLSOP, L. T.	
1022	Private	ALVIN, J. F.	
711	Private	AMY, W. H.	
818	Private	ANDERSON, C.	
2671	Private	ANDERSON, C. G.	Wounded
10	Private	ANDERSON, E. E.	Wounded
	Lieutenant	ANDERSON, F.	
9	Private	ANDERSON, F. P.	Killed in Action
54146	Private	ANDERSON, H. R.	
	Lieutenant	ANDERSON, J. C.	
1940	Private	ANDERSON, J. D.	
2417	Private	ANDERSON, J. K.	
51533	Private	ANDERSON, L. G.	
6401	Private	ANDERSON, R.	
	Captain	ANDERSON, R. C. N.	
2774	Private	ANDERSON, R. F.	Died of Wounds
6	Private	ANDERSON, S.	Wounded
819	Private	ANDERSON, W. H.	
3016	L/Corporal	ANDERSON, W. N.	Killed in Action
7	Private	ANDERSON, W. L.	
1300	Private	ANDREWS, E. J.	Wounded
3023	Private	ANDREWS, J. H. L.	
4493	Private	ANDREWS, L. J.	Wounded
820	Private	ANDREWS, R.	
51526	Private	ANGLISS, G. J.	
5968	Private	ANGWIN, J. H.	
1786	Private	ANNANDSON, W. R.	Wounded
	Lieutenant	ANNEAR, F. J. B.	
12239	Private	ANNETT, A. V.	Wounded
12	Private	ANTHONY, W. J.	
51527	Private	APLIN, P. H.	
711A	Private	ARCHER, A.	
64	Private	ARCHER, C. B.	
	Major	ARMFIELD, G. S.	
393	Sergeant	ARMFIELD, H. A.	
	2nd Lieutenant	ARMSTRONG, C. E.	Wounded
1612	Private	ARMSTRONG, H. P.	
2519	Private	ARMSTRONG, J.	

NOMINAL ROLL

Reg'tal No.	Rank	Name	Casualty
2518	Private	ARMSTRONG, J. V.	Wounded
7106A	Private	ARNOTT, H.	
2858A	Private	ARNOTT, R. G.	
3017	Private	ARTHUR, H. R.	
1207	Private	ASHBY, J. A.	
821	Private	ASHCROFT, I.	Wounded
822	Private	ASHTON, F. H. G.	
2775	Private	ASHWIN, A. C.	
7116	Private	ASTON, E. E.	
3018	Private	ASHWORTH, J.	
2773	Private	ATKINSON, J. H.	Wounded
1205	L/Corporal	ATKINSON, N.	Wounded
2768	Private	ATTENBOROUGH, E. J.	
3255	Private	ATTWOOD, L.	Wounded
	Lieutenant	AUGUST, J. S.	Gassed
13	Private	AUSTERBERRY, A.	Killed in Action
	Lieutenant	AYERS, A. E. W.	Wounded
1805	Private	AYRES, W. E.	
14	Corporal	BACKWAY, A. J.	Killed in Action
4515	Private	BAGULEY, E. B.	Wounded
5969	Private	BAHEN, F.	Wounded
2044	Private	BAILEY, G.	Killed in Action
400	Sergeant	BAILLE, J. McD.	Killed in Action
823	Private	BAIN, F. A.	Died of Wounds
399	Private	BAIN, J.	
824	L/Corporal	BAINBRIDGE, G.	
825	Driver	BAINBRIDGE, W. E.	Wounded
15	Private	BAKER, C. M.	
2784	Private	BAKER, G.	Wounded
5972	L/Corporal	BAKER, L. F.	Died of Wounds
5973A	Private	BAKER, P. G.	
795	Corporal	BAKER, W. F.	Died of Wounds
2525	Private	BALDWIN, C. H.	Wounded
3026	Private	BALLAN, N. P.	
1623	Private	BALLARD, C. H. S.	
2039	Private	BALLHAUSEN, L. G.	Wounded
1620	Private	BAMFORD, H. W. R.	
5973	Private	BANCELL, H. R.	Killed in Action
5974	Private	BANES, J.	Wounded

Reg'tal No.	Rank	Name	Casualty
16	Corporal	BANFIELD, C. V.	
55572	Private	BANGER, E. M.	
411	Private	BANKS, R.	Died of Wounds
3266	Private	BANNISTER, J.	
54621	Private	BARBER, E. F.	
	Lieutenant	BARBOUR, H. A.	
796	Corporal	BARCLAY, W.	Died of Wounds
1615	Private	BARDEN, F.	
2524	Private	BARDEN, L.	Wounded
18	Private	BARKER, H.	Died of Wounds
408	Private	BARKER, J.	Wounded
	Captain	BARKER, L. E. S.	Wounded
827	Private	BARNES, H. J.	
19	Private	BARNES, H. T.	
2043	Private	BARNES, J. W.	
410	Driver	BARNES, W.	
2781	Private	BARNES, W. P.	Killed in Action
1227	Corporal	BARR, A. E.	Wounded
1226	Private	BARR, G. H.	Killed in Action
802	Sergeant	BARRETT, W. H.	Killed in Action
1213	Private	BARRY, M. F.	Wounded
2042	Private	BARTELS, D. J.	
2788	Private	BARTLETT, F. S. K.	Killed in Action
5979	Private	BARTLETT, R. T.	
51543	Private	BARWOOD, H. O.	
1612	Corporal	BASCOMBE, F. N.	
51	Private	BASHAN, R. R.	
1792	Private	BASS, R. J.	Wounded
3019A	Private	BASSHAM, C.	Wounded
256	Corporal	BATES, E. W.	Wounded
1219	Sergeant	BATESON, R.	Wounded
1218	Corporal	BATTERSBY, H. D.	Died of Wounds
1239	Private	BAUGH, E. A.	Killed in Action
	2nd Lieutenant	BAUM, H. A.	
397	Private	BAXTER, A. C.	Wounded
828	Sergeant	BAXTER, G. A.	
3024	Private	BAYLE, A.	
3418	Private	BAYLIE, G. S.	
3265	Private	BAYNES, G. E.	

NOMINAL ROLL

Reg'tal No.	Rank	Name	Casualty
54622	Private	BEACH, C. W. H.	
20	Private	BEALE, J. H.	
2779	Private	BEALE, W. L.	Wounded
21	Private	BEAMES, R. E.	
	Lieutenant	BEAN, H. E.	
5977	Private	BEATON, F.	Wounded
1788	Private	BEATON, L. A.	Wounded
2283	Private	BEATON, W. T.	Died of Wounds
2539	Private	BEATTY, T. J.	Gassed
	Captain	BEAUCHAMP, L. L.	
	Lieutenant	BEAVIS, J. S.	Died of Wounds
2430	Private	BEE, S.	
1238	Private	BEECHAM, G. J. L.	Killed in Action
	Lieutenant	BEER, H. J. C.	
815A	Private	BEESON, A.	
1221	Private	BEGGS, T. H.	
1115	E.R. Sergeant	BELL, A. A.	
1617	Private	BELL, A.	
3264	Private	BELL, A. G.	
3031	Private	BELL, G. C.	
2036	Private	BELL, J.	Killed in Action
3030	Private	BELLCHAMBERS, H. A.	Killed in Action
23	Private	BENDALL, A. L.	
15141	Driver	BENN, F. W.	
2531	Private	BENNETT, A. R.	Killed in Action
25	Private	BENNETT, E. S.	
402	Private	BENNETT, J. E.	
3260	Private	BENNETT, J. W.	
2031	Private	BENNETT, L. G.	Killed in Action
2521	Private	BENNETT, W.	
51544	Private	BENNETTS, A. G.	
2771	Private	BENNINGTON, J. L.	Wounded
2538	Private	BENSON, H. R.	Wounded
2034	Private	BENSON, L. A.	
2786	Private	BERLINSKY, J.	
1211	Private	BERRY, G.	Wounded
53924	Private	BERRY, G. R. L.	
714	Private	BERRY, J. H. R.	Wounded
4504	Private	BERTEL, R. F.	

Reg'tal No.	Rank	Name	Casualty
17	Private	BESEMERES, H. V.	
26	Corporal	BEST, H.	
	Chaplain	BEST, J.	
3168	Private	BESTON, F. L.	Wounded
3262A	Private	BETHUNE, W. C.	
1618	Private	BETTS, G. V.	
2038	Private	BETTS, H. J. C.	Wounded
1858	Private	BEVIS, R. R.	Wounded
1229	L/Corporal	BIBBY, T. E.	Died of Wounds
3019	Private	BICKETT, H. J.	
3020	Private	BICKFORD, C. O.	
407	Sergeant	BICKNELL, G. H.	
829	Corporal	BIDDLE, W. B.	Wounded
27	Private	BIGGEN, E. H.	
781	Private	BIGNELL, A.	
3507	Private	BILLINGS, W. C.	
51536	Private	BINDER, H. J.	
	Captain	BINGLE, W. R.	Wounded
3268	Private	BINNS, J.	
4507	Private	BIRCHALL, J. A.	Gassed
33	Driver	BIRKETT, A. J.	Wounded
	Lieutenant	BIRRELL, S. H.	
3264	Private	BISHOP, F. H.	
1237	L/Corporal	BISHOP, P. A.	Wounded
1797	Private	BISHOP, S.	Wounded
831	Private	BISHOP, T. J. G.	Wounded
258	Private	BISHOP, W. C.	
1235	Private	BLACK, G. A.	Killed in Action
1234	L/Corporal	BLACK, G. C.	Wounded
2285	Private	BLACKBURN, A. G.	
257	Sergeant	BLACKBURN, C. R. H.	Wounded
51539	Private	BLACKEBY, H.	
1236	Private	BLACKNEY, J. A.	Killed in Action
28	Private	BLACKNEY, W. J.	
1224	Private	BLAIR, J. A.	Killed in Action
2527	Private	BLAIR, S. A.	Wounded
1798	Private	BLAIR, W. D.	
1223	Private	BLAIR, W. J.	Wounded
403	Private	BLAKE, S. L.	

Reg'tal No.	Rank	Name	Casualty
1624	Private	BLAND, J.	Wounded
	Major	BLAUBAUM, I.	
2395	Private	BLEE, C. H.	
832	Private	BLOOMER, H.	Wounded
6115	Private	BLOOMFIELD, P.	
3021	Private	BLUME, C. H.	Killed in Action
3022	Private	BLUME, F. C.	Wounded
29	Private	BLYTHE, G.	Wounded
3110	Private	BLYTHMAN, G. J.	Killed in Action
2286	Private	BLYTHMAN, H. W.	Wounded
2935	Private	BOARDMAN, H. K.	
	Lieutenant	BOASE, N. H.	
5970	Private	BOATFIELD, E. W.	Wounded
1220	Private	BOATMAN, C. H.	
1619	Private	BODDINGTON, J. H.	
2780	Private	BODY, W. E.	
2397	Private	BOEHM, E. B.	Wounded
2278	Private	BOLAND, H.	Wounded
24	Corporal	BOLDISTON, E. J.	Wounded
1801	Private	BOLITHO, J.	Killed in Action
4505	Private	BOLLOW, J. W.	
30	Private	BOLTON, C. H.	
3422	Private	BOLTON, J. E.	Died of Illness
2521	Private	BOLTON, N. E.	
4675	L/Corporal	BOLTON, R. H.	Died of Illness
3258	Private	BOLTON, R. T.	
5967A	Private	BOMFORD, J. W.	
3008	Private	BOND, J. R.	Died of Wounds
3257	Private	BOOTH, A. L.	Killed in Action
31	Private	BOOTH, B. H.	
	Captain	BOOTH, N. G.	Wounded
1222	Private	BOSLEY, J. A. V.	Killed in Action
32	Private	BOTT, T. E.	Wounded
3258	Private	BOTTEN, R. T.	
2536	Private	BOUGHTON, A.	Wounded
51537	Private	BOURKE, R. E.	
2396	Private	BOURKE, T.	Wounded
406	L/Corporal	BOWDEN, A. T.	Killed in Action
259	Corporal	BOWEN, J. A.	Killed in Action

Reg'tal No.	Rank	Name	Casualty
51540	Private	BOWER, G. A.	
3027	Private	BOWERING, S. C.	Wounded
1210	Private	BOWES, W. E.	
2523	Private	BOWLER, T. E.	
2526	Private	BOWLER, W. H.	
3267	Private	BOWMAN, F. W.	
5980	Private	BOWMAN, T. L.	Wounded
1216	Private	BOWTELL, V. B.	Died of Wounds
5504	Private	BOYCE, H.	
2222	Corporal	BOYD, A. E.	
3033	Private	BOYD, D.	
2041	Private	BOYD, J. C.	Killed in Action
2040	Private	BOYD, P. J.	Wounded
52258	Private	BOYD, M.	
3024	Private	BOYLE, A.	
3025	Private	BOYLE, G.	
1212	Private	BRACHER, J. E.	Killed in Action
2687	Private	BRADDOCK, A. J.	Gassed
51541	Private	BRADSHAW, G.	
2280	Private	BRADSHAW, S. G.	Killed in Action
396	Sergeant	BRADY, E.	Killed in Action
673	L/Corporal	BRADY, J. J.	
1233	Private	BRADY, P. F.	Wounded
1232	Private	BRADY, P. J. B.	
669A	Private	BRAGG, T. J. H.	Killed in Action
34	Private	BRAIDIE, H.	Wounded
2787	Private	BRAND, F.	Wounded
3259	Private	BRAY, A.	
2688	Private	BRAY, F. J.	Killed in Action
401	L/Corporal	BRAY, G. G.	Wounded
	Lieutenant	BRAY, T. R.	
4500	Private	BRAY, W. C.	Wounded
37	Private	BRAY, W. S.	
220	Private	BREALEY, W. J.	
35	Private	BREMNER, D. A.	Killed in Action
2281	Private	BRENNAN, L. D.	Gassed
1787	Sergeant	BRERETON, W. G.	
2037	Private	BRETAG, C. F.	Wounded
2284	Private	BREW, J.	Killed in Action

NOMINAL ROLL

Reg'tal No.	Rank	Name	Casualty
	Lieutenant	BREWER, L. J.	
1794	Private	BRIANEY, T.	Wounded
38	C.S.M.	BRIESE, N.	Wounded
36	Private	BRIGGS, H. C. W.	
1989	Private	BRILLIANT, J.	Gassed
1798	Corporal	BRINDLEY, J. G.	Wounded
833	Private	BRISTOW, A. B.	Wounded
3350A	Private	BROADHURST, P.	
1796	Private	BROCK, D. P.	Died of Wounds
	Lieutenant	BROCKSOPP, H. A.	Wounded
39	Corporal	BROCKWELL, C. H.	Died of Wounds
3028	Private	BRODIE, C. S.	
2691	Private	BRONSON, W. B.	Wounded
3032	Private	BROOK, E.	
409	Private	BROOKS, C.	Wounded
2785	Private	BROOKES, W. E.	
1195	Sergeant	BROOKSBANK, A.	
273	R.S.M.	BROUGH, W. T.	Wounded
42	Private	BROWN, A.	Gassed
1217	Private	BROWN, A. H.	
2032	Private	BROWN, A. R.	
2035	Private	BROWN, C. A.	
580A	Private	BROWN, C. J.	
2763	L/Corporal	BROWN, E. A.	
405	Private	BROWN, F. J.	Wounded
51545	Private	BROWN, H.	
2578	Private	BROWN, H. G.	
1799	Private	BROWN, J. A.	Killed in Action
1215	Private	BROWN, M. W.	Wounded
	Lieutenant	BROWN, O. R.	Wounded
41	Private	BROWN, T.	
2782	Private	BROWN, W.	
835	Private	BROWN, W. G.	
	Lieutenant	BROWNE, A. A.	Wounded
4665	Private	BROWNE, C. A.	
	Lieutenant	BROWNE, G. S.	
2789	Private	BROWNE, H. S.	
	Lieutenant	BRUCE, A. E.	Died of Wounds
1790	Private	BRUMBY, G. H.	

Reg'tal No.	Rank	Name	Casualty
1228	Private	BRUNTON, A. W.	Wounded
2030	Private	BRYANT, W. E.	
	Lieutenant	BRYDIE, W.	
836	L/Corporal	BRYSON, J. W.	
1225	L/Corporal	BUCHOLZ, R. N.	Wounded
3507A	Private	BUCHANAN, N. C. M.	
1789	Private	BUCHANAN, W. J.	Wounded
5971	Private	BUCKINGHAM, D. J.	Gassed
1231	Private	BUCKLE, R. G.	Died of Wounds
2689	Private	BUCKLEY, G. F.	
2534	Private	BUCKLEY, M. J.	
5981	Private	BUERCKNER, R. C.	Wounded
1230	Private	BULL, A. A.	Wounded
832	Private	BULL, H. F.	
1993	Private	BULL, R. R.	Killed in Action
1201	E.R. Sergeant	BULLUSS, J. I.	Wounded
1187	Corporal	BURBIDGE, C. C.	Killed in Action
837	Private	BURKE, E. M.	
3261	Private	BURKE, M. A.	
1198	C.S.M.	BURN, J. W.	
3263	Private	BURNELL, A.	
2528	Private	BURNELL, G.	Wounded
47	Private	BURNELL, W. G.	Wounded
1214	Private	BURNETT, H. G.	Wounded
3256	Private	BURNETT, T.	
3023	Private	BURNETT, T. F.	
404	Private	BURNIP, C. J. T.	
838	Private	BURNS, E. F.	Wounded
2282	Private	BURNS, R.	Wounded
2031	Private	BURNS, S. H.	
2690	Private	BURNS, W. J.	
	Major	BURROWS, H. O. A. D.	Gassed
1240	Private	BURROWS, T. H.	
48	Private	BURTON, A. E.	Wounded
2522	Private	BURTON, W.	
398	Sergeant	BUSH, H. F.	Killed in Action
40	Private	BUSCH, S. F.	
2422	Corporal	BUSSELL, J. H.	
2783	Private	BUTLER, G.	

Reg'tal No.	Rank	Name	Casualty
4010	Private	BUTLER, G. E.	Wounded
1795	Private	BUTLER, J. A.	Wounded
839	Private	BUTLER, P.	Died of Illness
	Captain	BUTLER, P. N.	Wounded
52	Sergeant	BUTSON, T. E.	Wounded
50	Private	BUTT, A. J. L.	
3034	Private	BUTTA, D.	
840	Private	BUXTON, H.	Wounded
1616	Sergeant	BUZOLICH, H.	Killed in Action
2403	Private	BYRNE, D. J.	Died of Wounds
53	Private	BYRNE, H.	Killed in Action
2435	Private	BYRNE, J.	Accid'ly Killed
3011	Private	BYRNE, J. T.	Wounded
2277	Private	BYRNE, T. P.	
841	Private	BYRON, J.	
1622	Private	BYRON, W. H.	
3414	Private	BYWATERS, R. W.	
2053A	Private	CADZOW, L. J.	Wounded
	Lieutenant	CAHILL, T. K.	Killed in Action
1634	Private	CAHIR, M. P.	
61	Sergeant	CAIRD, V. R.	
1248	Private	CAIRNS, D. B.	Wounded
1176	Sergeant	CAIRNS, L. D.	
1250	L/Corporal	CALDWELL, A.	
2692	Private	CALDWELL, A.	Wounded
1255	Private	CALDWELL, R.	Wounded
1628	Private	CALLAGHAN, A.	
51550	Private	CALWAY, W. H. E.	
60	L/Corporal	CALWELL, C. P.	
3170	Private	CAMERON, A. L.	
58	Private	CAMERON, A. R.	
1631	Private	CAMERON, C.	Died of Wounds
1258	Driver	CAMERON, D. S. N.	Wounded
1633	Private	CAMERON, H. R.	Died of Wounds
57	Private	CAMERON, J.	
1260	Private	CAMERON, J.	
2802	Private	CAMPBELL, A. A.	Wounded
2295	Private	CAMPBELL, C.	Wounded
4273	Private	CAMPBELL, C. S.	Wounded

Reg'tal No.	Rank	Name	Casualty
2059	Private	CAMPBELL, E. M.	
2290	Private	CAMPBELL, J. B.	
4524	Private	CAMPBELL, J. W.	Wounded
2793	Private	CAMPBELL, R.	
1637	Private	CAMPBELL, W.	
1632	Private	CAMPFIELD, J.	
427	Private	CANE, E. J.	
426	Private	CANDY, H. J.	Wounded
634A	Private	CANTLON, M. H.	
	Lieutenant	CANTWELL, A. R.	
1023	Private	CANTWELL, R.	
5999	Private	CAREY, H. J.	Wounded
2804	Private	CARGILL, H. G.	Wounded
675	Private	CARINE, J. W.	Wounded
2050	Private	CARLING, R. A.	
3419	Private	CARLISLE, H. P.	
2405	Private	CARLYON, S.	Wounded
2057	Private	CARMICHAEL, A. N. L.	Killed in Action
3270	Private	CARNEY, J. E.	
51557	Private	CARPENTER, H. R.	
55	Private	CARRICK, C. E.	Gassed
	Captain	CARRODUS, J. A.	
412	Corporal	CARROLL, F. F.	
2031A	Private	CARROLL, H. M.	
3276	Private	CARROLL, J. P.	
10592	Private	CARRUCAN, C. R.	Wounded
415	L/Corporal	CARTER, A. P.	Wounded
414	Sergeant	CARTER, C. H.	Killed in Action
65	L/Corporal	CARTER, F. H.	Wounded
2544	Private	CARTER, G. S. R.	Killed in Action
	Lieutenant	CARTER, R. T.	Wounded
3769	Private	CARTER, S. G.	Wounded
2027A	Private	CARTER, T.	
59	Private	CARTLIDGE, B.	
64	Sergeant	CARTLIDGE, C. E.	
1802	Private	CARTLIDGE, H.	Wounded
2292	Private	CASEY, P.	
2063	Corporal	CASIDY, F. W.	Wounded
417	Private	CASS, P.	

NOMINAL ROLL

Reg'tal No.	Rank	Name	Casualty
3041	Private	CASSIDY, G. H.	Killed in Action
842	L/Corporal	CASSIDY, P. L.	Killed in Action
66	L/Corporal	CAWLEY, A.	
	Hon. Captain	CERRUTTY, C. H.	
416	Sergeant	CHAMBERS, S. O.	Wounded
3042	Private	CHAMBERS, T. H.	
2296	Private	CHAMINGS, N.	
2693	Private	CHAMPION, F. C. L.	
422	Private	CHANDLER, W.	
425	Private	CHAPLIN, A. E.	Wounded
1636	Private	CHAPLIN, G.	Wounded
424	L/Corporal	CHAPLIN, H.	Killed in Action
	Lieutenant	CHAPMAN, J. H.	
2288	Private	CHAPPELL, H. T.	Gassed
843	Private	CHAPPELL, R.	
1172	C.Q.M.S.	CHAPPELL, T. H.	Wounded
51560	Private	CHARLES, C. F.	
1807	Private	CHARLES, W.	
3360	Private	CHARMAN, H. H.	
1247	Private	CHAROUNEAU, A. W.	
51555	Private	CHARTER, G. E.	
63	Sergeant	CHASE, L. P.	
62	Private	CHATFIELD, F. N.	
1942	Private	CHEESEMAN, T.	Wounded
1803	Private	CHEESEMAN, W.	Wounded
1630	Sergeant	CHEESEMAN, W. C.	
	2nd Lieutenant	CHENHALL, C. W. H.	
1626	Private	CHIBNALL, W. H.	
14240	Private	CHIDGEY, R.	
51562	Private	CHISLETT, F. A.	
	Lieutenant	CHRISTENSEN, C. P.	Killed in Action
2053A	Private	CHRISTENSEN, J. T.	
2803	Private	CHRISTENSEN, R. C.	
1032	Private	CHRISTIE, A.	Killed in Action
	Lieutenant	CLACK, V. V. K.	
1242	L/Corporal	CLARK, A.	Killed in Action
2436	Private	CLARK, A.	Wounded
5990	L/Corporal	CLARK, A. A.	Wounded
	Captain	CLARK, J. K.	Wounded

Reg'tal No.	Rank	Name	Casualty
390	Corporal	CLARK, L.	
423	Private	CLARK, W.	Killed in Action
2293	Private	CLARK, W. H. T.	
1244	Private	CLARKE, C. G.	
2796	Private	CLARKE, E. A.	Died of Wounds
2287	Private	CLARKE, G.	
3039	Private	CLARKE, J.	
2060	Private	CLARKE, J. J.	
67	L/Corporal	CLAYTON, C. G.	
69	T/Corporal	CLAYTON, E. F.	Died of Wounds
1252	Private	CLEARY, J.	Wounded
71	Private	CLEE, H.	
1072A	Private	CLEMENTS, A. F.	
2542	Private	CLENCH, C. P.	Wounded
2044	Sergeant	CLIFF, M. J.	Wounded
3038	Private	CLIFFORD, V.	Wounded
7341	L/Corporal	CLINGAN, J. W.	
70	Private	CLUES, J.	
2061	Private	COATES, O.	Wounded
3273	Private	COATS, J. C.	
3272	Private	COBBET, J.	
	2nd Lieutenant	COBDEN, C. M.	Killed in Action
844	Private	COCHRANE, W. F.	Wounded
68	Private	COCKERILL, C. C.	
5992	Private	COCKLE, W. C.	Died of Wounds
1635	Private	COCKROFT, A. J. B.	
2056A	Corporal	CODY, T.	Wounded
260	Corporal	COE, V. P.	
428	Sergeant	COFFEY, D. F.	
2888	Private	COFFEY, T.	
72	Private	COGHILL, J.	Wounded
845	Corporal	COGHLAN, W. M.	Wounded
413	Private	COLAHAN, A.	Wounded
3272	Private	COLBERT, J.	
2055A	Private	COLE, P. H.	Wounded
3278	Private	COLE, R. C.	
51551	Private	COLEMAN, A.	
2799	Private	COLES, W. H.	
2792A	Private	COLLING, R.	Wounded

NOMINAL ROLL

Reg'tal No.	Rank	Name	Casualty
2546	Private	COLLINS, J. J.	Wounded
	Lieutenant	COLLINS, T. J.	
1943	Private	COLLINS, W. T.	Wounded
	Lieutenant	COLLIS, C. H.	
78	C.Q.M.S.	COLLYER, A. C.	
2540	Private	COLTMAN, C. G.	Died of Wounds
76	L/Corporal	COLYER, A. L.	
2790	Private	COLWILL, W. J.	Killed in Action
5987	Private	COMBRIDGE, C. C.	Wounded
420	C.S.M.	COMRIE, A. N.	Wounded
643	Private	CONBOY, G. F.	Died of Wounds
3012	Private	CONDON, J.	
7192	Private	CONNELL, A. F.	
4997	Private	CONNELLY, W. F.	Died of Wounds
3043	Private	CONNER, A. H.	
3044	Private	CONNER, G. A.	Killed in Action
4525	Private	CONNOLE, W. F.	Killed in Action
1806	Private	CONNOLLY, A. J.	Wounded
3275	Private	CONNOLLY, J. H. J.	
53932	Private	CONNOLLY, T. J.	
3373	Corporal	CONNOR, W. D.	
1262	Private	CONROY, R. P.	
1197	L/Corporal	CONSIDINE, J.	
80	Sergeant	COOK, A. C.	Wounded
3418	Private	COOK, J.	
5985	Private	COOK, J.	Wounded
	Lieutenant	COOK, J. D.	Wounded
1257	Private	COOK, L. J.	Wounded
674A	Driver	COOK, R. W.	
1251	Sergeant	COOK, W. C.	
54165	Private	COOKSEY, D. R.	
5072A	Private	COOLLEDGE, A.	
84	Private	COOMBE, C. A.	Wounded
1254	Corporal	COOMBES, H.	Killed in Action
54168	Private	COONEY, C.	
1031	Private	COONEY, T. H.	Wounded
2055	Corporal	COOPER, E. A. H.	Wounded
2406	Private	COOPER, E. G. E.	
5986	Private	COOPER, O. G.	Wounded

Reg'tal No.	Rank	Name	Casualty
2054	Private	COOPER, P.	
2791	Private	COPLEY, S. J.	
5997	Private	COPPIN, W.	Wounded
85	Private	CORBETT, J.	Wounded
2543	Private	CORBETT, L. R.	
2294	Private	CORDELL, J. J.	Wounded
51553	Private	CORNWELL, R. G.	
	Lieutenant	CORRIGAN, J. L. T.	
555	Sergeant	COSSINS, J. F.	
421	Private	COSTELLO, J. L. R.	Killed in Action
87	Private	COSTELLO, W. D.	Wounded
77	Private	COSTELLOE, E.	
2800	L/Corporal	COTTRILL, F. E.	Died of Wounds
4523	Private	COUCH, W. J.	Killed in Action
1259	Private	COULSON, A. O.	
1256	Private	COULSON, J. R. S.	
3045	Private	COULSON, R. B.	
846	Private	COURT, H. G.	
2541A	L/Corporal	COUSINS, C. E.	
847	Private	COUTTS, A. E.	Wounded
848	Private	COUTTS, D. G.	Wounded
3037	Private	COUTTS, H. A.	
849	Private	COUTTS, R. H.	Died of Wounds
86	Private	COWAN, C.	Wounded
88	Sergeant	COWAN, D. B.	
2058	Private	COWAN, W. F.	Wounded
3269	Private	COWLING, P. R.	
2545	Private	COWPER, G. H.	Wounded
850	Private	COX, B.	
89	Private	COX, C.	
5991A	Private	COX, F. B.	Killed in Action
2056	Corporal	COX, G. H.	Killed in Action
803	L/Corporal	COX, W.	Killed in Action
419	Private	COXALL, A. B.	Wounded
1809	Driver	COXON, H.	
1808	Driver	COXON, W. E.	
2829A	Private	CRAIGIE, S.	Wounded
418	Private	CRACKNELL, J. E.	
2048	Private	CRAM, W. E.	

NOMINAL ROLL

Reg'tal No.	Rank	Name	Casualty
2798	Private	CRAMERI, J. C.	
3046	Private	CRAVEN, E.	Wounded
5990	Private	CRAWFORD, C.	
	Lieutenant	CRAYFORD, W. B.	
1891	Private	CRIBBES, G. M.	
2541	Private	CRICHTON, C. V.	Wounded
90	Private	CRIPPS, L. D. L.	
91	Corporal	CROCKFORD, B. E.	
851	Private	CROFT, W. F.	
1243	Sergeant	CROFT, W. J. H.	Wounded
146A	Private	CROMAY, J.	
852	A/Corporal	CROMWELL, C. A.	Gassed
853	Private	CRONIN, J. J.	
1261	Sergeant	CROOK, W. J.	Wounded
854	Corporal	CROPLEY, A. C.	Wounded
	Lieutenant	CROSS, D. B.	Wounded
2437	Private	CROSS, J. A.	Wounded
1253	Corporal	CROSTHWAITE, I. S.	Wounded
	Lieutenant	CROTTY, V. J.	Wounded
2795	Private	CROUCH, A. T.	
1985	Private	CROUCH, H.	
5983	Private	CROWSON, C. J. P.	
2048	Corporal	CROWE, P. W.	Wounded
2404	Private	CROWLEY, W.	
	Captain	CROWTHER, G. H.	
855	Private	CROY, J.	Wounded
2797A	Private	CULL, L. C.	Wounded
1249	Sergeant	CULLIVER, E. C.	Wounded
	Captain	CUMMING, W. R.	Wounded
2051	Private	CUNDY, F. J. G.	Wounded
1245	Private	CUNNINGHAM, A.	Wounded
5995	L/Corporal	CUNNINGHAM, A. J.	Wounded
51554	Private	CUNNINGHAM, C. L.	
1246	Private	CUNNINGHAM, C. S.	
51588	Private	CUNNINGHAM, H. T.	
2801	Private	CUNNINGHAM, J. H.	Killed in Action
856	Corporal	CUNNINGHAM, T.	Killed in Action
857	Private	CUPIT, G.	Killed in Action
858	Private	CUPIT, H.	

Reg'tal No.	Rank	Name	Casualty
51552	Private	CURNOW, C. T.	
1963	Private	CURRAN, D.	Wounded
6127	Private	CURRAN, E. W.	Wounded
3048	Private	CURRELL, W. J.	
859	Private	CURRY, J. P.	
3279	Private	CURRY, W. R.	
3047	Private	CURTAIN, T. R.	
2808	Private	DACK, C. W.	
642	Private	DALE, J. J.	Died of Wounds
2060	Private	DALTON, C.	Killed in Action
438	Sergeant	DALZIEL, J. W.	
2299	Private	DARE, N. E. V.	
861	Private	DARK, F. C.	Wounded
2066	Corporal	DARLING, R. G.	Killed in Action
1843	Private	DARLING, W. T.	Wounded
2303	Private	DART, F. J.	Wounded
2185	Private	DASHPER, W. J.	Killed in Action
2302	Private	DAVEY, A. R.	
51570	Sergeant	DAVEY, B. G.	
862	Private	DAVEY, J.	Wounded
	2nd Lieutenant	DAVIDSON, C. S.	Wounded
	Lieutenant	DAVIDSON, F. B.	Died of Wounds
435	Private	DAVIDSON, J.	Wounded
	Lieutenant	DAVIDSON, K. McM.	
804	Sergeant	DAVIES, B. R.	Wounded
6001	Private	DAVIES, C. J.	
3051	Private	DAVIES, C. W.	
	Lieutenant	DAVIES, D. R.	Wounded
	2nd Lieutenant	DAVIES, G. H.	
3052	Private	DAVIES, H. R.	
	Lieutenant	DAVIES, McF. C.	
95	L/Corporal	DAVIES, P. J.	Gassed
863	Private	DAVIES, T. H.	
1638	Private	DAVIES, W. C.	Wounded
2551	Private	DAVIS, C. H. W.	Wounded
1813	Private	DAVIS, E. A.	Wounded
3013	Private	DAVIS, F.	
94	Private	DAVIS, L. N.	
96	Private	DAVIS, P.	Killed in Action

NOMINAL ROLL

Reg'tal No.	Rank	Name	Casualty
2550	L/Corporal	DAVIS, S. C.	Gassed
432	Private	DAVIS, T.	
436	Private	DAVIS, T. W.	Wounded
	Captain	DAVIS, W. E.	
93	L/Corporal	DAVIS, W. H.	Killed in Action
5997A	Signaller	DAW, E. E.	Wounded
2762	Corporal	DAWSON, A. C.	Wounded
51569	Private	DAWSON, R. H.	
	2nd Lieutenant	DAY, A. C.	
3288	Private	DAY, G.	
434	Private	DEAN, F.	Wounded
2064A	Private	DEAN, H. L.	Wounded
2300	Corporal	DEAN, J.	Gassed
1645	Sergeant	DEAN, R. C.	
1190	Corporal	DEAN, W. H.	
1644	Private	DEANS, E. J.	
6008	Private	DEARY, J.	Gassed
431	Private	DECKER, W.	
6009	Private	DELAHOY, H. J.	Killed in Action
1268	Private	DELAHUNTY, J. A.	Wounded
430	Private	DELAMARE, A. H.	
2347	Private	DELANEY, J. J.	Killed in Action
1631	Private	DELL, G. C.	
2419	Private	DELLAR, T. G.	Gassed
3283	Private	DELLER, W. E.	
3165	Private	DEL MARCO, R. M.	
22182	Private	DE MACK, J. C.	
437	Private	DE MOUILPIED, W. G.	
51571	Corporal	DEMPSTER, A. C.	
1272	Private	DENHOLM, R. A. W.	Wounded
2429	Private	DENT, C. H.	
	Captain	DERAVIN, A. E.	Wounded
7126	Private	DE VALLE, A.	Wounded
7128	Private	DE VALLE, L. F.	
864	Private	DE VILLECURT, F.	
2548	Private	DEVINE, R. J. S.	
17301	Private	DEVIRS, J.	
51566	Private	DEW, P. V.	
433	Private	DEWAR, D.	Wounded

Reg'tal No.	Rank	Name	Casualty
3053	Private	DEWBURY, B.	
1265	Private	DICK, S.	Wounded
1639	Private	DICKENSON, A. R.	
1274	Private	DICKENSON, H.	
97	Private	DICKIE, T. W.	Gassed
2807	Private	DICKINSON, J. C.	Gassed
3035	Private	DICKINSON, R. S.	Wounded
3056	Private	DICKINSON, T. W.	Gassed
6010	Private	DICKSON, R.	
98	Sergeant	DILLON, A. A.	
51567	Private	DIMOND, R. J.	
865	Private	DINES, H. G.	Wounded
535	Private	DINSDALE, E.	
1273	Private	DIWELL, W. H.	Wounded
429	Private	DIXON, R.	
665	L/Corporal	DIXON, W. A.	
51568	Private	DOBBYN, O. J.	
2301	Private	DOBLIE, L.	Killed in Action
866	Private	DOBSON, L. M.	Wounded
1171	Driver	DODD, G. P.	
51573	Private	DODD, S. H.	
3280	Private	DODGE, F. W.	
1275	Private	DODGSON, R. H. W.	
1646	Private	DODSON, A. J.	
2064	Private	DONALD, C.	Wounded
2420	Private	DONALDSON, D.	
867	Private	DONALDSON E. A.	
2809	Private	DONELLAN, M.	
4028	Private	DONOHUE, G. H.	Wounded
169A	Private	DORAN, J. T.	Wounded
5998	Private	DOUGLAS, J. G.	Gassed
1810	Private	DOUGLASS, H. U.	
868	Private	DOUPE, H. F.	Died of Wounds
6011	Private	DOVASTON, A. G.	Wounded
6004	E.R. Sergeant	DOWDEN, B. L.	
869	Private	DOWLING, J.	Wounded
1264	Corporal	DOWN, L. J.	Killed in Action
2810	Private	DOWNES, R. H.	
870	Corporal	DOWNING, W. G.	Wounded

NOMINAL ROLL

Reg'tal No.	Rank	Name	Casualty
1266	Private	DOYLE, A. J.	
3010	Private	DOYLE, J.	Wounded
3167	Private	DOYLE, J.	
1267	Private	DRAFFIN, I.	
6132	Private	DRISCOLL, A. E.	Killed in Action
1311	Private	DRURY, D. F.	
2069	Private	DUCKMANTON, H. A.	
3284	Private	DUDLEY, L. R.	
1814	L/Corporal	DUFF, A.	Wounded
2694	Private	DUFFY, T.	Wounded
1271	Private	DUGGAN, C. J.	Wounded
4530	Corporal	DUGGAN, R.	Killed in Action
3420	Private	DUKE, C. J.	
2805	Private	DULLARD, T.	Wounded
3292	Private	DUNCAN, A. G.	
4529	Private	DUNCAN, L. L.	Killed in Action
2297	Private	DUNCAN, N. S.	
1269	Private	DUNKLY, A. T.	
2136	Private	DUNLOP, J. S.	Wounded
3050	Private	DUNLOP, T. K.	
5664	Private	DUNN, H. A.	
1642	Private	DUNN, L. V.	
3279	Private	DUNN, P.	
51572	Private	DUNN, P. H.	
1643	Corporal	DUNN, R. H.	
3379	Private	DUNNE, G. M.	Wounded
2806	Private	DUNNE, M. P.	Wounded
433A	Private	DUNSTAN, H. B.	
1627	Sergeant	DUNSTAN, J. H. C.	
	Lieutenant	DUNSTAN, J. R.	
2304	Private	DUNSTER, A. J.	Died of Wounds
2067	Private	DURAND, W.	Wounded
1270	Private	DUSCHER, S.	
1276	Private	DUXSON, H. H.	
2917B	Private	DWYER, W.	
1035	Private	DWYER, W. J.	Wounded
1811	Private	DYER, G.	Wounded
1815	Private	DYKES, W.	Wounded
567A	Corporal	DYSON, H. J. B.	

Reg'tal No.	Rank	Name	Casualty
871	Corporal	DYSON, J.	
99	Private	EADE, D. W.	Died of Wounds
3286	Private	EARLES, C. A.	
3287	Private	EASTICK, F. H.	
2552	Corporal	EASTWOOD, J. A.	Wounded
1943	Private	EDGAR, G. C.	Gassed
872	Private	EDGAR, G. S.	
443	Private	EDMENDS, A. R.	Wounded
100	S/Sergeant	EDSALL, W. E.	
2305	Private	EDWARD, A. D.	Wounded
	Lieutenant	EDWARDS, A.	Wounded
1281	Private	EDWARDS, B.	
2811	Private	EDWARDS, F. B.	Killed in Action
1649	L/Sergeant	EDWARDS, F. T. A.	Killed in Action
444	Private	EDWARDS, H. R.	Killed in Action
1648	Private	EDWARDS, P. L.	
793	L/Sergeant	EDWARDS, S. H.	Wounded
2072	Private	EDWARDS, T. E.	Wounded
1278	Private	EDWARDS, W.	
101	Private	EDWARDS, W. G.	
1280	Private	EDWARDS, W. J.	
102	Private	EGAN, D. E.	Wounded
103	Private	EGAN, F. A.	Wounded
2553	Private	EGAN, J. J.	
104	Private	ELDER, D.	
1817	Private	ELLEN, J. A.	Died of Wounds
2555	Private	ELLERY, C. N.	Gassed
51578	Corporal	ELLETSON, J.	
439	Corporal	ELLETT, A.	
446	L/Corporal	ELLIOT, J. D. W.	
441	Private	ELLIOTT, P. S.	Killed in Action
	2nd Lieutenant	ELLIS, A. R.	
442	L/Corporal	ELLIS, F. J.	
51574	Private	ELLIS, H. J.	
1277	Sergeant	ELLIS, J.	Wounded
440	L/Corporal	ELLSWORTH, G. W.	Died of Wounds
740	Private	ELSON, R.	Killed in Action
2070	Private	ELSTON, W. C.	Wounded
51577	Sergeant	ELSWORTHY, E. M.	

NOMINAL ROLL

Reg'tal No.	Rank	Name	Casualty
2073	Signaller	ELTZE, C. F.	Wounded
1279	Private	EMERY, R. J.	
105	Private	EMMERSON, A. E.	Wounded
1647	Private	EMMERSON, W. G.	
873	A/Corporal	EMMETT, A. R.	Killed in Action
445	Corporal	EMMETT, F. H.	Gassed
3058	Private	EMONSON, P. S.	Died of Wounds
2071	Private	ENDEAN, R. J.	Wounded
874	Sergeant	ENGBRIGTSEN, E.	
875	Private	ENGLEDOW, W. R. B.	
3288	Private	ERFURTH, C. C.	
876	Private	ERRY, G. B.	
693	Private	EUMAN, W. W.	
2770	Private	EVANS, C.	Wounded
3057	Private	EVANS, G. J.	Killed in Action
671	Private	EVANS, H.	
3285	Private	EVANS, H.	
6007	Private	EVANS, J. G.	Killed in Action
3059	Private	EWING, G. M.	
5072	Private	FACEY, D. R.	Killed in Action
3066	Private	FACEY, J.	Wounded
3345	Sergeant	FAGAN, R. H.	
2821	Private	FAIRBRASS, L.	
3300	Private	FAIRBROTHER, R. F.	
3061	Private	FALLSHAW, P. C.	
877	Private	FANNING, J.	
3291	Private	FARGHER, D. B.	Wounded
1826	Private	FARLEY, A.	Wounded
1824	Private	FARMER, A. R. G.	Wounded
449	Private	FARRIES, L. H.	
4537	Private	FARROW, W. C.	
2308	Private	FARROW, W. H. R.	
51A	Private	FAULKNER, H.	Wounded
2818	Private	FAWKNER, W.	
3064	Private	FELTHAM, G.	
6134	Private	FENWICK, A. R.	
450	L/Sergeant	FERGUSON, A.	
6019	Corporal	FERGUSON, G. A.	
1934	Driver	FERGUSON, G. J.	

Reg'tal No.	Rank	Name	Casualty
6020	L/Corporal	FERGUSON, J.	Wounded
447	Private	FERGUSON, R. D.	
2309	Private	FERGUSON, W. W. L.	Wounded
878	Private	FETHERSTON, J. J.	Wounded
	Lieutenant	FIDLER, G. A.	
3060	Private	FIDDES, E. A.	Wounded
3295	Private	FIELD, H. E.	
1822	Private	FIELDS, J. C. B.	Wounded
3296	Private	FIELDEN, W.	
51585	Private	FILES, C. J.	
2307	Private	FINCH, H. W.	
2311	Private	FINCH, J. A.	Wounded
2817	Private	FINEMORE, A. F.	
425A	Private	FINLAY, G.	Killed in Action
426A	Private	FINLAY, J.	Wounded
1821	Private	FINN, W. T.	
	2nd Lieutenant	FINSTER, A. A.	
108	Corporal	FISHER, F. H.	Killed in Action
51583	Private	FISHER, R.	
1825	Private	FISK, G. J.	Died of Illness
2816	Private	FITZGERALD, B.	
3293	Private	FITZGERALD, B. D.	
2306	Private	FITZGERALD, H.	Wounded
2684	Private	FITZGERALD, W. J.	
3065	Private	FITZPATRICK, F. J. J.	Wounded
2814	Private	FLEAY, A. F. J.	Wounded
	Lieutenant	FLEITER, E.	Wounded
1286	Private	FLETCHER, J. F.	
2820	Private	FLETCHER, W. A.	
2075	Sergeant	FLOCKHART, G. E.	Wounded
6120	Private	FLOCKHART, J.	
879	Private	FLOYD, W. J. E.	
2076	Private	FLYNN, J. V.	Wounded
1820	Private	FOGARTY, J.	Wounded
3789	L/Corporal	FOGARTY, W. M.	Wounded
3290	Private	FOLEY, R. E.	Wounded
1288	Private	FOLKES, G. A.	Wounded
1287	Sergeant	FOLKES, S. J.	Killed in Action
4036	Private	FOLLETT, C. E.	

NOMINAL ROLL

Reg'tal No.	Rank	Name	Casualty
1945	Private	FOOTE, T.	Wounded
2913	Private	FOOTE, W. L.	
2074	Corporal	FORBES, R. A.	Wounded
2077	Private	FORD, G. E. S.	
880	Private	FORD, H.	
1944	Private	FORD, H.	
453	Sergeant	FORD, J. M.	
261	Private	FORSTER, S.	Wounded
1285	Sergeant	FOSTER, C. A.	
2469	Private	FOSTER, W. R.	Wounded
1827	Private	FOUND, L. D.	Died of Wounds
5689	L/Corporal	FOUND, N.	Killed in Action
109	Private	FOWELL, W. J.	Died of Illness
452	Driver	FOWLER, P.	Wounded
3298	Private	FOX, A. M.	
3292	Private	FOX, E. A.	
1283	Private	FOX, T.	
881	Corporal	FOYLE, W. F.	Wounded
6025	Private	FRAMPTON, G.	Killed in Action
1282	Private	FRANCIS, F.	
1819	L/Sergeant	FRANCIS, H. C.	
508A	Private	FRANCIS, J. E.	
882	Private	FRANCIS, L. R.	Wounded
51586	Private	FRANK, P. C.	
448	L/Corporal	FRANKLIN, L. R.	Died of Wounds
3289	Private	FRASER, A. L.	
805	Corporal	FRASER, E. B.	Wounded
1653	Private	FRASER, R. J.	
3289	Private	FRASER, A. L.	
883	Private	FREARSON, C. R.	
1284	Private	FREELAND, W. H.	Killed in Action
1196	Sergeant	FRENCHAM, C. R.	
884	Private	FROUDE, W. H.	
451	Driver	FRY, J. J.	
	Lieutenant	FRYER, J. R.	Gassed
2813	Private	FULLER, G. A.	Killed in Action
3297	Private	FURLONG, E. L.	
51584	Private	FURNESS, J.	
1672	Private	FYANDER, C. T.	

Reg'tal No.	Rank	Name	Casualty
110	Sergeant	GALAGHER, L. S.	
885	Private	GALLAGER, N.	Killed in Action
2424	Private	GALLAGHER, F. S.	
1300	Private	GALLAGHER, J. F.	
	2nd Lieutenant	GALLAGHER, J. V.	
2197	Private	GAMMON, C. J.	
111	A/Corporal	GARD, H. T. G.	
3300	Private	GARDINER, C. A. T.	
3303	Private	GARDINER, C. M.	
2078	Sergeant	GARDINER, I. W.	
1297	Private	GARDNER, H. B.	Died of Wounds
	Lieutenant	GARRARD, C. E.	Killed in Action
1830	Private	GASKETT, W. J.	
886	Private	GAZZARD, H. E.	
887	Private	GEDDES, A.	
462	C.S.M.	GEDDES, R.	Wounded
51590	Private	GEDDIS, J.	
3304	Private	GEMMELL, J. G.	
3065	Sergeant	GEORGE, A. R.	
3070	Private	GEORGE, J. S.	Killed in Action
117	Private	GEORGE, N. L.	
1836	Private	GERDTS, R. A.	Killed in Action
3071	Private	GERMAINE, A. G.	
2499	Private	GERRING, A. S.	Died of Wounds
1293	Private	GEYER, E. T.	
1295	Private	GIBBON, T. W.	
113	Driver	GIBBS, S. B.	
2695	Private	GIBSON, A.	
2080	Private	GIBSON, C.	Killed in Action
2920	Private	GIBSON, C. E.	
1116	Private	GIBSON, H. J.	
2312	Private	GIBSON, P. W.	Wounded
4541	Corporal	GIESE, H.	
888	Private	GILBERT, A. E.	
889	Sergeant	GILBERT, L. V.	Wounded
676A	Private	GILBERT, S. H.	Killed in Action
1299	Private	GILDING, J. E.	
3068	Corporal	GILES, A. F.	
4674	Private	GILES, C. H.	

NOMINAL ROLL

Reg'tal No.	Rank	Name	Casualty
	Captain	GILES, C. L.	Wounded
3301	Private	GILL, F.	
2557	Private	GILLAN, E. E.	
1946	Private	GILLESPIE, C. J.	Wounded
1947	Private	GILLESPIE, N. J.	Died of Wounds
6027	Private	GILLIGAN, P.	Wounded
1292	Private	GILLIN, C. E.	
3068	Private	GILMORE, A. R.	Wounded
7018	Private	GILMORE, E.	Wounded
1291	Private	GILMOUR, W.	Wounded
6028	Private	GITSHAM, C. F.	Killed in Action
3308	Private	GLADMAN, F. E.	
114	Private	GLASSON, R.	Wounded
5101	Private	GLEESON, G.	Wounded
6028A	Private	GLEISNER, E.	
1834	Private	GLEISNER, F.	Wounded
3305	Private	GLENN, T. J.	
115	Private	GLENNON, T. R.	
2822	Private	GLOSSOP, C. H.	Wounded
3001	Private	GLOVER, F.	
891	Private	GLOVER, P.	Died of Wounds
116	Private	GLOVER, T.	Killed in Action
1191	Corporal	GOBLE, H. C.	
3067	Private	GODDARD, E. H.	
2825	Private	GODDARD, W. H.	
118	Private	GOLDBERG, C.	Wounded
119	Private	GOLLINGS, L. J.	Wounded
806	Sergeant	GOLDSBROUGH, P. E.	Gassed
2826	Private	GOMEZ, J.	
3072	Private	GOODE, W.	Killed in Action
6030A	Private	GOODGAME, A.	Wounded
892	Private	GOODWIN, J.	Wounded
2273	Private	GOOLEY, C. J.	Killed in Action
1294	Private	GORDON, C. R.	Killed in Action
1656	Private	GORDON, G. H.	Wounded
460	Corporal	GORDON, S. L.	Gassed
807	Sergeant	GOTHARD, W. N.	Wounded
6031	Private	GOUDEY, A.	Wounded
6121	Private	GOULD, E.	

Reg'tal No.	Rank	Name	Casualty
1837	Private	GOULD, F. R.	Killed in Action
2313	Private	GOWLAND, J. E.	
3525	Private	GOYNE, C. H.	
4665	Private	GRAFF, A.	
723A	Private	GRAHAM, E. H.	Wounded
2919	Private	GRAHAM, J.	
1296	Private	GRAHAM, R. J.	
3069	Private	GRANERI, J.	
3173	Private	GRANGER, J.	
1290	Private	GRANT, C. E.	
785	Sergeant	GRANT, H. J.	Wounded
3251	Private	GRANT, J. S.	
	Lieutenant	GRANT, L. E.	Killed in Action
893	Private	GRANT, R. K.	Gassed
4544	Driver	GRANT, W. McG.	
1829	Private	GRANTLEY, T. F.	Wounded
	Lieutenant	GRATION, J. W.	
281	Private	GRAY, D. A.	
2823	Private	GRAY, F.	Wounded
894	Private	GRAY, H.	Died of Wounds
635	Private	GRAY, H. J.	
	Lieutenant	GRAY, R. F.	
1289	Private	GRAY, S.	
1301	Private	GRAY, W.	
455	Private	GRAY, W. A.	Wounded
	Lieutenant	GRAYLING, F. L.	Wounded
2028	Private	GREEN, F. J.	
722A	Private	GREEN, H.	
2563	Private	GREEN, S. M.	Wounded
262	Private	GREEN, W. E.	
	Lieutenant	GREENAWAY, W. E.	Wounded
1298	Private	GREENBANK, J. L.	Killed in Action
6876	Private	GREENFIELD, R.	
	Lieutenant	GREENHALGH, A.	
1832	Private	GREENLEES, R.	
3304	Private	GREENWAY, F. R.	
3306	Private	GREENWAY, J. S.	
51594	Private	GREENWAY, S.	
895	Private	GREENWELL, W. J.	

NOMINAL ROLL

Reg'tal No.	Rank	Name	Casualty
3387	Private	GREENWOOD, J. T.	Died of Illness
896	Private	GREENWOOD, S. J.	Killed in Action
2556	Private	GREGORY, E. R.	Gassed
2696	Private	GREGORY, G. F.	Wounded
942A	Private	GRIFFIN, C.	Wounded
2410	Private	GRIFFIN, P. J.	
4543	Private	GRIFFITHS, H.	Died of Wounds
1837	Private	GRIFFITHS, J. G.	Wounded
51593	Private	GRIFFITHS, R. L.	
463	Private	GRIFFITHS, T. F.	Wounded
454	ER/WO.1	GRIFFITHS, W. E.	
3307	Private	GRIGG, F. G.	
897	Private	GRIGGS, F.	Gassed
4539	Private	GRONBECK, W. A.	Wounded
	Lieutenant	GRONDONA, L. St. C.	Wounded
1657	Private	GROSE, A. B.	
2824	Private	GROSE, W.	
808	L/Corporal	GROVES, J. L.	
2079	Private	GROVES, W.	
2313	Private	GROWLAND, J. E.	
1987	Private	GRUMMETT, C. J.	
2558	Private	GRUNDY, L. J. C.	Died of Illness
458	Private	GUBBY, W. J.	
2674	Private	GUILFOYLE, C. J. M.	Gassed
898	Corporal	GUINEA, J. L.	Killed in Action
1659	Private	GUINNEY, J.	Wounded
464	L/Corporal	GULL, R. S.	Wounded
	Lieutenant	GULLY, S. E.	Wounded
1835	Private	GUMMOW, J.	Gassed
122	Private	GUPPY, W. J.	Wounded
2561	Private	GURTH, F. E.	
885	Private	GURNEY, R. E.	
461	Private	GUTHRIE, J.	
2827	Private	GUY, E. R.	Gassed
	Lieutenant	GUYETT, A. E.	Wounded
7240	Private	GUYETT, N. F.	Wounded
54674	Private	GWILLIAM, F. S.	
1305	Driver	HAGE, T.	
	Lieutenant	HAIN, G. F.	

Reg'tal No.	Rank	Name	Casualty
1312	Sergeant	HAINES, V. R.	Wounded
11762	Sergeant	HAIR, S. G.	
4555	Private	HALE, H. E.	Died of Wounds
5401	L/Corporal	HALL, S. A.	
1209	Private	HALL, T. H.	
1321	Private	HALL, W. T.	Died of Wounds
2834	Corporal	HALLEY, A. N.	
3313	Private	HALLIDAY, P. W.	
3074	Private	HALLS, W.	
125	Private	HAM, R. L.	
1992	Private	HAMILL, A.	
1993A	L/Corporal	HAMILTON, A. L.	Wounded
1970	Private	HAMILTON, F.	Wounded
809	Sergeant	HAMILTON, J. H.	Wounded
2091	Private	HAMILTON, W.	
899	Private	HAMMON, H. T.	
668A	Private	HAMMOND, C. W.	Killed in Action
2031	L/Corporal	HANCOCK, R.	
51609	Private	HANCOCK, W. R.	
2841	Private	HANKS, A. C.	Killed in Action
2912	Private	HANLAN, S. C.	Wounded
1662	Private	HANLON, H. McD.	
1316	Private	HANNA, D.	
2829	Private	HANNIGAN, A. W.	Wounded
900	Private	HANNIGAN, M. J.	
3080	Private	HANRAHAN, T. P.	Wounded
2438	Private	HANSON, W.	Wounded
123	Sergeant	HARBECK, A. R.	Died of Wounds
2410	Private	HARBOURNE, M. J.	Killed in Action
6116	Private	HARDEN, R.	Wounded
901	Private	HARDIE, G. J.	
902	Private	HARDING, R. H.	
2318	Private	HARDING, W. A.	
2832	Private	HARDWICK, J. R. G.	Died of Illness
2321	Private	HARE, H. N.	
1024	Private	HARITONOFF, P.	
2090	Private	HARMAN, S. F.	
477	Private	HARPER, J. H.	Died of Illness
1310	Private	HARPER, R. H.	Killed in Action

NOMINAL ROLL

Reg'tal No.	Rank	Name	Casualty
6135	Private	HARRIP, J.	Wounded
1554A	Corporal	HARRIS, A. J.	Wounded
1850	Private	HARRIS, A. J.	Wounded
2195	Driver	HARRIS, E. H.	
6862	Private	HARRIS, E. W.	Wounded
1995	Private	HARRIS, G. H.	
2566	Private	HARRIS, H. B.	Wounded
51598	Private	HARRIS, H. H.	
903	Private	HARRIS, J.	Wounded
904	Private	HARRIS, J. W.	
790	Sergeant	HARRIS, J. N.	Wounded
1839	Private	HARRIS, L. D.	Killed in Action
905	Private	HARRIS, T.	
906	Private	HARRISON, L. J. M.	
1307	Private	HARRISON, R.	
2573	Corporal	HARRISON, R. L.	
797	Corporal	HARRISON, W.	
2089	Private	HARRISON, W.	Wounded
132	Private	HARRISON, W. A.	
1309	Private	HARRY, W. L.	Wounded
6144	Private	HARTWICK, W.	Wounded
6123	Private	HARVEY, A. J.	Killed in Action
3427	Private	HARVEY, A. W.	
2330	Private	HARVEY, G. T.	
3073	Private	HARVEY, H.	
124	Driver	HARVEY, H. R.	
468	Private	HARWOOD, C. C.	
2834	Private	HARWOOD, C. F.	
126	Private	HARWOOD, T. J.	Gassed
	Lieutenant	HASKEY, W. G.	
1849	Corporal	HASLAM, R. F.	
2086	Private	HASTIE, J. T.	
1882	L/Corporal	HATTAM, E.	Wounded
3077	Private	HAW, K. J.	
1302	Private	HAWKER, G. E.	
1665	Private	HAY, C.	Wounded
	Lieutenant	HAY, G.	Wounded
1846	Private	HAYDON, J. J.	Gassed
7254	Private	HAYES, E. W.	

Reg'tal No.	Rank	Name	Casualty
1661	Driver	HAYWARD, A. G. V.	
2675	Private	HAYWARD, A. J.	Wounded
2022	Private	HAYWOOD, E.	Wounded
3316	Private	HEANEY, G. H.	
51599	Private	HEARD, R. S.	
907	Driver	HEARNE, G. T.	
1322	Corporal	HEATH, S. V.	Killed in Action
2322	Private	HEBB, F. G.	Gassed
3317	Private	HEHIR, W. J.	
3075	Private	HEENAN, A. T.	Wounded
7357	Private	HEENAN, A. F.	Gassed
3164	Private	HEFFERNAN, L. A.	Killed in Action
1841	Private	HELLIAR, H. C.	
3321	Private	HELLYER, G.	
51601	Corporal	HENDERSON, A. J.	
2572	Private	HENDERSON, C.	
2587	Private	HENDERSON, C.	
6041	Private	HENDERSON, C. T.	
128	Corporal	HENDERSON, H. W.	Wounded
3318	Private	HENDERSON, J. A.	Wounded
466	Private	HENDERSON, R. C.	
	Lieut.-Colonel	HENDERSON, R. O.	Killed in Action
2101	Corporal	HENDERSON, R. S.	Wounded
	Captain	HENRY, A.	
1205	Driver	HENRY, C. E.	
2319	Private	HENNESSEY, G. S.	
908	Private	HENNESSY, T.	Gassed
51611	Private	HENRIKSEN, H.	
2838	Private	HEPBURN, N. J.	Wounded
	Lieutenant	HEPBURN, R.	Wounded
1844	Private	HERON, H. F.	
476	Private	HERRMANN, A. J.	Wounded
1304	Private	HERRMANN, E. O.	
	Captain	HESELTINE, S. H.	
467	Private	HESLOP, A.	
602	Private	HEWAT, J.	
909	L/Corporal	HEWITT, F. B.	Died of Wounds
129	Sergeant	HEWITT, T. S.	
2083	Private	HEWITT, W. B.	Killed in Action

NOMINAL ROLL

Reg'tal No.	Rank	Name	Casualty
177A	Sergeant	HEWLAND, C. J.	Gassed
3172	Private	HEYWOOD, A. E.	
3315	Private	HIAM, F. H.	
1313	Corporal	HICKFORD, J. C.	Killed in Action
4307	Private	HICKS, F.	Wounded
2831	Private	HICKS, J. F.	Wounded
1303	Private	HIGGINS, D. A.	
1663	Private	HIGHMAN, F.	
3076	Private	HILBURN, A.	Died of Wounds
2317	Private	HILDERBRANDT, L.	Wounded
51602	Private	HILL, A.	
1197	Private	HILL, C. A. W.	
2096	Private	HILL, C. P.	Wounded
910	Sergeant	HILL, F. G.	Wounded
895	Sergeant	HILL, G. M. C.	
51604	Private	HILL, H. S.	
2088	Private	HILL, L.	Wounded
678	Private	HILL, W. C. F.	
472	Private	HINCHCLIFFE, L. E.	
1153A	Private	HINDS, J. W.	Wounded
3320	Private	HIPPISLEY, A. V.	
3312	Private	HIPPISLEY, H. J.	
1666A	Private	HIRD, W. B.	Killed in Action
3083	Private	HITCHCOCK, G. M. J.	
133	Sergeant	HOBBA, A. H.	Wounded
3077	Private	HOCKING, T. H.	Wounded
2835	Private	HODDER, M. H.	Died of Wounds
2085	Private	HODGERS, J.	Wounded
2567	Private	HODGES, R. K.	
2315	Private	HODGES, W. J. T.	
469	C.S.M.	HODGETTS, L. F.	Wounded
3014	Private	HODGSON, P.	Wounded
2087	Corporal	HOGAN, E. W.	
2925	Private	HOGAN, F. H.	Gassed
51605	Private	HOGARTH, G. H.	
1664	Private	HOLLAND, L. A.	
911	L/Corporal	HOLLAND, R. G.	Wounded
1311	Private	HOLLEY, J.	
51606	Private	HOLLINGSWORTH, S. S.	

Reg'tal No.	Rank	Name	Casualty
2084	Private	HOLLIS, E.	Wounded
2635A	Private	HOLMES, A. F.	Wounded
478	Corporal	HOLMES, C. A.	Wounded
	Lieutenant	HOLMES, T. J.	
2250	Private	HOLMES, W.	
5391	Private	HOLSTON, W. O.	Wounded
1697	Private	HOLWELL, H. G.	
470	Private	HOLYHEAD, C. E.	
4060	Private	HOPE, L.	
912	Private	HOPKINS, F. A.	Wounded
2316	Private	HOPKINS, F. W.	
2697	Private	HOPKINS, H. J. M.	
2836	Private	HORAN, C.	
2839	Private	HORAN, E.	
2840	Private	HORAN, R.	Wounded
2570	Private	HORKINGS, R.	
54681	Private	HORNE, A.	
677A	Private	HORNE, G. G.	
1319	Corporal	HOROBIN, W.	
2830	Private	HORTON, W. J.	Wounded
R.1999	Private	HOSKING, T.	
2564	Private	HOSKINS, R. M.	Killed in Action
3310	Private	HOUSTON, C.	
2676	Private	HOWARD, A. W.	Wounded
3080	Private	HOWARD, H. F.	
3317A	Private	HOWARD, K.	
3078	Private	HOWE, W. H.	Wounded
473	Private	HOWELL, E. B.	Gassed
474	Private	HOWELL, E. J.	Died of Wounds
1667	Private	HOWELL, R.	
51600	Private	HOWES, T. E.	
130	L/Sergeant	HOWSE, C. W.	
	Lieutenant	HOWSON, B. C.	Wounded
475	Private	HOY, F. A.	
2764	Sergeant	HUBBARD, F. H.	Wounded
2102	Private	HUBBARD, L. H.	
6039	Private	HUDGSON, A. L.	
6113	Private	HUDLESTON, F.	Wounded
51607	Private	HUDSON, A.	

Reg'tal No.	Rank	Name	Casualty
1585	Private	HUDSON, J.	Wounded
7559	Private	HUDSON, R. I.	Wounded
2443	Private	HUGGET, H.	
3314	Private	HUGHES, A.	
131	Private	HUGHES, E. M.	
1318	Private	HUGHES, E. W.	Wounded
6999	Private	HUGHES, H.	Gassed
913	Private	HUGHES, H. N.	
2085	Private	HUGHES, H. W.	
1308	Private	HUGHES, J. R. E.	
1847	Private	HUGHES, T.	Killed in Action
1857	Private	HULGRAVE, H. A.	
51597	2nd Corporal	HULME, S. E.	
914	Sergeant	HUME, W. J.	Wounded
6040	Private	HUMPHREY, E.	
2766	Sergeant	HUMPHREY, C. F.	
479	Private	HUMPHREYS, W.	
1185	Corporal	HUNKIN, C. E.	Wounded
2409	Private	HUNT, D. F.	
915	Private	HUNT, E. G.	
2918	Private	HUNT, H. H.	
7012	Private	HUNT, J.	
471	Private	HUNTER, D. R.	Wounded
51608	Private	HUNTER, J. A.	
1317	Private	HUNTER, J. B.	
480	Corporal	HUNTER, J. W.	Wounded
1849	Private	HUNTER, W. R.	Died of Wounds
6022	L/Corporal	HUNTLEY, J. A.	
3079	Private	HURREN, J. A.	Wounded
2767	Private	HURST, C. P.	Killed in Action
1314	Private	HUTCHEON, A.	Wounded
1315	Private	HUTCHEON, A.	
134	Private	HUTCHINS, J. G.	Gassed
2320	Private	HUTCHINSON, E.	
	Major	HUTTON, C. R.	
2828	Private	HUTTON, W.	
263	Sergeant	HYDE, C.	
1306	Private	HYDE, E. E.	Wounded
908	Private	IBBOT, F. H.	

Reg'tal No.	Rank	Name	Casualty
916	Private	ILLIG, G. A.	
917	Private	ILLIG, S. G.	Gassed
4063	Private	INGLIS, F. N.	Killed in Action
51612	Private	INGRAM, J. W.	
2698	Private	IRELAND, E. R.	Wounded
1323	Private	IRELAND, W. C.	Wounded
10629	L/Corporal	IRETON, M. C.	
2574	Sergeant	IRONMONGER, H. C.	
2575	Private	IRVINE, H.	Killed in Action
51613	Private	IRVING, S. L.	
918	Private	IRWIN, A. J.	Wounded
482	Corporal	IRWIN, J. R.	Wounded
1052A	Private	IVORY, W. E.	
2567	Private	JACK, A.	Wounded
2095	Corporal	JACKA, E. L. K.	
51618	Private	JACKSON, G.	
26681	Corporal	JACKSON, J. W. H.	
1328	Private	JACKSON, S.	
6043	Private	JACKSON, S. J.	Wounded
1668	Sergeant	JACKSON, T. G.	Wounded
919	Private	JACKSON, W. J.	
1852	Driver	JAGGAR, C. C. K.	
7266	Private	JAMES, C. P.	
2324	Private	JAMES, E.	
135	Private	JAMES, G. H.	Wounded
485	Private	JAMES, H.	
	Lieutenant	JAMES, H. J.	
3085	Private	JAMES, R. T.	
3086	Private	JAMES, W. E.	
6029	Driver	JAMIESON, B.	
	Lieutenant	JAMIESON, E. A.	
6045	Private	JAMIESON, J. A.	Died of Wounds
487	Private	JEFFERY, A. E.	
4561	Private	JEFFERY, W. G.	Wounded
2723	Private	JEFFERYS, G.	
810	Corporal	JEFFERYS, N. V.	Wounded
3170	Private	JEFFERYS, T. H.	
136	Private	JENKINS, J.	Wounded
51621	Private	JENKINS, J.	

Reg'tal No.	Rank	Name	Casualty
5412	Private	JENKINS, N. L.	Wounded
1329	Private	JENKINS, S. S.	Gassed
51617	Private	JENKINS, W.	
1330	L/Corporal	JENKINS, W. C.	Died of Wounds
6293	Private	JENNETT, G. W.	Wounded
143	Private	JENNINGS, H.	
1331	Private	JENNINGS, L. R.	
297	Private	JEPSON, R. J.	
51619	Private	JERAM, S. L.	
2325	Private	JERROM, R. C.	
1669	Private	JEWELL, R. H.	Wounded
	Lieutenant	JEWKES, W. G.	Died of Wounds
489	Private	JOEL, M. S.	Wounded
6946	Private	JOHANNSEN, H. N.	
3324	Private	JOHANSSON, A. J.	
4694	Sergeant	JOHNSON, A. C.	
920	Private	JOHNSON, A. E.	Wounded
3325	Private	JOHNSON, A. R.	
2106	Private	JOHNSON, A. V.	
488	C.S.M.	JOHNSON, H.	Wounded
3322	Private	JOHNSON, J.	
1332	Private	JOHNSON, L. J.	Killed in Action
2845	Private	JOHNSON, T.	
3245	Private	JOHNSON, W. S.	Wounded
51623	Private	JOHNSTON, A.	
486	Private	JOHNSTON, J. E.	Wounded
	Lieutenant	JOHNSTON, R. A.	
679	Private	JOHNSTONE, A. G. E.	
743	Private	JOHNSTONE, C. W.	Wounded
51622	Private	JOLLIE, A.	
6292	L/Sergeant	JONES, A. B.	
2844	Private	JONES, A. E. C.	Wounded
3084	Private	JONES, C.	
915	Private	JONES, C. A.	
2323	Private	JONES, D. H.	Wounded
1326	Private	JONES, E. G.	
1325	Private	JONES, H.	
45084	Private	JONES, H. W. T.	
1324	Private	JONES, J. H.	

Reg'tal No.	Rank	Name	Casualty
6892	Private	JONES, J. H.	
921	Private	JONES, P.	Died of Wounds
484	Private	JONES, W.	
490	Driver	JONES, W. F.	Wounded
137	Private	JONES, W. J.	Killed in Action
6030	Private	JORDAN, A. J.	
8003	Private	JORGENSON, H. J.	
3087	Private	JUDGE, E. G.	
1327	L/Corporal	JULIAN, L.	Killed in Action
922	Private	JURY, W. C.	Wounded
2582	Private	KABLE, P. G.	Killed in Action
436A	Private	KANE, J.	
138	Private	KANE, J. W.	
1333	Private	KANE, N. L.	
923	Private	KARLLSTROM, G.	Died of Wounds
2411	Private	KAUFFMAN, M. O.	
	Captain	KAUFMAN, H.	
1670	Private	KAY, W. J.	Wounded
2098	L/Corporal	KEAM, W. M.	Wounded
6051	Private	KEARNEY, W.	
2097	Private	KEARNS, W. H. A.	Wounded
144	Private	KEATING, J. P. A.	Killed in Action
498	Private	KEEGAN, R. J.	Died of Wounds
51629	Private	KEENE, E. C.	
1335	Corporal	KEILLER, A.	
1334	Driver	KEILLER, T. F.	
2848	Private	KELLS, R. F.	
1671	Private	KELLY, A.	
922	Private	KELLY, A. N.	
495	Corporal	KELLY, J.	Wounded
1854	L/Corporal	KELLY, J.	Killed in Action
1855	Private	KELLY, J.	Gassed
3327	Private	KELLY, S.	
	Lieutenant	KENLEY, F. R.	
491	Driver	KENNEDY, J.	Wounded
924	Private	KENNEDY, J. J.	
	Lieutenant	KENNEDY, K. G.	
2099	Private	KENNEDY, P. A.	Wounded
2580	Private	KENNEDY, P. F.	Gassed

Reg'tal No.	Rank	Name	Casualty
2846	Private	KENNETT, S.	Wounded
139	Private	KENNY, E. J.	
497	Private	KENNY, J. P.	
6052	Private	KENT, A. A.	Killed in Action
51630	Private	KERBY, N.	
2412	Private	KERR, A. H.	
3332	Private	KERR, J. W. B.	
496	Driver	KEY, W. H.	
3089	Private	KICK, A. S.	
1948	Private	KILFOYLE, A. J.	Wounded
925	Private	KILLKELLY, J. P.	Killed in Action
2327	Private	KIMPTON, A. J.	Wounded
2413	Private	KINCADE, R.	
3091	Private	KINCADE, T. J.	Wounded
492	Private	KINDRED, G. H.	Wounded
51628	Private	KING, A. W.	
579	Private	KING, R.	Died of Illness
3328	Private	KING, T. J.	
6138	Private	KIPPING, A. J.	Wounded
4150	Corporal	KIRKPATRICK, G. A.	Died of Wounds
2100	Private	KIRWAN, P. E.	Wounded
145	Corporal	KISLER, W. J.	Killed in Action
493	Sergeant	KITCHEN, R. H.	Gassed
3088	Private	KNELL, W. G.	Wounded
42A	Private	KNIGHT, A. H.	
51627	Private	KNIGHT, G. G.	
499	Private	KNIGHT, H. H.	Wounded
51565	Private	KNIGHT, L. V.	
3090	Private	KNIGHT, T.	
2326	Private	KNIVETT, T. J.	Wounded
494	Sergeant	KOHLER, R. C.	
3326	Private	KRUG, C. W.	
1202	Sergeant	KYLE, L. G. C.	Killed in Action
2592	Private	LACEY, O.	
319	Sergeant	LACEY, V. R.	
2589	Private	LACOCK, J.	
508	L/Corporal	LAIDLOW, O. M.	Wounded
2594	Private	LAIRD, C.	Killed in Action
2595	Private	LALLY, P.	

Reg'tal No.	Rank	Name	Casualty
3092	Private	LAMB, C. H.	Killed in Action
1344	Private	LAMBERT, A.	
1859	Private	LAMBERT, E. W.	Wounded
	Captain	LAMBLE, R.	
2889	Corporal	LAMONT, W.	
2105	Private	LANDY, A. R.	Died of Wounds
3096	Private	LANE, G. A.	
507	Private	LANG, C. J.	Wounded
147	Private	LANGE, G. A	Wounded
146	Private	LANGE, P.	
927	Private	LANGFORD, D. S.	Wounded
811	L/Corporal	LANGTON, E. J.	Wounded
501	Private	LANIGAN, R. E.	Killed in Action
148	Private	LARKIN, T. M.	Gassed
733	Corporal	LARKIN, W. L.	
680	Private	LARSEN, O. S.	Gassed
2586	Private	LATTA, B. R.	Wounded
500	Private	LAURENT, A. E.	Killed in Action
928	Private	LAVARS, J. H.	
1221	Private	LAW, W. J.	
3818	Private	LAWLER, W. C.	
510	Private	LAWRENCE, F. G. W.	
2831A	Private	LAWRENCE, W. C.	Killed in Action
2101	Private	LAWRENCE, W. McL.	
2769	Private	LAWSON, S. T.	
2589	Private	LAYCOCK, J.	Wounded
10635	Private	LAYCOCK, W. T.	
1675	Private	LEAHY, J. D.	
	Lieutenant	LEE, A. J. B.	Wounded
512	Private	LEE, J. H.	
2699	Private	LEE, P. G.	
51635	Private	LEE, W. T. R.	
1861	Private	LEERSON, A. H.	Wounded
	Lieutenant	LE FEVRE, S.	Killed in Action
2849	Private	LEHEY, A. S.	
1996	Signaller	LEIDLE, L. H.	Gassed
3329	Private	LEIGH, L.	
509	Private	LEIGH, V. L.	Killed in Action
1856	Private	LEIGHTON, G. E.	

NOMINAL ROLL

Reg'tal No.	Rank	Name	Casualty
1857	Private	LEIGHTON, V. H. T.	Wounded
2587	Private	LEMON, H. A.	Wounded
511	Private	LENG, D.	
	Lieutenant	LENTON, R. M.	Wounded
1938	Private	LEPP, A. N.	Gassed
2588	Private	LESLIE, B. L.	
3331	Private	LEVEILLE, E.	
929	Private	LEVER, E. C.	
505	Sergeant	LEVY, A.	Killed in Action
4567	Private	LEWIS, C. W.	Died of Wounds
	Captain	LEWIS, E.	
2106A	Corporal	LEWIS, E. A.	
7256	Private	LEWIS, H. H.	
1875	Private	LEWIS, J. A.	
1331	Corporal	LEWIS, J. A.	
930	Private	LEWIS, W. C.	Wounded
1029	Private	LIDDICOAT, C. J.	Wounded
6537	Private	LIDSEY, A. W. J.	
2329	Private	LIERSCH, G. A.	Killed in Action
3094	Private	LILLEY, A. E.	
513	Private	LILLEY, J.	
1030	Private	LIMBOM, G.	
	Lieutenant	LINDEN, O. R.	
3332	Private	LINDSAY, A. A. J.	
1339	Private	LINDSAY, J. R. R.	Wounded
	Hon.Lieutenant	LINDSAY, W.	
2853	Private	LINTHORNE, F.	
2107	Private	LIPPIATT, C. M.	Killed in Action
2852	Private	LLOYD, F. H.	Wounded
1021	Private	LLOYD, J.	Killed in Action
3166	Private	LOAS, J.	
1337	Private	LOATES, A. T.	
2599	Private	LOCK, W. H.	
	Lieutenant	LOCKHART, N. J.	
1674	Private	LOFTS, A.	
1672	Private	LOFTS, A. L.	
151	Private	LOGAN, D. L.	Wounded
152	Private	LOMAS, H.	
3093	Private	LONG, A. G.	

Reg'tal No.	Rank	Name	Casualty
503	Private	LONG, R. J.	
1341	Arm. Sergeant	LONGTHORN, F. W.	
3095	Private	LONIE, W. H.	Wounded
153	Private	LONSDALE, S. W.	
6059	Private	LOOKER, E. A.	Killed in Action
504	Sergeant	LOONEY, O. J.	Wounded
3095	Private	LORD, A. F.	
3333	Private	LORD, A. R.	
154	Sergeant	LORENSINI, W. R.	Died of Illness
519	Private	LORIMER, R. A.	
1676	Private	LORRIMAN, G. W.	
12339	Private	LOTHIAN, J. G.	
2184	Private	LOUTTIT, J.	Wounded
2585	Private	LOVE, C. B.	Wounded
1336	Private	LOVETT, L. C.	Wounded
2934	Sergeant	LOW, J. S.	
1343	Private	LOWE, A. E.	Wounded
1340	L/Corporal	LOWE, F.	Wounded
2593	Private	LOWE, N. L.	Wounded
	Lieutenant	LOWE, W. B.	
2104	Private	LOWE, W. E.	
6294	Private	LOWEN, P. A.	
2181	Sergeant	LOXTON, C.	Wounded
2108	Private	LUMSDEN, J.	Died of Wounds
1346	Private	LUNN, P. F. J.	
1347	Private	LUNN, S. H. L.	
7052	Private	LUNT, A. J.	Wounded
2591	Private	LUNT, E.	
1338	Private	LUSHER, A. L.	Wounded
2700	Private	LYNCH, J. J.	Killed in Action
155	Sergeant	LYNCH, P. J.	Killed in Action
2851	Private	LYNN, R. J.	Wounded
506	Sergeant	LYONS, J.	Wounded
1677	Private	LYTHGO, F. W.	
3330	Private	LYTHGO, R. M.	Wounded
1874	Private	MABBITT, N. B.	Died of Wounds
2916	Private	MACEY, F. L.	
3252	Sergeant	MACDERMOTT, W. E.	
2608	Private	MacGEACHIE, A. N.	Wounded

NOMINAL ROLL

Reg'tal No.	Rank	Name	Casualty
266	Private	MacGREGOR, D. M.	Wounded
156	L/Corporal	MACKAY, D.	Gassed
	Lieutenant	MACKAY, D. G.	Died of Wounds
265	L/Corporal	MACKAY, G. R.	
3347A	L/Corporal	MACKAY, K. M.	
1687	Private	MACKAY, R.	
	Lieutenant	MACKAY, R.	
	Lieutenant	MACKENZIE, D.	Wounded
51612	Private	MACKINTOSH, R. F.	
2188	Corporal	MacLEAN, D.	Wounded
2099A	Private	MacVEAN, W. H.	Wounded
178	Private	MAGILL, J. G. N.	Wounded
2331	Private	MAGILL, L. G.	Gassed
3348	Private	MAGSON, W.	Wounded
1867	Private	MAGUIRE, P. T.	Killed in Action
636	Private	MAIDMENT, G. N.	Wounded
940	Private	MAIN, E. E.	Wounded
1350	Private	MAKEHAM, C. R.	
2439	Private	MAKIN, W. E.	
2109	Corporal	MALIN, L. J.	Died of Wounds
2602	Private	MALLETT, C. F.	
3343	Private	MALLETT, H. E.	
941	Private	MALLETT, L. G.	
2110	Sergeant	MALONE, M.	Wounded
2111	Private	MALONEY, L.	
1358	Private	MALONEY, J.	
1357	Private	MANN, C. A.	Wounded
3171	Corporal	MANN, L.	
3526	Private	MANSFIELD, V. W. P.	
2765	L/Corporal	MANSON, W. N. E.	Died of Wounds
1956	Private	MAPLEBACK, J. J.	
2866	Private	MARFLEET, W.	
672	Private	MARION, G.	
2116	Private	MARNER, A. J.	Killed in Action
2117	Private	MARNER, J. S.	Wounded
2118	Private	MARNER, R. G.	Wounded
	2nd Lieutenant	MARQUIS, S. C.	
729	Private	MARSH, D. M. W.	
3097	Private	MARSHALL, A. E.	

Reg'tal No.	Rank	Name	Casualty
942	Private	MARSHALL, C. S.	Wounded
3343	Private	MARSHALL, G.	
521	Private	MARSHALL, G.	Killed in Action
2335	Private	MARSHALL, J. T.	
943	Private	MARTIN, A. C.	
1355	Private	MARTIN, A. P.	
944	Private	MARTIN, F. J.	Wounded
523	Private	MARTIN, F. S.	
179	Private	MARTIN, G.	Killed in Action
945	Private	MARTIN, J. A.	
2868	Private	MARTIN, J. C.	
526	L/Sergeant	MARTIN, R. G.	
1683	Private	MARTIN, T. W.	Killed in Action
1950	Private	MARTIN, T. W.	Killed in Action
54002	Private	MARTIN, W. J.	
517	Private	MARTLAND, L. C.	Wounded
2603	L/Corporal	MASCORD, P. J.	Wounded
	Lieutenant	MASON, C. T.	
3337	Private	MASON, W. H.	
158	Private	MATHESON, J. McP.	Wounded
2432	Private	MATHESON, M. A.	
6063	Private	MATHESON, W. H.	Wounded
51657	Private	MATSON, H. J.	
3169	Private	MATTHEWS, A. L.	
2402	Private	MATTHEWS, H.	
159	Private	MATTHEWS, L. W.	Wounded
4136	Sergeant	MATTHEWS, R. J.	Killed in Action
2598	Private	MATTHEWS, W. H.	Wounded
160	Private	MATTHEWS, W. J.	Died of Wounds
3101	Private	MAULDON, J. A.	Wounded
3338	Private	MAXHAM, A. R.	
946	Private	MAXWELL, G. E.	Wounded
947	Corporal	MAXWELL, H. G.	Wounded
948	Private	MAXWELL, L. A.	Killed in Action
	Lieutenant	MAXWELL, M.	Wounded
1869	Private	MAYES, W. K.	
3344	Private	MAYNARD, C. J.	
6065	Private	MAYNARD, E. H.	Wounded
2112	Private	MEADE, E. J.	Wounded

Reg'tal No.	Rank	Name	Casualty
2862	Private	MEADS, E.	
7061	Private	MEADOWS, B.	Wounded
2332	Private	MEAGHER, J. P.	Killed in Action
1975	Private	MEEHAN, P.	
3108	Private	MELDRUM, L. R.	
6067	Private	MELLISH, E. J.	Killed in Action
7060	Corporal	MENAGH, R. A. H.	
3102	Private	MEREDITH, G.	
949	Private	MEREWEATHER, F. A.	
1868	Private	MEREWEATHER, W.	Wounded
162	Private	MERIFIELD, W.	Died of Illness
2597	Private	MERKEL, M.	Wounded
3347	Private	MEYER, L. A.	
3876	Private	MICALLEF, S. P.	
	Captain	MIDDLETON, D. F.	
518	L/Corporal	MILDREN, A. A.	Killed in Action
519	Private	MILDREN, C. J.	
950	Private	MILDREN, W.	
951	Corporal	MILES, E. J. L. B.	Wounded
2861	Private	MILES, F. T.	Died of Wounds
	Lieutenant	MILES, H. F.	Killed in Action
3336	Private	MILES, H. H.	
1680	Private	MILES, L. R.	
2113	Private	MILES, W. R.	Wounded
1678	Private	MILLAR, R. J.	
1871	Private	MILLARD, W.	Wounded
2768	Private	MILLEN, R. W.	
164	Private	MILLER, A. F.	Died of Illness
812	Private	MILLER, A. H.	
1348	Private	MILLER, A. P.	
3098	Private	MILLER, A. T.	Wounded
1359	Corporal	MILLER, C.	
1353	Private	MILLER, C. V.	
1686	Private	MILLER, F.	
165	Corporal	MILLER, G. D.	Wounded
1862	L/Corporal	MILLER, H.	
2863	Private	MILLER, J.	
2915	Private	MILLER, R. J.	
1685	Private	MILLER, S.	

Reg'tal No.	Rank	Name	Casualty
1351	Private	MILLER, W. F.	Wounded
952	Private	MILLERSHIP, R. L.	
166	C.Q.M.S.	MILLS, B. H.	
1901	Private	MILLS, H. P.	Wounded
1863	Private	MILLS, V. J.	
1356	L/Corporal	MILLWARD, H. W. J.	
939	Corporal	MILNER, A. E.	
953	Private	MILNER, C.	Gassed
954	Private	MILTON, C. F.	
7034	Private	MISSEN, J.	
525	Private	MITCHELL, C.	
	Lieutenant	MITCHELL, F. R.	Wounded
2701	Private	MITCHELL, J. T.	
6068	Private	MITCHELL, R. E. H.	Killed in Action
955	Private	MITCHELL, T. T.	Wounded
2414	Private	MITCHELL, W. E.	Killed in Action
167	Private	MITCHELL, W. J.	Wounded
51654	Private	MOLLOY, P. J.	
168	L/Sergeant	MOLLOY, W. L.	Killed in Action
1358	Private	MOLONEY, J.	
1352	Private	MOLONEY, W. P.	
319	Private	MONAHAN, P. J.	
51649	Private	MONAHAN, R.	
18738	Private	MONAHAN, R. S.	
789	C.S.M.	MOORE, A. R.	Killed in Action
515	L/Sergeant	MOORE, G. F.	Wounded
267	Private	MOORE, H. W. G.	Died of Illness
1349	Private	MOORE, L.	
169	Private	MOORE, R. J.	Wounded
3422	Private	MOORE, R. M.	
	Chaplain	MOORE, W. A.	
2333	Private	MOORE, W. H.	Killed in Action
51650	Private	MORAN, W.	
4206	Private	MORAN, W.	
956	Private	MORCOM, H. R.	
3443	Private	MORCOM, R. S.	
2114	Private	MORECOMBE, W.	Wounded
514	Private	MORELAND, H. F.	Wounded
2200	Private	MORGAN, C. H.	Wounded

Reg'tal No.	Rank	Name	Casualty
958	Private	MORGAN, D. O.	
6779	Private	MORGAN, E.	Wounded
6318	Private	MORGAN, T. H.	Wounded
4571	Private	MORGAN, W. L.	
1951	L/Sergeant	MORIARTY, F.	
6069	Private	MORLEY, G. W.	Wounded
51651	Corporal	MORLEY, W.	
520	Private	MORLEY, W. L.	Wounded
171	Private	MORLEY, W. S.	
4088	Private	MORONEY, L. F.	
1361	Private	MORPHETT, H. G.	
722A	Private	MORRIS, E. G.	
959	Private	MORRIS, F.	
1679	Private	MORRIS, F. P.	
2330	Private	MORRIS, J. R.	Died of Illness
3106	Private	MORRIS, S. W.	
960	Private	MORRIS, W. C.	
2193	Private	MORRISON, A. J.	Wounded
2867	Private	MORRISON, U. A. DeB.	
2116	L/Sergeant	MORRISON, E. Mc.	
2432	Private	MORRISS, A. C.	
172	Private	MORRISSEY, J.	
1736	Private	MORRISSEY, J.	
961	Private	MORROW, H.	Wounded
	Lieutenant	MORROW, H. G.	
175	Private	MORTON, J. C.	
	Lieutenant	MORTON, J. H.	
173	Private	MORTON, L.	Killed in Action
1962	Private	MOSELY, H.	Killed in Action
3107	Private	MOSS, E. H.	
1682	Private	MOTT, C.	
2421	Private	MOTT, R. J.	Wounded
3439	Private	MOTTERAM, R. H.	
1873	Private	MOTTRAM, J. F.	Wounded
1681	Private	MOUNSEY, F.	
2864	Private	MOUNTFORD, J. E.	
3341	Private	MOXOM, N. L.	
962	Private	MOY, A. W.	Died of Wounds
477A	Private	MOY, C. J.	Wounded

Reg'tal No.	Rank	Name	Casualty
174	Private	MOYES, W.	
524	L/Corporal	MOYLAN, B. A.	Wounded
	Lieutenant	MOYLE, F. H.	
3334	Private	MUDFORD, R. S.	
2127A	Private	MUIR, G. F.	Killed in Action
2596	Private	MULHOLLAND, E.	Gassed
2401	Private	MULLANE, L.	Killed in Action
2334	Private	MULLER, E. A.	
2117	Private	MULLEY, E. W.	Wounded
516	Private	MULLINS, J. F.	
4572	Private	MULVAHIL, J. A.	Killed in Action
2118	Private	MUNRO, D.	Died of Wounds
1025	Private	MUNRO, J.	
51653	Private	MUNRO, M.	
2199	Private	MUNRO, W.	Wounded
963	Private	MURDOCH, J. L.	
3106	Private	MURPHY, G.	
3105	Private	MURPHY, J. M.	
1360	Driver	MURPHY, J. P.	Killed in Action
3100	Private	MURPHY, M. T.	Wounded
176	Private	MURPHY, T. F.	
1367	Private	MURPHY, T. J.	
	Captain	MURRAY, A. J.	
3421	Private	MURRAY, C. W.	
2911	L/Corporal	MURRAY, F. J.	Wounded
2865	E.R. Sergeant	MURRAY, W. H.	
177	Private	MURRELL, A. L.	
3099	Private	MURRELL, H. E.	Killed in Action
3346	Private	MUSTER, E.	
522	Private	MUTCH, E. J.	
1870	Sergeant	MUTTON, R. H.	
6783	Private	MYALL, A.	Wounded
681	Private	MYERS, G. E.	
964	Private	MYERS, L. G.	
2336	Private	McADAM, C. L. H.	Killed in Action
2682	Private	McALISTER, D.	Died of Wounds
7381	Private	McALISTER, A. M.	
7351	Private	McALLISTER, G. J.	
3113	Private	McALLISTER, J. A.	Wounded

Reg'tal No.	Rank	Name	Casualty
3117	Private	McALLISTER, K.	Wounded
1366	Sergeant	McANALLY, G. F.	Killed in Action
	Lieutenant	McARTHUR, A. D.	Wounded
799	Sergeant	McARTHUR, N. A.	Wounded
188	S/Sergeant	McBAIN, A. K.	
5493	Private	McBAIN, J. H.	
530	Private	McCABE, J.	
536	Corporal	McCALLUM, A. J.	Died of Wounds
541	Private	McCANN, E. H. M.	Wounded
3185	Private	McCARTHY, C. A.	Gassed
2424	Private	McCARTHY, F.	Wounded
527	Private	McCASHNEY, J. H.	Wounded
	Lieutenant	McCAUL, A. C.	
2855	Private	McCAW, G. H.	Wounded
931	Private	McCLEERY, A. C.	
932	Private	McCLOSKEY, J. E.	
538	Private	McCLYMONT, C. R.	
534	Private	McCOLL, A. J.	Died of Wounds
187	Private	McCOLL, R. C.	Gassed
3109	Private	McCONACHY, L. J.	
933	Private	McCONACHY, S. L.	Killed in Action
2856	Private	McCONNELL, W.	
1690	Private	McCORMACK, W. R.	
180	Private	McCUBBIN, W. A.	
2272	Signaller	McCULLOCH, E. H.	Wounded
6549	Private	McCULLOCH, R. G.	Wounded
2763A	Private	McCULLOCH, B. O.	Wounded
2609	Private	McCURDIE, J.	
2854	Private	McDAVITT, G. L.	
2337	Corporal	McDONALD, A.	Wounded
6072	Private	McDONALD, A.	
1368	Private	McDONALD, C. K.	
2415	Private	McDONALD, C. P.	
6062	Driver	McDONALD, E. R.	
1189	Corporal	McDONALD, H.	
	Lieutenant	McDONALD, H. N. R.	Wounded
2120	Corporal	McDONALD, I.	Killed in Action
940	Private	McDONALD, L.	
934	Private	McDONALD, N.	Wounded

Reg'tal No.	Rank	Name	Casualty
3342	Private	McDONALD, W.	
51644	Private	McDONALD, W. F.	
1692	Private	McDONALD, W. J.	
3427	Private	McDONALD, W. J.	
3345	Private	McELHINNEY, D. R.	
1432	Sergeant	McELHINNEY, G. M.	
1694	Private	McERVALE, J. L.	
1695	Private	McERVALE, I. T.	
3118	Private	McEVOY, A.	
6074	Private	McEVOY, T.	Wounded
	Lieutenant	McEWAN, F. J.	Wounded
2858	Private	McEWAN, T.	
181	Private	McFARLANE, D.	
51639	Private	McGOWAN, G. D.	
935	Private	McGRATH, J. W.	Wounded
2860	Private	McGRAW, J.	
3110	Private	McGREE, W. F.	
540	Private	McGREGOR, A. D.	
539	Private	McGREGOR, G. A.	
2857	Private	McGREGOR, H. R.	Wounded
535	Sergeant	McGREGOR, W. T.	Wounded
3111	Private	McGUIRE, T. W.	
2121	Private	McHARG, A. G.	Killed in Action
51645	Private	McINTOSH, D.	
537	Private	McINTYRE, E. H.	
1872	Private	McINTYRE, J. R.	
3207	Sergeant	McINTYRE, P. J.	
2122	Private	McIVER, C. G.	Died of Illness
2611	Private	McKAY, D. L.	Killed in Action
3112	Private	McKAY, R. M.	Wounded
3115	Private	McKAY, W. L.	
5711	Private	McKEAN, H. H.	Wounded
1370	Private	McKECHNIE, J. N.	Wounded
4587	Private	McKENNA, T. J.	Killed in Action
1363	L/Corporal	McKENRY, J.	
2123	Private	McKENRY, J. H. G. S.	Wounded
2605	Sergeant	McKENZIE, A.	Wounded
268	Private	McKENZIE, A.	
2859	Private	McKENZIE, A.	Killed in Action

Reg'tal No.	Rank	Name	Casualty
2914	Private	McKENZIE, A. A.	Killed in Action
6078	Private	McKENZIE, A. W. F.	Wounded
532	Private	McKENZIE, D. D.	Killed in Action
1362	L/Corporal	McKENZIE, R. G.	Died of Wounds
184	Private	McKENZIE, W.	
3339	Private	McKENZIE, W. H.	
1369	Private	McKERRY, F. D.	
528	Private	McKINNEY, G. W.	
529	Private	McKINNEY, J. J. H.	
1877	Private	McLAINE, D. J.	Killed in Action
936	Private	McLAREN, E.	
182	Private	McLAREN, J.	Died of Wounds
1879	Private	McLAUGHLIN, C. M.	Wounded
533	Private	McLAUGHLIN, P. A.	
937	Private	McLAUGHLIN, T.	Wounded
51647	Private	McLEAN, A. R.	
51646	Private	McLEAN, D. H.	
1689	Private	McLEAN, N. L.	Killed in Action
2338	Private	McLEAN, R. N.	Killed in Action
2124	Private	McLELLAN, J.	Wounded
1878	Private	McLEOD, H. H.	Wounded
4583	Private	McLINDEN, A. D.	Wounded
51643	Private	McMAHON, J.	
6055	L/Corporal	McMAHON, J. J.	
2606	Private	McMAHON, O.	Gassed
1691	Private	McMAHON, T.	Wounded
1880	Private	McMASTER, D.	Wounded
1881	Private	McMASTER, D.	
3116	Private	McMASTER, R. J.	
1693	Corporal	McMILLAN, J.	Wounded
1364	Private	McMULLIN, G.	Killed in Action
1365	Private	McMURTRIE, G.	Wounded
2604	Private	McNALLEY, J.	Wounded
2612	Private	McNAMARA, J. W.	Wounded
451A	Private	McNAMARA, P.	
2340	Driver	McNAMARA, T. J.	Died of Illness
2610	Private	McNEVIN, W. A.	
938	Private	McNISH, J.	Killed in Action
4586	Private	McNIVEN, A.	

Reg'tal No.	Rank	Name	Casualty
1883	Private	McPHERSON, A. S.	
1952	Private	McROSS, C. M.	Wounded
51640	Private	McROSTIE, J. N. J.	
939	Private	McWATERS, P.	Wounded
	Lieutenant	NARIK, E. F.	
2677	Private	NASH, E. S. R.	
3345	C.S.M.	NATHAN, P. J. H.	
3122	Private	NAYLOR, J.	Wounded
51661	Private	NAYLOR, J. H.	
391	L/Corporal	NAYLOR, J. J.	Died of Wounds
1884	Private	NAYLOR, W. T.	Killed in Action
1885	Private	NEAL, A.	Wounded
543	Private	NEANDER, J.	Wounded
1997	Private	NEGRI, R. W.	Wounded
	Lieutenant	NEILSON, P.	Wounded
546	L/Corporal	NELSON, C. P.	Wounded
3120	Private	NELSON, D.	
193	Sergeant	NELSON, J. DeM.	Wounded
3121	Private	NEVILL, W. J.	Killed in Action
2423	Sergeant	NEVILLE, W. L.	
3350	Private	NEWCOMBE, A. P. H.	
3354	Private	NEWCOMBE, E. G.	
2125	Private	NEWELL, E. R.	Died of Wounds
1697	Private	NEWEY, C. H.	
2422	Private	NEWEY, N. C.	
1696	Private	NEWERY, L. P.	Wounded
2613	Private	NEWLYN, F. A.	Wounded
194	Corporal	NEWMAN, G. A. A.	
3351	Private	NEWMAN, W. J.	
1703	Private	NEWSON, J.	
195	L/Corporal	NEWTON, A.	
1700	Private	NEWTON, C. H.	Killed in Action
3540	Private	NEWTON, F. O.	
2343	Private	NEWTON, L. C.	
2699	Sergeant	NEWTON, N.	
196	Private	NEWTON, W. J.	
4588	Private	NICHOLAS, C. E.	
	Lieutenant	NICHOLES, W. P.	Killed in Action
965	Private	NICHOLLS, G. E.	

Reg'tal No.	Rank	Name	Casualty
1866	Corporal	NICHOLLS, W. J.	Wounded
3119	Private	NIELSEN, V. L. W.	Killed in Action
1886	Private	NIMMO, J. A.	
544	Private	NINNIS, F. L.	
547	Private	NOLAN, J.	
542	Private	NOLAN, J.	
2130	Corporal	NOLL, H. A.	
51662	Private	NOONAN, J. J.	
197	Corporal	NOONAN, W. J.	Wounded
51663	Private	NORMAN, A.	
192	Private	NORTHCOTT, C. N.	Wounded
198	Sergeant	NORTHCOTT, R. R.	
7052	Private	NORTON, H. B.	
545	Private	NORTON, J. E.	
1953	Private	NORRIS, A. V.	Wounded
2342	Private	NOTTING, F. G.	
3839	Signaller	NOWLAN, L. T.	Wounded
1698	Private	NUNN, P.	
3349	Private	NUTH, W. T.	
51675	Private	OAKFORD, P.	
3124	Private	OAK, R. J.	
549	Private	OAKLEY, J. J.	
51670	Private	OAKLEY, W. L.	
2872	Private	OATLEY, G. McK.	
51671	Private	OATS, B. J.	
51668	Private	O'BRIEN, A.	
655A	L/Corporal	O'BRIEN, D. M.	
199	Private	O'BRIEN, J.	Killed in Action
389A	Private	O'CALLAGHAN, S. J.	
	Lieutenant	O'CARROLL, J. P.	
550	Corporal	O'CONNELL, D. D.	
1254	Private	O'CONNOR, D. T.	
2869	Private	O'CONNOR, F. J.	
2871	Private	O'CONNOR, J.	Wounded
1371	Sergeant	O'CONNOR, P. A.	Wounded
	Lieutenant	O'DEE, A. H. J.	
51672	Private	O'DEE, C. B.	
2344	Private	O'DOHERTY, H. K.	Gassed
6326	Private	O'DONOGHUE, D. J.	Wounded

Reg'tal No.	Rank	Name	Casualty
548	Sergeant	OEHM, N. W.	
2127	Private	OGDEN, J. M.	Gassed
1889	L/Corporal	O'KEEFE, W.	
551	Sergeant	OLIN, A. A.	Killed in Action
	Lieutenant	OLIVER, J. D.	Killed in Action
553	Sergeant	OLIVER, J. J.	
1204	Corporal	O'LOUGHLIN, T. C.	Wounded
966	Private	OLSEN, J. R.	Wounded
2618	Corporal	OLSON, A. V.	Wounded
2621	Private	O'MARA, S.	Wounded
2619	Private	O'NEALE, L.	Died of Illness
1888	Private	O'NEILL, H.	
637	Private	O'NEILL, J. S.	
3423	Private	ONSLOW, J. G.	
3007	Private	ORDERS, F. A.	
1887	Private	ORME, G.	Killed in Action
782	Corporal	ORMISTON, C.	
	Hon. Captain	ORNSTEIN, S. P.	
667	Private	O'RAFFERTY, M.	
272	L/Corporal	O'RORKE, H. M.	Wounded
1957	Corporal	ORR, F. J.	
1372	Private	ORR, T. S.	Wounded
552	Private	ORRICK, H. A. A.	
2933	Private	OSBORN, G. S.	Died of Wounds
51667	Private	OSBORNE, H. J.	
51669	Private	OSBORNE, J. A.	
967	Private	OSBORNE, S. E.	Wounded
3125	Private	O'SHANNESSY, V. R.	
2620	Private	O'SHEA, J. A.	
6327	Private	OUCHIRENKO, J.	Wounded
968	Private	OULD, H.	Wounded
969	Private	OVERALL, P.	Wounded
	Lieutenant	OVERTON, R. H.	Wounded
1373	Private	OWEN, J.	
6109	Private	OWENS, B.	Killed in Action
4592	Corporal	OWINS, T. G.	Killed in Action
2630	Private	PACKHAM, F. G.	
2128	Corporal	PACKHAM, H. C.	Gassed
3362	Private	PADGETT, A. W.	

NOMINAL ROLL

Reg'tal No.	Rank	Name	Casualty
970	Private	PAGE, A. W.	Wounded
2189	Sergeant	PAGELS, E. A.	Wounded
	Lieutenant	PAINTER, E. A.	
201	Corporal	PALMER, J. R.	Wounded
3128	Private	PALMER, R.	
4596	Private	PALMER, W. J.	
	Lieutenant	PALSTRA, W.	
2346	Private	PAPWORTH, J. L.	
554	Private	PARFREY, W. T.	
3357	Private	PARKE, J. H.	
54024	Private	PARKER, J. A.	
1898	L/Corporal	PARKER, P. G.	
1377	Private	PARKINSON, A. G.	
682	Private	PARMITER, J. J. W.	
2703	L/Corporal	PARRISH, A. E.	
202	Private	PARROT, L. H. C.	Wounded
971	Private	PARSONS, H.	
767	Private	PARSONS, J. H.	Wounded
4595	Private	PARTRIDGE, W.	
561	Private	PATCHETT, P. F.	
2880	Private	PATERSON, A.	
	Lieut.-Colonel	PATERSON, A. T.	Wounded
639	Private	PATERSON, G.	Killed in Action
2876	Private	PATERSON, H.	
2882	Private	PATERSON, J. D.	Wounded
	Lieutenant	PATERSON, W. J.	
1958	Private	PATIENCE, A.	
638	Private	PATRICK, R. A. H.	Died of Wounds
562	Private	PAYNE, R.	
51680	Private	PAYNE, R.	
2129	Private	PAYNTER, J. W.	Wounded
2874	L/Corporal	PEARCE, F. C.	
1954	Private	PEARCE, T. G. D.	Wounded
2130	Private	PEARSON, G. F.	Wounded
2622	Private	PEARSON, J.	Wounded
2879	Private	PEDLER, J. P.	
51679	Private	PEEL, A. J.	
51678	Private	PEIRCE, L. R.	
2131	Private	PEOPLES, J.	Wounded

Reg'tal No.	Rank	Name	Casualty
203	Private	PEPPERELL, C. G.	
1379	Private	PERCIVAL, C. E.	Wounded
563	Private	PERMEWAN, R. H. T.	Wounded
3358	Private	PERRIE, C. G.	
1375	Private	PERRY, A. D.	
2878	Private	PERRY, B. T.	
3360	Private	PERRY, F. R.	
3366	Private	PERRY, H.	
2624	Private	PERRY, L.	Died of Illness
1378	Private	PERRY, W. G.	
2347	Private	PETERS, A.	
204	Private	PETERSON, T	
557	Private	PETTETT, W. H.	
972	Private	PETTIFER, J.	Wounded
2132	Corporal	PHELAN, F. S.	Wounded
2887	Corporal	PHILLIPS, A. S.	
2202	Private	PHILLIPS, C.	Killed in Action
974	C.S.M.	PHILLIPS, D. A.	Wounded
975	Private	PHILLIPS, F.	
976	Corporal	PHILLIPS, F. I.	
3297	Private	PHILLIPS, G.	Wounded
2685	Private	PHILLIPS, H. V.	Wounded
2068	Private	PHILLIPS, T. D.	Wounded
	2nd Lieutenant	PHILLIPS, T. P.	
1896	Private	PHILLIPS, W. G.	Died of Wounds
205	Private	PHILLIPS, W. H.	Wounded
206	Private	PHILLIPS, W. R. H.	Wounded
2625	Signaller	PICKERING, E. J.	Gassed
3359	Private	PICKETT, C. T.	
6081	Private	PICKFORD, A.	Killed in Action
977	Private	PICKFORD, L. J.	Killed in Action
473A	Private	PIERSON, W. F.	Wounded
3363	Private	PIKE, C. S.	
1704	Private	PINFOLD, A. F.	
2704	Private	PLATT, J.	
565	Private	PLUSH, W. H.	
2877	Private	POHLSON, G. A.	
2873	Private	POLLARD, J.	
	Major	POLLARD, L. L.	

NOMINAL ROLL

Reg'tal No.	Rank	Name	Casualty
1897	Private	POLLOCK, W. G.	Killed in Action
558	Private	POLLOCK, W. H.	
3365	Private	PONTIN, G. V.	
564	Private	POPE, B. A.	
1891	Private	PORTER, J. R.	Wounded
269	Private	PORTER, R. J.	Wounded
3127	Private	PORTER, V. A.	Died of Wounds
1894	Private	PORTER, W.	Wounded
560	Private	POST, A. G.	Wounded
3364	L/Corporal	POTTER, G. L.	
1991	Private	POTTER, S. C. M.	
1374	Sergeant	POTTER, W. J.	
2875	Private	POW, A.	
978	Private	POWELL, D.	
	Lieutenant	POWELL, W. R.	Wounded
3355	Private	POWER, A. J.	
2345	Sergeant	POWER, F. T.	
1990	Private	PRAETZ, H. F.	
1705	Private	PRATT, J.	
559	Private	PRATT, J. M.	Wounded
979	Private	PREECE, H. P.	Killed in Action
	Lieutenant	PRENTICE, J. M.	Wounded
3130	Private	PRESCOTT, J. L.	Wounded
2893	Private	PRESHNER, M.	
980	Private	PRESTON, A. E.	Wounded
1376	Private	PRESTON, H. W.	
209	Private	PRESTON, J.	Wounded
1706	Private	PRESTON, S. B.	Wounded
566	Private	PRICE, E. A.	Wounded
2623	Private	PRICE, F.	Wounded
	Lieutenant	PRICE, H. J.	
3131	Private	PRICE, J.	Killed in Action
2884	Private	PRICE, W. G. N.	
210	Private	PRICKETT, J.	Wounded
683	Private	PRIESTMAN, F. J.	Wounded
2881	Private	PRINCE, H. J.	Wounded
4350	Private	PRITCHARD, C. R. W.	Died of Wounds
51681	Private	PROBIN, W. E.	
7284	Private	PUGH, F. R. H.	

Reg'tal No.	Rank	Name	Casualty
5891	Private	PUGH, J. W.	Died of Wounds
1893	Private	PULBROOK, J. G.	Wounded
3129	Private	PUMMEROY, A. C.	Wounded
3356	Private	PUNCH, A. E.	
1895	Private	PUNSHON, J. M.	Wounded
981	Private	PYKE, O.	Wounded
2886	S/Sergeant	QUEALY, W. V.	
4601	Private	QUICK, R.	Died of Illness
2885	Private	QUILL, T. J.	Wounded
3784	Private	QUIN, A. J.	
2348	Private	QUIN, W. C.	Killed in Action
567	L/Corporal	QUINN, A.	Wounded
211	Private	QUINN, A.	Wounded
1380	Private	QUINN, J. G.	
1381	Private	QUINN, M. A.	
2706	Private	QUINTON, H. A.	Killed in Action
2705	Private	QUINTON, W. J.	Died of Wounds
2355	Private	RAINSFORD, J.	Wounded
2626	Private	RAMSAY, A.	Wounded
	Lieutenant	RAMSAY, C. J. A.	Killed in Action
1905	Private	RANDALL, H. J.	Wounded
	Lieut.-Colonel	RANKINE, R.	
1709	Private	RANSON, V. L.	Wounded
4278	Private	RASMUSSEN, H. W.	
213	Corporal	RATHGEBER, F.	Wounded
212	Private	RATHGEBER, J. H.	Killed in Action
3374	Private	RATTRAY, G. W.	
4357	Private	RAWLE, F.	Wounded
51689	Private	RAYMER, L. E.	
1389	L/Corporal	REA, T. A.	Wounded
214	L/Sergeant	READ, A. G.	
51693	Private	READE, J. G.	
2628	Private	READER, T.	Wounded
3370	Private	REAH, H. M.	
570	Private	REDFEARN, J.	
578	Private	REDFERN, A. R.	
1707	Private	REDFERN, W. A.	
2888	Private	REDMAN, J.	
6087	Private	REEVES, J. J.	Wounded

NOMINAL ROLL

Reg'tal No.	Rank	Name	Casualty
1385	L/Corporal	REID, A. W.	
982	Private	REID, C. J.	
215	Sergeant	REID, E.	
4604	Private	REID, G. M.	
2357	Private	RENTOUL, A. J.	
582	Private	REYNOLDS, H. C.	Wounded
579	Private	REYNOLDS, W. J.	Wounded
51694	Private	RHODES, H. A.	
3140	Private	RHODES, J. S.	Wounded
2134	Private	RHOOK, A. J.	Wounded
2135	Private	RHOOK, H. J. W.	Died of Wounds
1899	Private	RIALLAND, A.	Wounded
1710	Private	RICE, H. G.	
1384	Private	RICE, J. W.	
3239	Private	RICH, S.	
2890	Private	RICHARDS, E. W.	Killed in Action
573	Private	RICHARDS, H. H.	Wounded
572	R.S.M.	RICHARDS, J. T.	Killed in Action
2425	Private	RICHARDS, P. C.	Killed in Action
	Lieutenant	RICHARDS, W.	Wounded
983	Private	RICHARDSON, E.	
576	Private	RICHARDSON, J. H.	
577	L/Corporal	RICHARDSON, R. C.	Wounded
2633	Private	RICKETTS, C. F.	Died of Wounds
	Lieutenant	RICKETTS, C. S. B.	Gassed
2681	Private	RICKETTS, R.	
2678	Private	RICKWOOD, G. H.	Wounded
581	Private	RIDD, J.	Gassed
984	Private	RIDDIFORD, C. V.	
585	L/Corporal	RIDDOCH, J.	
2349	Private	RIDGE, H.	Wounded
3372	Private	RIDGEWAY, W.	
561A	L/Corporal	RIDGWELL, J. E.	Killed in Action
2350	Private	RIGBY, W. A.	Gassed
2353	Private	RILEY, G.	Wounded
2182	Private	RINGIN, A.	Wounded
2358	Private	RIORDAN, E. J.	
1266	Sergeant	RISELEY, W. T.	
2360	Private	RITCHIE, A. W.	Wounded

Reg'tal No.	Rank	Name	Casualty
3424	Private	ROBENS, N. S.	Wounded
1902	Private	ROBINS, W.	
583	Corporal	ROBERTS, B. J.	Wounded
2627	Private	ROBERTS, F. H.	Wounded
1904	Private	ROBERTS, F. W.	
	Captain	ROBERTS, L.	Killed in Action
580	L/Corporal	ROBERTS, O.	Died of Wounds
3141	Private	ROBERTS, S. R.	
2441	Private	ROBERTS, T. P.	
1391	L/Corporal	ROBERTS, W. H.	Wounded
2887	Private	ROBERTSON, A.	Wounded
1383	Private	ROBERTSON, G. H.	
684A	Private	ROBERTSON, G. W.	
3133	Private	ROBERTSON, J.	
1708	Driver	ROBERTSON, J. H.	
6088	Private	ROBERTSON, P. L.	Killed in Action
985	Private	ROBERTSON, S. H.	Wounded
2428	Private	ROBERTSON, W.	
3367	Private	ROBERTSON, W. D.	
1902	Private	ROBINS, W.	Wounded
3006	Private	ROBINSON, A. B.	Killed in Action
51688	Private	ROBINSON, C. H.	
986	Private	ROBINSON, E.	
51690	Private	ROBINSON, F. T.	
	Lieutenant	ROBINSON, G.	
	Lieutenant	ROBINSON, H.	Wounded
584	Private	ROBINSON, J.	
586	C.Q.M.S.	ROBINSON, J. C.	
51686	Private	ROBINSON, R.	
987	Private	ROBINSON, T. G.	Wounded
2889	Corporal	ROBINSON, W.	
640	Private	RODGERS, G. D.	Wounded
1386	Sergeant	ROGAN, J. J.	Wounded
2138A	Private	ROGERS, A.	
3137	Private	ROHAN, J.	
2136	Private	ROLFE, H.	
1906	Private	ROLFS, J.	
4603	Private	ROLLINSON, G. W.	Wounded
571	Private	ROLLS, D.	

NOMINAL ROLL

Reg'tal No.	Rank	Name	Casualty
1906	L/Corporal	ROOK, V. A.	Wounded
4605	Private	ROONEY, W. J. S.	
2629	Private	ROSE, H. T.	Wounded
569	Corporal	ROSE, H. V.	Wounded
3138	Private	ROSEWALL, A. E.	Wounded
1387	Corporal	ROSEWARNE, C.	
2137	Private	ROSEWARNE, G. L. G.	
1977	Private	ROSS, A. McL.	Wounded
2138	Sergeant	ROSS, D. A.	Wounded
2180	Private	ROSS, D. S.	
551A	Private	ROSS, D. S.	Wounded
216	Private	ROSS, E.	Killed in Action
2351	Private	ROSS, G. T.	
	Captain	ROSS, H. E. C.	
3368	Private	ROSS, J. W.	
1390	Private	ROSS, M. J.	Killed in Action
1382	Private	ROSSER, A. E.	
2145	Private	ROSSER, C. E.	Wounded
217	Private	ROSSER, H. W.	Wounded
568	Sergeant	ROSSER, T.	
	Lieutenant	ROSS-SODEN, H.	
6569	Private	ROUSE, G. R.	Killed in Action
3134	Private	ROUTLEDGE, G.	
7365	Private	ROWATT, L. A.	Killed in Action
51685	Private	ROWE, E. D.	
1050	Private	ROWE, G. R.	
574	Private	ROWE, J. A.	
6091	Private	ROWE, N. H.	Wounded
2630	Private	ROWE, S. T.	Wounded
2356	Private	ROWE, T.	Wounded
791	Sergeant	ROWELL, A.	
2702	Private	ROYSTON, F. J.	
988	Private	RUBY, F. A.	Wounded
3139A	Private	RUSE, G. J.	
	Lieutenant	RUSHBROOK, N. J.	
2352	Private	RUSSELL, H. E.	Killed in Action
3145	Private	RUSSELL, R. P.	
1840	Private	RUSSELL, S. M. G.	
3135	Private	RUST, W. J.	

Reg'tal No.	Rank	Name	Casualty
219	Private	RUTHERFORD, A. R.	
3371	Private	RUXTON, S. V.	
1388	Private	RYAN, J.	
6073	Private	RYAN, J. C.	
489A	Private	RYAN, J. J.	
575	Private	RYAN, M. P.	Wounded
7315	Private	RYAN, P. L.	
51691	Private	RYAN, R. L.	
2139	Private	RYAN, T.	
2354	Private	RYDAR, B.	
220	L/Corporal	RYMER, J.	Died of Illness
3376	Private	SACKS, B. S.	
593	Private	SAFSTROM, C.	
2634	Sergeant	SALEEBA, C. J.	
596	L/Corporal	SALONEN, U. L.	Killed in Action
589	Private	SAMUELS, S.	Killed in Action
2376	Private	SANDERS, J.	Wounded
2646	Private	SANDERSON, C. V.	
988	Private	SANDERSON, J. E.	
1330	Private	SANDFORD, C. G.	
1188	Private	SANDFORD, W. R.	Wounded
603	Private	SANDS, W.	Wounded
2442	Private	SANDY, E.	
221	Private	SANFORD, T. A.	
3384	Private	SANGWELL, H. R.	
2140	Private	SARGENT, J.	
1405	Private	SARGENTSON, C. E.	Died of Wounds
601	Driver	SARTAIN, F.	
989	Private	SAUNDERS, E.	Wounded
4124	Private	SAUNDERS, R. W.	
990	Private	SAWYER, C. P.	Wounded
3388	Private	SCHMAHL, G. L.	
3374	Private	SCHMAHL, V. H.	
3377	Private	SCHMIDT, W. C.	
2141	L/Corporal	SCHNEIDER, R. E.	Wounded
2364	Private	SCHULZ, L. O.	
2365	Private	SCHULZ, O. G.	
1717	Private	SCHUTT, E. J.	Gassed
409	L/Sergeant	SCOTT, A.	

Reg'tal No.	Rank	Name	Casualty
2934	Private	SCOTT, D. McG.	Wounded
4594	Private	SCOTT, G. R.	Died of Illness
2362	Private	SCOTT, H.	
51699	Private	SCOTT, L. J.	
594	Driver	SCOTT, N.	Wounded
597	Private	SCOTT, W. E. J.	
2142	L/Corporal	SCOTT, W. J.	
3378	Private	SCRIVEN, J. E.	Gassed
3384	Private	SCRIVEN, J. E.	
270	Private	SCRIVENER, A.	
4125	Corporal	SEARL, S. N. S.	
1397	Private	SEARLE, L.	Wounded
3134	Private	SELL, J. H.	
	Lieutenant	SENIOR, A. W.	Wounded
991	Corporal	SENNETT, H. J.	
2143	Private	SEVIOR, P. O.	Wounded
2147	Private	SEWELL, H. C. R.	
2638	Private	SEYMOUR, J. W.	Wounded
1401	Private	SHALDERS, H.	Wounded
2190	Private	SHARMAN, J.	Wounded
2144	Private	SHARP, S.	Killed in Action
2637	Private	SHARPE, C. E.	Killed in Action
2366	L/Corporal	SHARPIN, G. N.	Wounded
602	L/Corporal	SHARROCK, C.	Killed in Action
2145A	Private	SHAW, A.	Killed in Action
2363	Private	SHAW, A. B.	
2635	Private	SHAW, A. J.	Wounded
598	Private	SHAW, A. W.	Wounded
	Lieutenant	SHAW, F. M.	
6095	Private	SHAW, G. A.	
51697	L/Corporal	SHAW, J. J.	
222	Private	SHAW, S. J.	
223	L/Corporal	SHAW, W. S.	Wounded
2146	Private	SHEAHAN, J. C.	
3387	Private	SHEARER, R. N.	
992	Private	SHEARWOOD, L. M.	
2636	Private	SHEATHER, E. L.	Killed in Action
2147	Private	SHEEHAN, D. M.	Wounded
2368	Private	SHEEHAN, J.	Wounded

Reg'tal No.	Rank	Name	Casualty
3380	Private	SHELLY, J.	
4126	Private	SHELTON, J. V.	
4661	Private	SHEPHERD, W. F.	Wounded
1394	Sergeant	SHERIDAN, M.	Wounded
1722	Private	SHIMMIN, J. N.	
4611	Private	SHINEBERG, H.	Wounded
736	Private	SHINNICK, W. G.	
3391	Private	SIDEBOTHAM, G.	
607	Private	SIEMERING, W. F.	Wounded
3383	Private	SIMMONDS, W.	
224	Sergeant	SIMMONS, R. H.	
605	Private	SIMPKINS, H. L.	Wounded
	Lieutenant	SIMPSON, B. J.	
1400	Sergeant	SIMPSON, E. J.	Died of Wounds
	Lieutenant	SIMPSON, J. A.	
2148	Private	SIMPSON, W. L.	
1284	Private	SIMS, D. C.	
3373	Private	SIMS, W. L. J.	
7320	Private	SINCLAIR, C. V.	Wounded
608	Private	SINCLAIR, D. E.	
2643	L/Corporal	SINCLAIR, O. V.	
2648	L/Corporal	SINCLAIR, R.	Wounded
3150	L/Corporal	SISELY, H. R.	
225	Corporal	SKEATS, J.	Gassed
590	Corporal	SKEHAN, A.	Wounded
2149	Private	SKURRIE, A. S.	
1713	Private	SKURRIE, R. H.	Wounded
1716	Private	SLATER, H. A.	Died of Illness
1721	Private	SLATTER, J. E. H.	
1916	Private	SLEEP, C. R.	Wounded
1917	Private	SLEEP, L. R.	Wounded
1402	Private	SLOAN, R. G. H.	
2150	Private	SMART, E. G.	Wounded
2377	Private	SMEDLEY, G. W.	Wounded
3375	Private	SMELGA, J.	
1913	Private	SMILIE, R.	Wounded
1392	Private	SMITH, A.	Wounded
1395	Driver	SMITH, A.	
587	L/Corporal	SMITH, A. H.	

NOMINAL ROLL

Reg'tal No.	Rank	Name	Casualty
2396	Private	SMITH, A. P. W.	
226	Private	SMITH, A. S. H.	
227	Private	SMITH, E.	
6074	Private	SMITH, E. E.	
1712	Private	SMITH, F. G.	
599	Private	SMITH, F. H.	
51704	Private	SMITH, F. T.	
787	Sergeant	SMITH, G.	Wounded
591	Corporal	SMITH, G. D.	Wounded
2639	Private	SMITH, G. E.	
641	L/Corporal	SMITH, G. H.	
1918	Private	SMITH, H. C.	
3379	Private	SMITH, H. S.	
737	Private	SMITH, J.	
2372	Private	SMITH, J.	Wounded
2146	Private	SMITH, J.	Wounded
2899	Private	SMITH, J.	
606	Private	SMITH, J. H.	
3139	Private	SMITH, L. H.	Wounded
2151	Private	SMITH, L. J.	Killed in Action
1026	L/Corporal	SMITH, L. R. G.	
600	L/Corporal	SMITH, N. W.	Died of Wounds
2375	Private	SMITH, P.	
3390	Private	SMITH, P. C.	
3147	Private	SMITH, P. J.	
	Captain	SMITH, P. L.	Died of Wounds
51709	Private	SMITH, T.	
2196	Private	SMITH, V. W.	Wounded
994	Sergeant	SMITH, W.	Wounded
51710	Private	SMITH, W. B. C.	
995	Private	SMITH, W. L.	Killed in Action
2369	Private	SMITH, W. M.	Wounded
22220	Private	SMITH, W. S.	
228	Private	SMITH, W. T.	Died of Illness
51707	Private	SMYTH, H. G.	
2092	Private	SMYTH, R.	Killed in Action
1393	Private	SMYTHE, J. H.	Killed in Action
592	Private	SOADY, B. L.	Wounded
2640	Private	SOMMER, S. W. P.	Died of Wounds

Reg'tal No.	Rank	Name	Casualty
2708	Private	SOUTER, W.	Wounded
	Captain	SOUTHBY, H.	Killed in Action
1718	Private	SPARK, T. M.	
595	Private	SPARKS, W. H.	
996	C.Q.M.S.	SPARNON, W. H.	
1396	Driver	SPEARY, T.	
51695	Private	SPEDDING, B.	
	Lieutenant	SPEERING, K. D.	Killed in Action
51700	Private	SPEIRS, A. J.	
14497	Private	SPENCER, A.	Died of Wounds
19826	Private	SPENCER, E.	Killed in Action
2707	Private	SPERRING, J. W.	Wounded
1955	Private	SPICER, G. A. E.	
2641	Private	SPICER, G. L.	Wounded
51716	Private	SPIERS, J. H. A.	
51705	Private	SPILLER, H. C.	
4615	Corporal	SPITTY, C. P.	
3538	Private	SPOTTISWOOD, R.	
51701	Private	SPRAKE, R. G.	
3425	Private	SPRATLING, L. G.	Wounded
6596	Corporal	SPUZEN, E.	
6099	Private	STACEY, S.	Died of Wounds
2642	L/Corporal	STACK, J. B.	Gassed
3146	Private	STAFF, E. J.	
51698	Private	STAFFORD, G. V.	
3148	Private	STAIT, C. H.	Killed in Action
3382	Private	STANBRIDGE, G. E.	
1910	Corporal	STANDEN, J. V.	Died of Illness
2644	Private	STANLEY, A. E.	Wounded
3149	Private	STANLEY, J. C.	
762A	Private	STANTON, V.	Wounded
588	Private	STATTON, H. D.	
3145	Private	STEARNES, H. C.	Wounded
51706	Private	STEELE, C. R.	
3613	Corporal	STEELE, W. G.	
3389	Private	STEFFENSEN, C. W. A.	
927	Private	STEPHEN, D.	
6411	Private	STEPHEN, D.	
2893	Private	STEPHENS, C.	

NOMINAL ROLL

Reg'tal No.	Rank	Name	Casualty
1919	Private	STEPHENS, D. H. A.	Wounded
2153	Sergeant	STEPHENS, F. A.	
2367	Private	STEPHENS, J. B.	Killed in Action
4653	Private	STEPHENS, J. S. G.	Wounded
3315	Private	STEPHENS, M.	
230	C.S.M.	STEPHENS, W. H. B.	
231	Driver	STERRITT, G. A.	
2657	Private	STEVENS, H. W.	
2374	Private	STEVENS, J.	
1711	Private	STEVENS, L. T.	Died of Illness
685A	Private	STEVENS, W. C.	Wounded
51708	Private	STEVENS, W. H.	
1719	Sergeant	STEVENSON, A. J.	Died of Wounds
2155A	Private	STEVENSON, E. R.	Killed in Action
1715	Private	STEVENSON, T. E.	Wounded
1399	Private	STEWART, A. A.	Killed in Action
232	Private	STEWART, A. E.	Killed in Action
3381	Private	STEWART, C. G.	
2894	Private	STEWART, H. J.	Killed in Action
	Captain	STEWART, J.	
1398	Private	STEWART, T.	Killed in Action
5687	Private	STEWART, W. G.	
51712	Private	STRICKLAND, J. S.	
233	Sergeant	STODDART, G. H.	Wounded
2371	Private	STOKES, F. T.	
1403	Private	STONE, O.	Wounded
6141	Private	STONE, R. W.	Wounded
2643	Private	STONEMAN, G.	
997	Corporal	STORER, L. J.	Killed in Action
1404	Corporal	STORER, O. T.	Wounded
6638	Sergeant	STOREY, C.	Wounded
2370	Private	STOTT, W.	
1199	Sergeant	STRAFORD, C. W.	Wounded
5797	Private	STRAFORD, V. W.	Wounded
2895	Private	STRAHAN, H. E.	Wounded
2156	Private	STRAHAN, J. G.	
235	Private	STRANGE, W. H.	Died of Wounds
51715	Private	STREATER, J.	
6085	Private	STREET, R.	Died of Wounds

Reg'tal No.	Rank	Name	Casualty
51702	Private	STROUD, N. V.	
6083	Private	STRUHS, R. A.	Wounded
58910	Private	STYGALL, J. T.	
2896	Private	SUGG, C.	
51713	Private	SUGG, H. N.	
1027	Private	SULLIVAN, J. J.	Wounded
998	Private	SULLIVAN, W.	
2031	Private	SUMMERS, G. A.	Died of Wounds
3144	A/Sergeant	SURMAN, J. W.	
51703	Private	SURRY, A. L.	
1714	Private	SUTHERLAND, W. W.	
2264	Private	SUTTON, F. J. M.	Wounded
3385	Private	SUTTON, W. J.	
687	Private	SWAIN, R. C.	
7054	Private	SWANSON, J. W.	
604	Private	SWEET, G. A.	
51711	Private	SWIFT, J.	
236	Private	SYDER, F. W.	
2647	Private	SYMONS, W. B.	Wounded
999	Private	SYPOTT, J.	
1000	Private	TALBOT, N. R.	
3153	Private	TARRAN, A. L.	
2901	Private	TATE, N. W.	Killed in Action
3396	Private	TAVENOR, P. F.	
2158	Private	TAYLOR, A. A.	
1921	Private	TAYLOR, A. W.	Killed in Action
237	Private	TAYLOR, G.	
1725	Private	TAYLOR, G. H.	
2904	Private	TAYLOR, H.	
1409	Private	TAYLOR, J. L.	Wounded
1408	Private	TAYLOR, J. T.	
3393	Private	TAYLOR, L. E.	
612	Private	TAYLOR, T. T.	
1407	Private	TAYLOR, W. R.	Wounded
2159	Private	TELFER, A.	Killed in Action
1918A	Private	TELFER, A. L.	
1413	Private	TENNANT, W. C.	
1052	Private	TEPPER, E. A.	
1922	Corporal	TERRELL, T. S.	

NOMINAL ROLL

Reg'tal No.	Rank	Name	Casualty
2160	Private	THACKER, S. F. C.	Died of Wounds
609	Private	THEWLIS, J. S.	Gassed
4625	Private	THOM, J. W.	Wounded
2649	Private	THOMAS, C. W.	
610	Private	THOMAS, N. H.	Killed in Action
4381	Private	THOMAS, P. V.	
2433	Private	THOMAS, R. C.	
614	Private	THOMAS, S. J.	Killed in Action
1410	Sergeant	THOMAS, W. N. B.	Wounded
1200	Corporal	THOMLINSON, J.	Wounded
54055	Private	THOMPSON, E.	
1411	Private	THOMPSON, J. H.	Killed in Action
4170	Private	THOMPSON, W.	Wounded
2650	Private	THOMPSON, W. G.	
4654	Private	THOMSON, A.	Gassed
6143	Private	THOMSON, A.	Wounded
1001	Private	THOMSON, H. E.	Wounded
6097	Corporal	THOMSON, J. P.	
4631	Private	THOMSON, W. M.	
51718	Private	THORNTON, C. H.	
2161	L/Corporal	THORNTON, R. S.	Died of Wounds
7060	Private	THROWER, E. L.	
2902	Private	TICHBORN, E.	Died of Illness
238	Private	TIETGENS, A. H.	
2183	Private	TILLETT, A. G.	Wounded
3290	Private	TIMBS, J. B.	
1406	Private	TIMMS, A. E.	
51717	Private	TIMMS, W. H.	
3247A	Private	TIPPETT, L.	
3151	Private	TOCKNELL, E. R.	
	Lieutenant	TODD, J. C.	
613	Private	TOEBELMANN, A.	
2652	Private	TOMS, E. W.	Died of Illness
616	Private	TONKIN, F.	Wounded
3317	Private	TONKIN, L. E.	Wounded
690	Private	TOOHER, W. J.	
1002	A/Corporal	TOOHEY, H.	
615	Private	TOOLE, A. H.	Wounded
2941	Private	TOY, A. E.	Wounded

Reg'tal No.	Rank	Name	Casualty
2653	Private	TRAFFORD, G. R.	Wounded
51721	Private	TRAHAIR, W. J.	
1926	Private	TRAINOR, H. J.	Wounded
	Lieutenant	TRANGMAR, A. J.	Killed in Action
2409	Private	TREGANOWAN, L. L.	
2382	Private	TREGANOWAN, W. T.	
1003	Private	TREKARDO, G. H.	Wounded
2162	Private	TRENGOVE, A. R.	Wounded
1723	Corporal	TRENGOVE, J. H.	Died of Illness
2379	Private	TRENWITH, C. A.	
2380	Private	TRETHEWEY, R. V.	Wounded
2383	Private	TRIBE, J. H.	
2654	Private	TRUNK, A.	
2381	Private	TUCKER, E. E.	Wounded
	Major	TUCKER, S. E.	Gassed
3394	Private	TUCKER, V. R.	
3154	Private	TUCKER, W. G.	
240	Private	TUDOR, H.	
241	Private	TURNBULL, J. C. McN.	Died of Wounds
1004	Private	TURNBULL, J. P.	Wounded
2191	Private	TURNER, F.	Killed in Action
2378	Private	TURNER, J. A.	Wounded
2655	Private	TURNER, J. E. M.	
1924	Private	TURNER, W. F.	Killed in Action
1412	Private	TURNHAM, R.	
3395	Private	TURRELL, T. C.	
4629	Private	TUTTLE, J.	Died of Wounds
6106	Private	TWATT, J.	Killed in Action
1726	Corporal	TYERS, J. N.	Wounded
2384	Private	UEBERGANG, F. E.	Wounded
3397	Private	UNWIN, H. G.	
1414	L/Corporal	URQUHART, J.	
	Lieutenant	URQUHART, T. H.	
	Lieutenant	VAN ASSCHE, H.	
723	Private	VANCE, C. O. B.	
242	Private	VARCOE, P. H. R.	
2163	Sergeant	VAUGHAN, C. F.	
1005	L/Corporal	VAUGHAN, R. D.	Killed in Action
243	Corporal	VAUGHAN, T. H.	Wounded

NOMINAL ROLL

Reg'tal No.	Rank	Name	Casualty
2164	Private	VAUGHAN, W. L.	Wounded
1415	Private	VEAL, C. V.	Wounded
618	Private	VEAL, L. M.	Wounded
1006	Private	VEYSEY, E. H.	
2387	Private	VICARS, H.	
617	Private	VICTOR, E.	Died of Wounds
2386	Private	VIZARD, R. G.	
3253	Sergeant	VOIGHT, F. A. K.	
51725	Private	VOIGT, F. J.	
3401	Private	WADDEN, R. J.	
2198	L/Corporal	WADDINGHAM, G. E.	Died of Wounds
2680	Private	WADE, F. J.	Wounded
3400	Private	WAILES, H.	
1418	Private	WALDRON, A. W.	
2665	Private	WALKER, A. H.	
	Lieutenant	WALKER, H. J.	Wounded
244	Sergeant	WALKER, R. T.	Wounded
15521	Private	WALL, T.	Killed in Action
	Lieutenant	WALL, W.	
2656	Private	WALLACE, A. B.	Killed in Action
2434	Corporal	WALLACE, A. C.	Wounded
2660	Private	WALLACE, H.	Killed in Action
6101	Private	WALLACE, W. A.	
2669	Corporal	WALLACE, W. I. H.	Wounded
4391	Private	WALLER, W. S.	
3161	Private	WALLIS, A. C.	
625	Private	WALSH, W. J. M.	
1929	Private	WALSHE, D.	
1007	Sergeant	WALTER, E. E.	
2165	Private	WALTERS, F.	Killed in Action
2657	Private	WALTON, C. D.	
2390	Private	WALTON, F. H.	Wounded
1427	Private	WANKE, A. R.	Wounded
2909	Private	WARD, F. T.	
627	Private	WARD, H. G.	
2271	Corporal	WARD, H. R.	
2166	L/Corporal	WARD, J.	Died of Wounds
1193	Corporal	WARDLAW, J. S.	Wounded
6114	Private	WARDLAW, T. F.	Wounded

Reg'tal No.	Rank	Name	Casualty
	Lieutenant	WARE, H. J.	Wounded
1008	Private	WARING, F. W.	Wounded
54752	Private	WARING, H. H.	
1988	Sergeant	WARLAND, H.	Wounded
245	Private	WARNE, C. F. P.	
743	Private	WARNER, C. W.	
1734	Private	WARREN, E. B.	
2659	Private	WASHER, G.	
2393	T/Sergeant	WATERS, L.	Killed in Action
2167	Private	WATERS, M. W.	Wounded
1009	Private	WATERS, T. P.	
4656	Private	WATERSTON, J. W.	
1028	Private	WATERTON, C. D.	Wounded
1430	Private	WATHEN, W. G.	Wounded
1931	Private	WATKINS, D. J.	Wounded
1010	Sergeant	WATKINS, G. E.	
2168	Private	WATSON, A.	Wounded
434	Corporal	WATSON, A. H.	
51732	Private	WATSON, E. W.	
741	Private	WATSON, H.	Wounded
246	Private	WATSON, J. A.	Wounded
2170	Private	WATSON, T.	Killed in Action
4146	Private	WATT, W.	Killed in Action
2171	Private	WATTERS, E. McD.	Wounded
2658	Private	WATTERS, J.	
51737	Private	WATTS, A. W.	
3156	Private	WATTS, E. J.	
1727	Private	WATTY, J.	
248	Private	WEARMOUTH, J. W.	Killed in Action
3398	Private	WEBB, C. S.	
3160	L/Corporal	WEBB, F. H.	Killed in Action
629	Private	WEBB, S. C. W.	Wounded
51734	Private	WEBB, W. H.	
2392	Private	WEBER, T. R.	
1011	Private	WEBSTER, F. T.	Died of Illness
1053	Private	WEBSTER, G. L. M.	
	Captain	WEGENER, J. F. W.	
6111	Corporal	WEIR, J. A.	Wounded
1012	L/Corporal	WELDON, R. J. M.	Wounded

NOMINAL ROLL

Reg'tal No.	Rank	Name	Casualty
	Lieutenant	WELLS, A. W.	
619	Private	WELLS, C. E.	
621	Private	WELSH, J. T.	
1013	Driver	WELSH, R. O.	
2908	Private	WESTHEAD, G. A.	
2709	Sergeant	WESTLEY, G. E.	
1933	Private	WHALEBONE, H.	
3244	Private	WHELAN, M. J.	
1426	Private	WHIFFIN, P. C.	
3159	Private	WHINFIELD, S. B.	
	Lieutenant	WHITE, B.	Died of Wounds
1014	Sergeant	WHITE, B. P.	Wounded
432A	Private	WHITE, C. H.	
1937	Private	WHITE, C. T.	
11800	Private	WHITE, D. J.	
2391	Private	WHITE, E. J.	Killed in Action
51738	Private	WHITE, F.	
3399	Private	WHITE, H. K.	
6113A	Private	WHITE, J. D.	Died of Wounds
800	T/Sergeant	WHITE, J. T.	
6918A	Private	WHITE, R. G.	
622	Corporal	WHITE, T. D.	Wounded
250	Private	WHITE, T. W.	Wounded
1421	Private	WHITE, W. G.	Killed in Action
2661	Private	WHITE, W. H.	
249	L/Corporal	WHITE, W. J.	Wounded
1927	Private	WHITEFIELD, H. J.	
3408	Private	WHITEHEAD, H. A.	
1732	Private	WHITFIELD, C. T.	Wounded
4663	Private	WHITFIELD, H.	Wounded
6124	Private	WHITFORD, V. H.	Wounded
251	Private	WHITTEN, T.	
110	Sergeant	WICKS, H. R.	
3157	Private	WICKS, R. A.	
3412	Private	WIGG, S.	
1930	Private	WIGHT, G.	
2922	Private	WIGNALL, S.	Wounded
3409	Private	WILCOCKS, R.	
2192	Corporal	WILKES, A. E.	

Reg'tal No.	Rank	Name	Casualty
706	Corporal	WILKIN, H. V.	
6117	Private	WILKINS, G. W.	Wounded
2665	Private	WILKINSON, A. J. S.	
628	Private	WILKINSON, F. H.	
1015	Private	WILKINSON, H.	Wounded
6116A	Corporal	WILKS, R. C.	Wounded
624	Private	WILLATON, J. S.	Wounded
2906	Private	WILLCOCKS, H. R.	Wounded
2904	Private	WILLIAMS, A.	
2921	Private	WILLIAMS, A. G.	
1429	Private	WILLIAMS, A. H.	
2415	Private	WILLIAMS, A. J.	
2427	Private	WILLIAMS, C. A.	
1016	Private	WILLIAMS, E. A.	Killed in Action
2907	Private	WILLIAMS, F.	
252	Private	WILLIAMS, F. J.	Wounded
3487	Private	WILLIAMS, G. C.	Wounded
	Lieutenant	WILLIAMS, H. T.	Gassed
1731	Private	WILLIAMS, H. W.	
1416	Private	WILLIAMS, J. A.	
1729	Private	WILLIAMS, J. E.	
2173	Corporal	WILLIAMS, J. F.	Wounded
7098	Private	WILLIAMS, J. H.	
51743	Private	WILLIAMS, L. A.	
1934	Private	WILLIAMS, L. H. C.	Died of Wounds
1417	Private	WILLIAMS, T. W.	Wounded
2175	Private	WILLIAMS, W.	Wounded
1428	Sergeant	WILLIAMS, W. H.	Wounded
1731	Corporal	WILLIAMS, W. H.	Wounded
6111A	Private	WILLIAMSON, E.	
2174	Private	WILLIAMSON, J.	Killed in Action
620	Private	WILLIAMSON, W. G.	Wounded
801	Sergeant	WILLIMOTT, R. A.	Wounded
51740	Private	WILLMOTT, A. A.	
51739	Private	WILLS, W. S.	
1017	Private	WILSON, A.	Wounded
623A	Private	WILSON, A. E.	
670	Private	WILSON, A. R. E.	Wounded
2903	Private	WILSON, B. O.	Wounded

NOMINAL ROLL

Reg'tal No.	Rank	Name	Casualty
2663	Private	WILSON, B. E.	
2662	Private	WILSON, C. C.	
1314	Driver	WILSON, C. P.	
2176	Private	WILSON, F.	Wounded
1203	C.Q.M.S.	WILSON, F. H.	
626	Private	WILSON, J.	Wounded
685A	Private	WILSON, J.	
1423	Private	WILSON, J. C.	Wounded
46	Private	WILSON, J. D.	
1425	Private	WILSON, J. R.	
253	L/Corporal	WILSON, P. L.	Wounded
3410	Private	WILSON, P. L.	
2664	Private	WILSON, S. C.	Killed in Action
51742	Private	WILSON, S. M.	
51735	Private	WILSON, W. M.	
3486	Private	WINROW, E.	
1419	Private	WINSALL, A. V. E.	Died of Illness
1422	Driver	WINSALL, L. V. E.	
2905	Private	WINTERHALTER, G. A.	Killed in Action
1936	Private	WISE, F. J.	Wounded
3156	Private	WISE, M. R.	
	Captain	WOLSTENHOLME, R.	
254	Private	WOMERSLEY, V.	Wounded
3162	Corporal	WOOD, J.	
2177	Private	WOOD, J. W.	Wounded
299	Corporal	WOOD, L. A.	
3407	Private	WOOD, R. A.	
51731	Private	WOODALL, H.	
598	Private	WOODHEAD, L. A.	
3167	Private	WOODLAND, H. H.	
2666	Private	WOODLEY, W. R.	Died of Illness
3155	Private	WOODS, C. J.	
3411	Private	WOODS, J. E.	
1424	Private	WOODS, J. R. G.	Wounded
1420	Private	WOODS, W. A.	Wounded
1728	Private	WOODWARD, E. S.	Killed in Action
1435	L/Corporal	WOOLCOCK, N. B.	
51736	Private	WOOLLARD, S. W.	
3402	Private	WORKMAN, H. W.	

Reg'tal No.	Rank	Name	Casualty
1018	L/Corporal	WORRALL, C. S.	Wounded
2388	Corporal	WORTHINGTON, R. J.	Wounded
3158	Private	WRIGHT, A.	
271	Private	WRIGHT, F. C.	
255	Private	WRIGHT, J. A.	Wounded
2426	Private	WRIGHT, W.	Killed in Action
1935	Private	WYNNE, R.	Killed in Action
1431	Private	YANNER, P. J.	Gassed
1019	Private	YATES, W. J.	Killed in Action
3415	Private	YELLAND, H. B.	
2178	Private	YOUNG, D.	Wounded
1020	R.Q.M.S.	YOUNG, G.	
1939	Private	YOUNG, J.	Gassed
2179	Private	YOUNG, J.	Died of Wounds
	Lieutenant	YOUNG, R. H. R.	
2026	Private	YOUNG, R. J.	Wounded
632	Driver	YOUNG, W. L.	
3163	Private	YOUNGER, E.	Wounded
2668	Private	YURAK, O.	
	Lieutenant	ZELMAN, E. H.	
2394	Private	ZEUSCHNER, E. A.	
3416	Private	ZIERK, H. T.	

INDEX

Index

Abbeville ... 241
Accroche Wood ... 212
Adderley Street, Capetown ... 41
Africa ... 39, 40
African Coast ... 38
A.I.F. ... 19, 20, 21, 23, 25, 29, 32, 62, 123, 171, 181, 247, 248
    Army Medical Corps ... 144, 158
    Army Service Corps ... 124
    Artillery, 3rd Divisional ... 57, 89, 102, 174, 176
    Battalions:
        2nd ... 232
        4th ... 232
        15th ... 129
        16th ... 202, 207, 208
        20th ... 208
        21st ... 171
        22nd ... 200
        24th ... 173, 207
        26th ... 205
        33rd ... 99, 175, 186, 222, 229
        34th ... 118, 119
        37th, 31, 32, 55, 60, 61, 74, 75, 76, 80, 83, 84, 85, 87, 91, 92, 99, 120, 124, 126, 130, 137, 139, 158, 167, 171, 173, 174, 175, 192, 198, 203, 205, 224, 225, 227, 228, 229, 232, 241.
        38th, 31, 32, 60, 87, 91, 92, 130, 137, 139, 140, 174, 187, 192, 194, 209, 210, 211, 219, 222, 229, 230, 231, 236, 237, 239.
        40th, 31, 32, 60, 83, 87, 90, 92, 93, 105, 117, 124, 130, 137, 139, 143, 144, 145, 146, 155, 169, 170, 174, 188, 189, 199, 219, 227, 230, 232, 237, 239.
        41st ... 91, 128, 129, 203
        42nd ... 92, 211, 214
        43rd ... 91, 101, 205
        44th ... 92, 111, 211, 226
    Brigades:
        6th ... 200
        9th, 117, 128, 155, 186, 195, 198, 202, 211, 216, 221, 222.
        10th, 19, 30, 31, 32, 53, 56, 61, 87, 98, 130, 137, 139, 144, 146, 147, 148, 172, 180, 181, 182, 186, 188, 195, 197, 201, 211, 216, 219, 220, 221, 225, 227, 228, 235, 241, 247, 248.

A.I.F.: Brigades *(continued)*—
    11th, 122, 128, 138, 159, 191, 195, 211, 215, 225, 230, 237.
    15th 216
  Corps:
    Australian 164, 202, 212, 213, 220, 221
    1st Anzac 164
    2nd Anzac 98
  Demobilization Regt.:
    10th 248
  Divisions:
    1st 133, 212, 220, 221, 225
    2nd 138, 211, 212, 221, 228, 231
    3rd, 19, 21, 29, 49, 56, 58, 62, 74, 76, 91, 108, 121, 126,
        132, 138, 164, 171, 188, 202, 211, 212, 213, 220, 221,
        225, 228, 231, 234, 247, 249.
    4th, ... 121, 193, 194, 212, 215, 221
    5th 210, 212, 221
  Engineers:
    Divisional 133, 205
    10th Field Company 87, 227
  Headquarters: Horseferry Road, Westminster ... 52, 100
  Light Trench Mortar Battery 53
  Quota 45 248
  Training Battalion:
    10th 54
    Tunnellers 107, 165
Air Force, British (See British Expeditionary Force).
Aire 179
Albert 21, 193
Aldershot 239, 249
Aldred, Cpl. A. B. C. 27
Aldred, L/Sgt. H. T. S. 145
Allan, Lieut. P. V. 25
Allied Army 176
Allonville 200, 201, 202
Allsop, Capt. L. T. 194, 218, 237, 240
Amesbury 47, 49, 62
Amiens, 19, 21, 27, 180, 181, 191, 192, 194, 200, 201, 204, 207, 212
Amiens-Albert Railway 192, 193
Amiens Defence Line 219
Ancre River 191, 193, 194, 207
Anderson, Pte. E. E. 154
Andrews, Pte. L. J. 218
Anscroft Avenue 107, 114, 115
Anton's Farm 107, 113, 115
Anzac 164
Anzacs 29

INDEX

Armentieres, 69, 71, 74, 75, 80, 81, 82, 83, 84, 88, 91, 92, 94, 95, 99, 100, 108, 112, 117, 127.
Armentieres, The Agony of ... 127
Armfield, Major G. S. ... 71, 87
Armistice ... 195, 241, 244, 247
Army Rest Area ... 130
Arquaire Wood ... 213
Arques ... 97
"Ascanius," H.M.A.T., A.11, 33, 34, 35, 36, 37, 38, 39, 40, 42, 43, 44, 45, 46, 47.
Atlantic ... 43
August, Lieut. J. S. ... 25, 27, 208
Australia, 21, 23, 27, 29, 30, 32, 38, 41, 53, 56, 58, 100, 156, 213, 246, 250.
Australian Federal Elections (See Elections).
Austrians ... 38
Authie ... 182
Avenue Farm ... 115, 118
Avon Valley ... 59

Bailleul ... 69, 95, 96, 130
Bailleul Railway Station ... 130
Ballarat ... 30, 31, 32, 33, 51
Barbed Wire Square, Armentieres ... 73
Barrett, C. ... 26
Base Records Staff ... 26
Basutos ... 39
Bates, Cpl. E. W. ... 143
Bay of Biscay ... 46
Bayenghem-les-Seninghem ... 177, 179
Bayonvillers ... 220
Bean, Dr. C. E. W. ... 23, 26
Beauchamp, Capt. L. L. ... 26, 106, 240, 247
Beavis, Lieut. J. S. ... 169, 208
Belgian Coast ... 136
Belgian Croix de Guerre ... 105, 168
Belgian Frontier ... 133, 134
Belgium ... 132, 160
Bellevue Spur ... 154
Bendigo ... 30, 31
Berlin Wood ... 145
Best, Chaplain J. ... 241
Betlheem Farm ... 121
Bight, The ... 37
Bingle, Capt. W. R. ... 85
Birdwood, Field-Marshal Sir W. R. ... 21, 26, 164, 170, 175, 201, 202
Bishop, L/Cpl. P. A. ... 224

Black Line	115, 118, 119
Black, L/Cpl. G. C.	140
Blangy-sur-Bresle	243, 244, 247
Blangy Tronville	201, 202, 203, 205
Blaringhem	132, 133
Blaubaum, Major I.	115, 144, 158, 159, 240
Blue Factory, Armentieres	99
Bois Laleau	182
Bois l'Abbe	203, 205, 206
Bollow, Pte. J. W.	218
Bony	19, 233, 234, 236, 237, 239
Booth, Capt. N. G.	168
Bouchavesnes	229
Bouillancourt-en-Sery	25, 243, 244, 245, 246, 247, 248
Boulogne	164
Boyles Farm	124, 125
Brady, Sgt. E.	142
Bray Road	216
Bray-sur-Somme	19, 221, 222, 223, 227
Bresle River	243
Brighton	34
Bristol Castle	124
British Isles	47, 52
British Colonisation in Africa	41
British Expeditionary Force:	
Air Force	111, 147
Army:	
1st	62
4th	180, 207
5th	202
Battalions:	
Dorsetshire	219
1st King's Own Yorkshire Light Infantry	239
Manchester Regiment	148
25th Northumberland Fusiliers	86
4th Tyneside Scottish Regiment	92
Brigades:	
24th	165
50th	219
102nd	92
198th	148
Divisions:	121, 212
8th	165
58th	212
66th	148, 156
Engineers:	
Royal, 184th Tunnelling Company	173

INDEX

British Expeditionary Force: Engineers *(continued)*—
    Special Companies ... 101
    Transport Services ... 179
    Transport Services, Inland Water ... 97
British Navy ... 43, 46, 65
Broodseinde ... 19, 135, 144, 148, 151, 163
Broodseinde Ridge ... 134, 137, 142, 143, 151
Brooke, Rupert ... 249
Brooksbank, Sgt. A. ... 26
Brown, Lieut. O. R. ... 211, 214, 215, 220, 245
Brown Line ... 234, 235
Browne, Lieut. G. S. ... 26
Bucholz, L/Cpl. R. N. ... 168
Buire ... 192, 195, 201, 249
Bulford ... 49, 56, 57
Bunhill Row ... 115
Burn, C.S.M. J. W. ... 217
Burnt Farm ... 86
Busmenard ... 245, 246
Bussu ... 233
Bustard ... 60
Bustard Inn ... 59

Caestre ... 180
Calais ... 65
Cameron, Pte. C. ... 105
Camon ... 207
Canadian Corps ... 212
Canadian Divisions ... 212
Canadian Troops ... 160
Cape Colony ... 38
Cape Town ... 38, 39, 40, 41, 43
Cape Verde Islands ... 45
Cardonnette ... 200, 201, 202, 205, 207
Catacombs ... 107, 110, 111, 171, 173
Catelet, le ... 234, 239
Ceylon Wood ... 225
Channel Ports ... 176, 197
Charing Cross Dressing Station ... 110
Chateau Rose ... 73
Chateau Wood ... 225, 226
Chief of the Cape Town Police ... 43
Christensen, Lieut. C. P. ... 128
Clarke, Cpl. L. ... 169
Cleary, Pte. J. ... 25
Clery-sur-Somme ... 19, 228, 229, 230, 231
Cobden, Lieut. C. M. ... 211, 214, 215, 220

Coe, Cpl. V. P.	224
Coffey, Sgt. D. F.	197, 227, 232
Coisy	220
Coliseum, Ballarat	32
Comforts Fund, Australian	83, 111
,, ,, Brigade	172, 245
Comines	119
Commonwealth, The (See Australia).	
Connelly, Major E.	160
Conscription Referendum	171
Coo-ees, The	170
Corbie	214
Corio Bay	34
Coutts, Pte. D. G.	219
Cowan, Sgt. D. B.	217
Cowgate Sector	92
Crater, The	167, 174
Crayford, Lieut. W. B.	227
Croix du Bac	172
Cromwell's Ironsides	56
Cunningham, Pte. A.	194
Curlu	227, 228, 231
Davidson, Pte. J.	233
Davies, Sgt. B. R.	25
Dead Horse Corner	171, 175
"Demosthenes," H.M.A.T.	40, 42, 46
Department-du-Nord	69, 98
Deravin, Capt. A. E.	240
Dernancourt	193
De Seule	172
De Seule Area	124
Desvres	160, 164
Devil's Peak	39, 41
Devon	46, 47
Devonport	47
Dichlorlthyl Sulphide	125, 126
Discomforture Trench	228
Distinguished Conduct Medal	102, 144, 170, 229, 230, 236
Distinguished Service Order	148, 249
Dog Trench	235
Donohue, Pte. G. H.	170
Doullens	181, 182
Douve Farm	115, 118, 121
Douve, River	115, 118, 119, 121
Douve Valley Camp	124
Dover	65

INDEX

Dover, Straits of	65
Downs, The (See Wiltshire Downs).	
Dranoutre	130
Drionville	132
Duggan, Cpl. R.	190
Duncan's Post	235
Dunne, Pte. M. P.	131
Durrington	56, 58
Ebblinghem	97
Ecole Professionale, Armentieres	87, 88
Eddystone Lighthouse	46
Education Service	244
Edwards, Sgt. F. T. A.	223
Elections, Australian Federal	100
Ellis, 2/Lieut. A. R.	144, 158
England	21, 46, 47, 49, 53, 55, 65, 86, 135, 173, 174, 250
English Channel	46, 65, 66
Epinette Sector	99
Equator	44
Erquinghem-Lys	94, 95, 96
Eu, Foret de	243
Europe	40
Exeter	47
Exeter, Mayoress of	47
Federal Parliament House (See Parliament House).	
Ferguson, Sir R. M. (See Viscount Novar).	
Flanders	49, 62, 68, 73, 98, 105, 122, 127, 135, 176, 188
Flanders Plain	124
Fleiter, Lieut. E.	87, 91
Folkes, Sgt. S. J.	239
Fortieth Battalion Association	27
Framerville	219
France,	21, 25, 29, 61, 62, 65, 67, 68, 69, 97, 135, 160, 164, 195, 203, 243, 246, 249, 250.
Frankston	34
Franvillers	183, 200
French Army—3rd Regiment of Zouaves	203
French Front	135
Gallipoli	29, 249
Gallipoli Landing	198
Gamaches	248
Garrard, Lieut. C. E.	230
Gazzard, Pte. H. E.	25
Gellibrand, Major-General Sir John	202, 249

George V., His Majesty the King 56, 57, 58, 220
Gerdts, Pte. R. A. 144
German Army:
    Bavarians 104, 146
    5th Bavarian Regiment 103
    Divisions 161, 197
    18th German Fusilier Regiment 232
    13th German Infantry Regiment 209, 211
    Jaeger Regiment 194
    Prussians 100
    Secret Service 88
    Uhlan Patrols 181
German Raiders 37
Gibbs, Philip 127
Giblin, Major 155, 156
Giles, Capt C. L. 84, 232, 235
Gillemont Crescent 237, 239
Gillemont Farm 234, 235, 236, 237, 238
Gillemont Trench 236
Glisy 202, 205
Godley, Lieut.-General 96, 98
Governor-General of Australia (See Viscount Novar).
Grand Sec Bois 96
Gration, Lieut. J. W. 144, 199
Gravenstafel Switch 140, 143
Great Britain 29, 135
Green Line 234
Green Point 40
Green Route 113
Gressaire Wood 221
Grey Farm 115, 118
Grey Farm Line 115, 118
Grinton, Cpl. 230
Grondona, Lieut. L. 87
Groot Schuur 41
Guinea, Gulf of 44
Guizancourt Farm 234
Gull, L/Cpl. R. S. 194
Guyett, Lieut. A. E. 157, 205, 222

Haig, Field-Marshal Sir Douglas 132, 161, 177, 197, 201
Haines, Sgt. V. R. 236
Half Past Eleven Square, Armentieres 72
Hamburg Farm 153
Hamel 207, 211
Hamelet 232
Hamelet Wood 233

INDEX

Hampton Court	53
Handel Copse	233, 234
Happy Valley	222
Harris, Pte. H. B.	25
Hasted House	107
Havre, Le	63, 65, 67, 69, 247, 248
Havre, Le—Gare Maritime	67
Hazebrouck	96, 97, 179, 180
Hazel Wood	213, 216, 220, 221
Heads, The	34
Heath, Cpl. S. V.	158
Heilly	185, 186, 187, 188, 195, 200
Heilly Road	183
Hem	230
Hem Railway Station	228
Henderson, Lieut.-Col. R. O., 92, 114, 136, 148, 188, 190, 204, 227, 229, 233, 235, 236, 237.	
Hervilly	232
Hervilly Wood	232
Heuringhen	181, 182
Hewland, Sgt. C. J.	217
Hillside Camp	124, 129, 130
Hill 63	106, 107, 125, 165, 173, 174, 176
Hindenburg	176
Hindenburg Line	21, 231, 233, 234, 239
His Majesty's Fleet of Troopships (See Troopships).	
Hobba, Sgt. A. H.	25
Hocquincourt	241, 243
Hodgetts, C.S.M. L. F.	142
Holmes, Cpl. C. A.	226
Horse Show	126
Hospice, Armentieres	99
Hottentots	39
Houplines	74, 76, 86, 99, 101
House of Commons, Members of	175
Houses of Parliament, London	52
Hoy, Pte. F. A.	25
Hubbard, Sgt. F. H.	25
Hume, Sgt. W. J.	142, 157
Hunter Avenue	107
Hunter, Pte.	158
Hussar Farm	151, 159
Hutton, Major C. R.	91, 231
Hyde Park Corner	107, 110, 165
"Ici"	195
Indian Army	63

Indian Ocean	37
International Posts	203
Ireton, L/Cpl. M. C.	25
Italian Front	135
James, Lieut. H. J.	25, 26, 154, 240
Jenkins, L/Cpl. W. C.	193
Jess, Brig.-General C. H.	241
Jewkes, Lieut. W. G.	85
Johnson, C.S.M. H.	26
Johnston, Pte. J. E.	208
Johnston, Lieut. R. A.	239
Kaffirs	39, 40, 41
"K" Track	137, 152, 159
Keepaway Farm	123
"Kent," H.M.S.	45
Kitchener, Lord	38
Kitchener's Army	29
Kluck	69
Kortepyp Camp	175
La Chapelle d'Armentieres	86, 93
"Laconia," H.M.S.	40, 42, 43, 46
La Creche	124
La Flaque	219
L'Hallue River	207
Lamble, Capt. R.	26, 106, 107
La Motte	164
Lamotte-Brebiere	202
Land's End	46
Larkhill	49, 50, 51, 53, 55, 57, 58, 62
Larkhill, No. 7 Camp	47, 50
"Larne," T.B.D., No. 57	46
Ledinghem	131
Le Fevre, Lieut. S.	218, 224, 225, 229
Levy, Sgt. A.	169, 190
Lille	81, 119
Lille Forts	122
Lindsay, Lieut. W.	240
Lindsay, Pte. J. R. R.	73
Lion's Head	39
Lock House, Armentieres	73
London	52, 126
London General Omnibus (See Omnibus).	
Longavesnes	234
Long, Bishop	201
Loxton, Sgt. C.	25, 224, 225

Lumbres	132, 176, 177, 179
Lys Canal	122
Lys, River	71, 112, 122
Makeham, Pte. C. R.	103
Mann, Pte. C. A.	143, 193
Marconi Installation	38
Marett Wood	188, 194, 196, 198
Marner, Pte. A. J.	193
Marsh, Pte. D. M. W.	224
Martin, Mr. Justice Russell	26
Martin, Pte. T. W.	105
Mason, Lieut. C. T.	245
Matthews, Sgt. R. J.	218
"Medic," H.M.A.T.	40, 42, 44
Melbourne	30, 31
Mellish, Pte. E. J.	157
Mericourt Chateau	192
Mericourt L'Abbe	188, 192, 194, 195, 200
Merris	69, 70, 71, 164
Messines, 96, 101, 107, 109, 120, 121, 122, 123, 124, 126, 127, 128, 148.	
Messines, Battle of	19, 20, 106, 109, 114, 116, 119
Messines Hill	113, 120
Messines Road	123
Messines Ridge	102, 108, 109, 126
Middleton, Capt. D. F.	144
Miles, Cpl. E. J. L. B	142
Miles, Lieut. H. F.	198, 199
Miles, Major	244
Military Cross	91, 120, 144, 170
Military Cross, Bar	160
Miller, Pte. W. F.	144
Military Medal	94
Mitchell, Pte. T. T.	224
Monash, Lieut.-General Sir John, 19, 20, 26, 56, 57, 202, 207, 212, 213, 220, 237.	
Monde-Court-Pas	182
Mons	63
Mont de Lille	95
Moore, Chaplain W. A.	241
Morbecque	108, 122, 133, 148
Morcourt	216
Morlancourt	199, 210
Morton, Pte. L.	142
Mount Kemmel	124
Mud Lane	107, 115
Murray Wood	224

Mustard Gas (See Dichlorlthyl Sulphide).
McDonald, Lieut. H. N. R. 232
McEwan, Lieut. F. J. 25, 158, 208, 209
McLinden, Pte. A. D. 223
McMahon, L/Cpl. J. J. 144
McNicoll, Brig.-General W. R. 60, 61, 181, 216, 227, 241

Natal 39
National Gallery, London 53
Navy, British (See British Navy).
Neal, Pte. A. 218
Negate Farm 164
Neilson, Lieut. P. 26
Neptune 44
Nether Wallop 55
Neuve Eglise 96, 123, 124, 171, 172, 173
New Zealand Division 121, 138
New Zealanders 120, 121, 142, 145, 154, 155
New Zealand Regiment 71
Nieppe 71, 105, 107, 111, 112, 122, 123
Nieppe, Forest of 164
Nieppe, Pont De 71, 112, 113
Nivelle, General 135
Nore 65
Normandy 68
Nouveau Monde 95, 96
Novar, Viscount 32

O'Brien, L/Cpl. D. M. 226
Olin, Sgt. A. A. 157
Olson, Cpl. A. V. 170
Omnibus, London General 183
Oosthove Farm 111, 112, 114, 119
"Ophir," H.M.S. 45
Orcheston 55
Orders, Pte. F. A. 193
Otway Light 34
Overton, Lieut. R. H. 199

Pagels, Sgt. E. A. 154
Palmer's Baths 173
Palstra, Lieut. W. 120
Paris 69, 126, 176, 180
Parliament House, Federal 31, 32
Parrish, L/Cpl. A. E. 25, 156
Partridge, Pte. W. 144
Pas 182

INDEX

Pas-de-Calais 96, 97, 98, 130, 164, 177
Passchendaele 19, 132, 142, 151, 158, 159, 161, 163
Passchendaele Ridge 21, 131, 148, 151, 152, 160
Paterson, Lieut.-Colonel A. T., 25, 26, 27, 93, 114, 115, 118, 119, 120, 155, 156, 159, 160, 186, 187, 190, 195, 199, 201, 204, 239, 245, 248, 249.
Payne, Major L. H. 227, 228
Peronne 228, 231, 241
Peronne Road 216
Petit Difques 97, 98, 99
Phillips, Cpl. F. I. 145
Picardy 49
Pilot Ship 34
Ploegsteert 101, 102
Ploegsteert Corner 114
Ploegsteert Wood ... 101, 105, 106, 113, 114, 165, 168, 171, 173
Plumer, General Sir H. O. 97, 130
Plymouth Sound 47
Pont de Nieppe (See Nieppe, Pont de).
Pont Remy 241
Poperinghe 134
Port Medical Officer, Cape Town 39
Port Melbourne 33
Portuguese 45
Postel, Mons. F. 244
Potijze 137
Powell, Lieut. W. R. 25, 156
Prentice, Lieut. J. M. 218
Price, Lieut. H. J. 26
"Princess Victoria" Admiralty Channel Transport 63, 65
Prospect Hill 234
Prowse Point 167, 173, 174
Proyart 216, 219, 220
Prussians (See German Army).
Pulbrook, Pte. J. G. 105

Queenscliff 34
Quelmes 98
Querrieu 207

Racine Dump 168
Rainecourt 219
Rambures 244
Rancourt Road 230
Rankine, Lieut.-Colonel R. 30, 71, 87
Ravebeek Creek 154
Rawlinson, General 220

Red Cross Staff	171
Red Lodge	165, 167, 174, 175
Reeves, Pte. J. J.	224
Regimental Aid Post	115, 144, 237
Renescure	97
Rhodes, Cecil	41
Rhodes' Memorial	41
Ribemont-sur-l'Ancre	186, 187, 194, 195
Richards, Pte. P. C.	169
Richardson, Pte.	158
Roberts, Lord	97
Roberts, Capt. L.	54, 103
Roberts, Pte. T. P.	226
Roisel	232
Rollestone	57, 62
Romarin	170, 171
Romarin Camp	168
Ronces Wood	231, 232, 233
Ronssoy	235
Ross, Cpl. D. A.	93, 94
Roulers Road	137
Royal Military College, Sandhurst	32
Rue Du Bois	86, 93
Russia	135
Russian Front	161
Russian Success	38
Sailly Laurette	215, 221
Sailly le Sec	221
Saint Adresse, Le Havre	66
Salisbury	49, 56
Salisbury Plain	19, 47, 49, 53, 55, 56, 57
Sandhurst Royal Military College (See Royal Military College).	
Sandringham	34
Sanvic, Le Havre	66, 67
Schnitzel Farm	119, 120, 121
Scott, L/Cpl. W. J.	145
Scrivener, Pte. A.	194
Seaforth Farm	107, 113
Sea Point	42
Senlecques	131, 164
Senior Officers' School, Aldershot (See Aldershot).	
Sennett, Cpl. H. J.	26
Sercus	180
Seymour	30, 31
Shaw, Lieut. F. M.	26, 217, 219
Sheehan, Pte. J	26, 145

Sheridan, Sgt. M.	188
Show Grounds, Ballarat	30
Smith, Capt. P. L.	85, 93, 107
Smith, L/Cpl. L. R. G.	193
Solent	63
Somme	21, 179, 180, 181, 184, 188, 195, 210, 221, 225, 228, 240
Somme River	191, 202, 207, 208, 211, 212, 214, 221, 225, 227, 228
Somme Valley	177, 182, 203
Sorrento	34
South Africa (See Africa).	
South African Ports (See Africa).	
South America	59
Southampton	61, 62, 63
South Coast, England	46
Spencer Street Railway Station	31
Sports Meeting, Brigade	124, 207
Sports Meeting, 3rd Divisional	58
St. Eloi	173
St. Emilie	233, 234, 239
St. Goud Trench	229
St. Kilda	34
St. Martin Au Laert	99
St. Omer	97, 99, 130, 181
St. Paul's, London	53
St. Pierre	132
St. Quentin	176
St. Quentin Canal	21
St. Quentin, Mont	228, 231
St. Sylvestre-Cappel	133
St. Vast	207
St. Vincent	45
St. Yves	102, 167, 173
St. Yves Avenue	166
Steenwerck	87, 99, 105, 165, 176, 177
Steenwerck Railway Station	165, 172
Steenwoorde	134
Stephens, Pte. J. B.	105
Stewart, Capt. R.	119
Stewart, Capt. J.	26, 54
Stoddart, Sgt. G. H.	145
Stonehenge	49, 51, 52, 56
Strombos Horn	74
Suzanne	224, 225, 226, 227
Suzanne Church	226
Swazis	39
Table Bay	38, 39, 40, 41, 42, 43

Table Mountain	39
Tailles Wood	221
Tank Camp	130
Tasmania	30, 31
Thievres	183
Tidworth	49, 57
Tilleul Road	115
Tincourt	232
Tissage Dump	75
Toronto Avenue	102
Tower of London	53
Treux	192, 195, 201, 249
Troopships, His Majesty's Fleet of	35, 42
Tucker, Major S. E.	114, 115
Ulna Avenue	121
Ulrica Avenue	118
United Kingdom	52
United States of America Army:	
27th Division	234
129th Regiment	210
131st Regiment	210
Ushant	65
Vaire Wood	207, 208, 210, 211
Vaux Wood	227
Vecquemont	208
"Verdun of Flanders" (See Ypres).	
Victor, Pte. E.	170
Victoria	21, 30, 173
Vieux Berquin	164
Ville-sur-Ancre	189, 192, 193, 199
Villers-Bretonneux	193, 195, 202, 203, 205, 207, 210, 216, 220
Villers-Bretonneux, White Chateau	203
Villers Faucon	234
Villers Line	211
Vlamertinghe	134, 148, 152, 160
Von Kluck (See Kluck).	
Wallon Cappel	180, 181
Walter, Sgt. E. E.	229, 230
Wardrecques	181
Ware, Lieut. H. J.	208
Warfusee-Abancourt	213, 214, 220
"Warilda," H.M.A.T.	42
Waring, Pte. F. W.	102
Warneton	123, 125, 128, 129, 169, 174

INDEX

Waterloo, London ... 52
Watkins, Sgt. G. E. ... 26, 27, 103, 104
Watkins, Lieut. G. H. ... 26
West Baths ... 94
Westminster Abbey ... 52, 53
Westminster Bridge ... 52
White, Lieut. B. ... 73
White, Major-General Sir C. B. B. ... 23, 24, 26
Williamstown ... 34
Wiltshire Downs ... 49, 57, 58
Windmill, The ... 128, 129
Winnezeele ... 133, 134, 177, 180
Wizernes ... 131
Woodford ... 59
Wulverghem ... 173
Wytschaete ... 121, 161, 173

Y.M.C.A. ... 50, 51, 67, 82, 111, 172, 181, 233, 244
Ypres, 21, 108, 117, 126, 127, 128, 133, 134, 135, 136, 152, 159, 160, 161, 170.
Ypres, Battle of ... 122, 132, 161, 170
Ypres Salient ... 109, 135, 160

Zelman, Lieut. E. H. ... 158
Zoological Gardens, Groot Schuur ... 41
Zoteux ... 131, 132, 160, 163, 164
Zulu ... 39

www.ingramcontent.com/pod-product-compliance
Lightning Source LLC
Chambersburg PA
CBHW070006010526
44117CB00011B/1439